CW00952135

Our Own Dear Queen

Our Own Dear Queen

by

Piers Brendon

Secker & Warburg
London

First published in England 1986 by
Martin Secker & Warburg Limited
54 Poland Street, London W1V 3DF

Copyright © 1986 by Piers Brendon

British Library Cataloguing in Publication Data

Brendon, Piers
    Our own dear Queen.
    1. Great Britain – Kings and rulers
    I. Title
    941'.009'92   DA28.1

    ISBN 0–436–06814–1

Set in Great Britain in Lasercomp Plantin, 11 on 13pt.

Printed and bound in Great Britain
by Richard Clay (The Chaucer Press) Ltd,
Bungay, Suffolk

To
REX and GUDULA
with love

Contents

'How different, how very different, from the home life of our own dear Queen!'

The comment attributed to a Victorian matron in the audience during Sarah Bernhardt's melodramatic portrayal of Cleopatra

Acknowledgements

It is standard practice at the beginning of books about royalty *not* to mention the names of those who have been of the greatest assistance. Some authors even go so far as to deny that certain details were provided by certain people. I shall not imitate them. However, in order to protect my sources I must, alas, adhere to the convention of secrecy, which helps to preserve the mystique of monarchy. I am grateful to the 'Buckingham Palace spokesmen' who were indiscreet enough to confide in me, but they must remain anonymous so that they will not be ostracized in the highest circles, or even whisked off to the Tower.

I may, though, acknowledge the generous aid of those less close to the throne, who are not, of course, responsible for the use I made of it. Susanna Scott-Gall did some excellent research on my behalf. Philippa Gibson sent me some extremely interesting correspondence. Willie Hamilton MP talked to me freely, frankly and amusingly about his views and his experiences as Britain's leading republican. Michael Murphy, Brian Outhwaite and Norman Stone directed me towards valuable sources of information. Andrew Best, Steve Cox, Peter Grose and Richard Overy read the text and made helpful criticisms and suggestions. So did my wife Vyvyen, who disagrees with my conclusions. Nevertheless, she and my two sons have been an inestimable source of strength and comfort during the many arduous months of research and writing.

One

The Royals Capture Washington

During the autumn of 1985 Americans began to work themselves into a lather of excitement over the forthcoming visit of Prince Charles and Princess Diana of Wales. In Washington, particularly, the imminent arrival of the world's most famous and glamorous couple provoked an ecstasy of anticipation. Throughout the capital, named after the revolutionary hero who had defeated the tyranny of King George III, purged the new nation of hereditary privilege and personally refused a crown, people scrambled for a chance to pay homage to the royal pair. In order to meet the Prince, and still more the Princess, socialites and politicians engaged in intrigues which might have brought a blush to the cheek of Richard Nixon. 'This is one of those events that if you're not invited,' said Sheila Tate, Nancy Reagan's former press secretary, 'you'll plan to be away for the weekend so no one will know.' Having achieved nothing with her importunate telephone calls, Joan Collins apparently tried to attract attention by getting married again. More ordinary folk made real sacrifices in order to witness what was coming to be known as the 'Chuck and Di Show'. For her birthday Judy Preston of Lansing, Michigan, was offered a car or a trip to Washington: she unhesitatingly chose to take the chance of glimpsing 'the royals'. As their advent drew nigh the pace of preparation quickened. All over Washington life-size pictures of the visitors began to appear. Peter Rocha, a graphic artist, completed his singular portrait of the Princess of Wales, made up of ten thousand jellybeans – the favourite candy of Ronald Reagan. In a hospice which she was to visit the pet cockatoo was taught to whistle 'God Save the Queen'.

Celebrity breeds publicity and *vice versa*. So expectations rose and press coverage increased in tandem. However, American journalists were frustrated to discover that almost no authentic information was available about the true character of the future King and Queen of Great Britain. Their public functions are an open book – rather a prosaic one – but their private life is a mystery. No one who breathes a word about it ever gets another chance to do so. No American, not even Barbara Walters, would be allowed to interview them. And transcripts of the few carefully stage-managed English interviews that have been given are discreet to the point of banality. British newspapermen were no help. Though catering busily to the insatiable appetite for royal gossip, Fleet Street's *crème de la scum*, as they brashly call themselves, deal in trivia, speculation or unabashed fantasy, mostly expressed in tones of fulsome adulation. As a disgusted *Washington Post* correspondent wrote, 'they must leap to Diana's every long-lashed blink, scribble to her every murmur, thrill to every nuance in her newest frock, rise to the dissemination of every pregnant rumour'. Nor did American newshounds find much to help them in the countless royal books, which have less in common with biographies than with almanacs. Stephen Barry's account of his *Royal Service*, for example, disproved the old adage that no man can be a hero to his valet – nevertheless, these unctuous and insipid reminiscences cannot be published in Britain. All told, the Washington press corps concluded, Buckingham Palace was more tight-lipped than the Kremlin.

In desperation they fell back on a long, tart article (which caused outrage in Britain) written by the English editor of *Vanity Fair*, Tina Brown, in October 1985. It was designed to satisfy the 'intense curiosity' which American readers felt about how the royal relationship had developed between the fairy-tale wedding and their present visit to the United States. Tina Brown asserted that a 'curious role reversal had taken place in the marriage'. Princess Diana, 'the shy introvert unable to cope with public life, has emerged as the star of the world's stage', while Prince Charles had increasingly withdrawn into his peculiar 'inner world'. She was 'the mouse that roared'. The apparently demure ingénue turned out to be a tenacious Sloane Ranger, one who had been emotionally toughened as a child by her parents' messy divorce – her home life had been shattered when her mother went off with a wallpaper tycoon. Now Diana gloried in her fame and was obsessed by her image. Having no inner resources or intellectual curiosity, she was only happy in the limelight. Out of it she spent hours poring over her press cuttings, or shopped compulsively, or danced by herself interminably to the music of Dire Straits or Wham! played on her Sony Walkman.

By contrast, Charles, for the first time in his life something less than the centre of attention, had been able to retreat from the hearty extrovert role which circumstances had forced on him ever since his days at the exercise-mad school at Gordonstoun. In truth 'a lonely, eccentric figure haunted by self-doubt', he had behaved for years like an 'Action Man'. His official life had been one long Outward Bound course and his private activities with 'a battery of ballsy blondes' were scarcely less energetic. Now the pressure was off. He could afford to relax, even to engage in a 'postadolescent rebellion against the Teutonic boorishness of Prince Philip', who thought his eldest son 'a wimp'. So Charles reverted to his natural self, becoming a reclusive house-husband, 'a fish-and-fowl freak', a devotee of alternative medicine, a mystic manqué who tried to 'make contact on a Ouija board with the shade of his beloved "Uncle Dickie" Mountbatten'. Despite their differences in age, taste and character, however, Charles and Diana were not destined to drift apart. Indeed, the royal romance, like less elevated ones beloved of women's magazines, was surely going to have a happy ending. A shrewd writer, with her eye firmly fixed on the market-place, Tina Brown concluded her abrasive piece of lèse-majesté on an emollient note. Prince Charles was 'in just the kind of mood to fall in love with a nursery-school teacher in flat shoes who's kind to guinea-pigs and babies. If he looks hard enough, she's still there.'

Perhaps sceptical about this fairy-tale finale, perhaps reflecting that Tina Brown is scarcely on intimate terms with the royal pair (she seems to have been introduced to them twice, though she does know Charles's biographer Anthony Holden), American journalists did not swallow her story whole. They were further dissuaded by the television interview which the Prince and Princess gave to Sir Alastair Burnet, much of which was shown by the American Broadcasting Company. Evidently its intention was to contradict the import of Tina Brown's article without, of course, dignifying it by a mention. Thus Charles denied that he was interested in the occult, that he favoured anything more than an 'open-minded approach' to 'complementary medicine', and that he was 'a complete vegetarian'. Diana declared that 'fashion isn't my big thing at all', that she was horrified by the amount about her in the newspapers, and that 'my role is supporting my husband . . . the most important thing is being a mother and a wife'. It did not seem to matter that the Princess was known to have been coached for her part by Sir Richard Attenborough, director of *Gandhi*. It was apparently irrelevant that the Prince qualified every statement into bland inoffensiveness – squirming and grimacing with anxiety, agonizing over what to call his wife and referring to her once as 'another person', he stumbled so much that there had to be constant re-takes. Nor did it seem to signify that Burnet behaved as though he were addressing two slightly feeble-minded deities. The programme was not even invalidated by having been put together with the care and skill of the glossiest advertising commercial. For it contained immensely popular touches – Charles's acknowledgement that he probably was becoming a bit eccentric with age and that 'it must be absolute hell living with an ancient old thing like me', the tiff about whether they had tiffs, the revelation that Diana had not enjoyed the wedding, finding it 'terrifying', their playing with the children. All told, the film appeared to convey the reality of royalty. So the journalists had to think again.

In the event, they could not resist warming up some of Tina Brown's tastier morsels. But these were served as gossip rather than fact. *Newsweek* speculated excitedly: 'At 36, he is becoming an eccentric wood hippie, obsessed with spiritualism and organic gardening. At 24, she has blossomed into a self-absorbed, clothes-mad combination of Madame Bovary and Joan Collins.' *Time* went a stage further, updating the royal saga from Cinderella to 'Palace Dallas': 'The Princess, once known as shy Di, has been transformed into "Dynasty Di"; and Prince Charles, once dubbed Action Man for his intrepid sky- and skin-diving, has become a hermetic, mystical crank.' Other journals made much play with the concept of 'Dianisty'. The word conveyed regal glamour in vivid terms, the language of soap opera now being more universal even than that of fairy-tale, and it suggested that the Prince and Princess were the stuff of which fantasy was made. The truth was, of course, that no one could find out what

Charles and Diana were really like. As *Time* wryly concluded: 'They are world-class illusionists . . . hinting at intimacy while keeping their distance.'

That, indeed, is their métier. For public ignorance is crucial if the mystique of monarchy is to be preserved. As the Victorian constitutional theorist Walter Bagehot wrote, secrecy is 'essential to the utility of English royalty as it now is. Above all things our royalty is to be reverenced, and if you begin to poke about it you cannot reverence it. When there is a select committee on the Queen, the charm of royalty will be gone. Its mystery is its life. We must not let in daylight upon magic.' The magic of Charles and Diana is that they are well known yet unknown. They thus become screens onto which the public can project their own preoccupations, living icons whose significance lies in the eye of the beholder. Commentators can read into them what they please. Witness Suzanne Lowry's comment on Princess Diana:

> In her stillness and beauty and limited intellectual range, Diana appears as the affluent society's perfect wife. A creature to desire, chase, catch and tame, then to shelter and impregnate and cover with the protective umbrella of home, status and all good things that a man on the right track in a consumerist world can provide. She is the first convincing princess of the video age, symbolizing . . . golden girlhood, romantic sexuality – just as Brigitte Bardot stood for more torrid, lustful liberated sex in her generation. But because Diana also represents the return of the wifely ideal, built on powerful passivity and dependence, the sex princess is much more powerful than the sex kitten or the delectable piece of fluff.

Perhaps . . . or perhaps not. It is possible to inscribe any theory on a *tabula rasa*. Knowing almost nothing worth knowing about the royal couple, people can imagine what they like.

During the 'months of preparation, anticipation, hoopla and hype' citizens of the United States permitted their imaginations to run riot. As the *Washington Post* reported, 'Anglomania has seized the capital and for weeks now Washingtonians have been boning up on their royal etiquette.' Among other things they discovered that the correct form of address on first meeting Charles and Diana, is 'Your Royal Highness', after which it is safe to say 'Sir' or 'Ma'am'. On the delicate question of whether to bow or curtsy, however, Lady Wright, wife of the British ambassador, advised: 'As Americans you please yourself.' But the rule was firm on the matter of physical contact. 'Royals' may touch commoners – indeed, the royal touch was once supposed to cure scrofula and other diseases that common flesh was heir to – but commoners may not touch royals, still less slap them on the back. (Nancy Reagan did not go that far, but she did breach the convention by putting her arm round the Princess's waist.) Armed with such etiquette, and determined to be polite without being subservient, the inhabitants of the capital prepared to be captivated.

So, at 8.40 on the morning of Saturday 9 November the Royal Australian Air Force jet which had brought Charles and Diana from their nineteen-day antipodean tour, via Hawaii, touched down at Andrews Air Force base. The royal couple, she as svelte and glossy as a model girl, wearing a scarlet costume with a white collar and a pill-box hat, he sporting a bald patch and a self-conscious grin, and dressed in a dark suit, stepped down onto the red carpet which had just been hand-picked free of lint. They were greeted with cheers and cries of 'Princess, Princess'. Then, in the bright sunshine, they made their way down the edge of the large crowd. Many of those who had gathered to welcome them waved Union Jacks, provided by the British embassy. Others had brought presents, ranging from flowers to puppets labelled 'Prince William' and 'Prince Henry', which their mother graciously accepted and expertly passed on to a lady-in-waiting. The response to royal smiles, waves, handshakes and occasional hugs for the children verged on the delirious. One young woman exclaimed: 'I just died.' And after the couple had passed, hordes of reporters swooped on each dazzled child who had talked to them 'as if checking out the results of contact with King Midas'. The press reflected the prevailing spirit of rapture. One headline blared: 'The British Have Landed And Washington Is Taken.' Another story elaborated on this predictable theme: 'On Aug. 24, 1814, the British took Washington with sea power, muskets and 3,500 troops. In mid-November, 1985, they conquered it again – this time with 7,000 pounds of luggage and a smile that could melt the Rock of Gibraltar.'

After twenty minutes Charles and Diana were whisked away by helicopter to the British embassy. Then, with barely a pause, they drove to the White House in the ambassador's silver Rolls-

Royce, the Prince of Wales's standard, which features harps and lions, fluttering in the breeze. Another red carpet, this one vacuumed five minutes before their arrival by a presidential aide, and then warm greetings from Ronald and Nancy Reagan at the door of the South Portico. As though to disarm criticism about her earlier extravagances, the First Lady was wearing a subdued beige wool dress with wide suede belt and gold choker. But the President really caught the eye. Outshining Diana herself, he was dressed in a green, red and blue plaid jacket which, according to the BBC's court correspondent, bore a marked resemblance to the carpet at Balmoral Castle. The 'most famous foursome in the world' then took coffee, cinnamon toast and sweets in the West Hall. Having exchanged gifts and pleasantries, the royal couple returned to the embassy for a tree-planting ceremony and lunch. Then, despite their weariness, they embarked on a hectic round of engagements.

The Prince visited the American Institute of Architects and the Octagon House, where he inspected the Treaty of Ghent, signed there after the Anglo-American War of 1812. In the crowd outside, a university student held up a banner which said 'Happy (Almost) Birthday Charles' – the Prince would be thirty-seven on 14 November. Meanwhile Diana called at a hospice for the elderly and dying. She met, among others, ninety-five-year-old Letitia Whitty, who said: 'When I was six and a half, my father took me to the streets to see Queen Victoria passing. I wouldn't wave at that ugly old woman.' When an even older resident remarked that she would shortly be celebrating her hundredth birthday, the Princess replied: 'Some people will use any excuse to have a party.'

In the evening, after a rest, the royal couple themselves went to a party, a select little banquet for seventy-nine guests, at the White House. This was the occasion when President Reagan made his celebrated 'flub', introducing the Princess of Wales first as 'Princess David', then as 'Princess Dian'. But Charles too made a little gaffe. He forgot to propose a toast and had to rise to his feet again to do so. Still, the occasion was deemed a stunning success. The Princess flirted gently with Clint Eastwood and danced energetically with John Travolta, who afterwards affirmed that 'she has style and rhythm'. The British press interpreted this as 'She's a great little mover,' and it frothed excitedly over Diana's 'Saturday Night Fever'. The *Sun* announced that 'the pair wowed Washington with their boogie bombshell'. And the *Mirror*, whose dedicated 'royal watcher' James Whitaker had not been present and freely admitted to 'jazzing the story up', gave a detailed account of how the Princess and 'the snake-hipped disco king . . . went through a routine that had everybody gasping'. Most guests, however, had been unable to satisfy their curiosity about what the couple were really like. A small incident illustrated their hunger for knowledge. Someone described the whooshing noise a hot-air balloon makes as it ascends. 'When the shhhhh sound hissed through the dining room, overtly signifying what many were secretly thinking, the guests stopped eating and talking and swivelled towards the Reagans and the royal couple. "When we found out what it was, everyone began giggling,"' recalled another guest. '"It showed that we were all really listening with a third ear."' The *New York Times* headlined its report: 'When the Royal Pair Talk, You Can Hear a Tiara Drop.'

After Saturday Night Fever came Sunday morning church. Diana had begun the day with a solitary eight o'clock dip in the St Alban's Boys' School swimming pool. And since well before dawn a line of people, eventually half a mile long, had queued outside Washington's Gothic cathedral. Three thousand had to remain outside, where they chanted 'Diana! Diana!' But the two thousand who managed to obtain pews heard Charles read the first lesson. It was taken from Isaiah and prophesied a peaceable place where the redeemed walk, with everlasting joy upon their heads. The congregation, its collective mind obviously fixed more on earthly crowns than heavenly ones, observed that the royal couple behaved impeccably throughout. They dutifully stood, sat and knelt, Charles on a hassock needle-pointed by his grandmother and given to the cathedral as a war memorial, at the appropriate times. Across the aisle from them, by contrast, Vice President Bush and his wife talked during the Gloria.

When the service was over the Prince and Princess spent ninety minutes touring an exhibition entitled 'Treasure Houses of Britain' at the National Gallery. Charles was a patron of this show, which consisted of 700 works of art and furnishings from 200 British country houses, and it was the official reason for his visit. As always on this trip, security was tight and police with dogs were everywhere. The crowd, some of whom were in Washington for the Redskins game, got little more than a glimpse of Diana's navy blue and white outfit and her flying saucer hat, which sometimes threatened to take off in the autumn breeze. But Donald E. Petersen, chairman of the Ford Motor Company, which had helped to sponsor the exhibition, received the Prince's personal thanks. And he was gratified to hear from the Princess that she enjoyed driving her red convertible Ford Escort. Charles found the show, which was packed with precious heirlooms, books, tapestry, silver, furniture, jewellery, china and works by Holbein, Titian, El Greco, Rembrandt, Rubens and others, 'quite dramatic'. He then pleased reporters by taking part in the first impromptu press conference he had held for years. He confirmed that his wife had enjoyed dancing with John Travolta – the matter was 'threatening to take on global importance', according to the *New York Times*, eclipsing even the burning question of whether the Princess swathed her legs in stockings or brown-gel. Charles also explained how he overcame jet lag: 'It's all in the breeding, you know.'

The royal couple next flew by helicopter to the magnificent country estate of Anglophile Paul Mellon at Upperville (where else?), Virginia. His family had accomplished the characteristic American transformation from robber barons to philanthropists – one of his forebears had made the celebrated pronouncement that it was impossible to run a steel works without machine-guns. Now Mellon laid on a sumptuous party for the royal visitors. His guest list was so small, select and secret that journalists reckoned a leak-prone government could take lessons in security from him. After lunch they all wandered round the grounds, visiting the stables and admiring the gardens. Having thus spent 'a very relaxed, cosy time' enjoying the countryside, the Prince and Princess were ready for another banquet, this time at the British embassy.

Here the guests were important rather than merely famous, political leaders rather than 'show business personalities'. As the royal press secretary Michael Shea announced defensively, 'No dancing, and Mr Travolta has not been invited, and this is not intended as a snub.' However, the proceedings were enlivened by an inventive menu – a fish mousse called 'Terrine "Charles"' and a hazelnut and strawberry confection christened '"Diana's

Delight" Pudding' – and by a spirited rendering from a choir of embassy staff and others of Noël Coward's 'The Stately Homes of England', updated to suit the occasion. 'We only keep them up for Americans to rent,' ran the ditty, a mildly satirical 'commercial' for 'The Treasure Houses of Britain', which were said to be 'otherwise known as the national nest egg'. One of the stately homes 'historically boasted two viscounts and a duchess, three monarchs and a ghost, though the lavatory makes you fear the worst and didn't appeal to Randolph Hearst, it was used by Charles the First (this guy's ancestor) and later by George the Fourth on a journey north'.

After all the weekend glitz and ritz, as the American newspapers liked to call it, the Prince and Princess moved sharply down-market on Monday morning. They paid a visit to J. C. Penney's suburban department store. The shops in this chain were originally, as the name suggests, little more than penny bazaars and they have a long way to go even now before getting into the same league as Harrods or Bloomingdale's. But they were selling a wide range of British exports which the Prince was keen to promote – though he denied being a travelling salesman. Penney's had made elaborate preparations to greet the visitors. The store provided 5,000 red-and-white balloons for the cheering crowd, which was, however, restricted to the car park. They laid on red roses, Union Jacks, a red carpet and even store detectives dressed up in the red tunics and white cross-belts of Royal Guards – Penney's public relations officers had wanted them to wear Beefeater costumes but the security chief baulked at asking men to wear red tights.

When Charles and Diana had entered the store people in the crowd rushed forward, squealing with delight, and pressed their noses against Penney's plate glass windows. The royal couple were shown an elaborate display of British goods, including the Royal Mint Stamp Collection, a doll of Queen Elizabeth I, replicas of the Crown Jewels, and a white-and-beige Rolls-Royce Silver Shadow balanced on four Wedgwood coffee cups. It was the Princess, though, in her slim-fitting cream wool suit, who was the focus of attention. Reporters were delighted when a royal flush mantled her cheeks as Charles asked if a bed was king or queen sized, adding: 'Is the king the large size?' They were frustrated when she bent down out of their view to look under the

Rolls-Royce. They were transfixed when she paused in front of a maternity outfit, and unbelieving when the shop assistant maintained that 'her real interest was in novelty fleece tops' featuring bears and ducks. They were intrigued by her view that double-breasted suits flattered men and at once began to prophesy a fashion revolution. It was so evident that Diana was getting all the attention that one man in the throng they passed outside the store commiserated with the Prince. Charles was the real royalty; he had the blood 'for crying out loud'; and he was getting 'a bum rap'. The Prince replied: 'Well, flattery will get you everywhere. Thank you.'

The rest of the day was a frantic rush of engagements. Before lunch there was a reception at the British embassy for 170 Washington notables, including Barbara Walters. After it the Prince went to the Library of Congress where he saw early American documents, including the Virginia Plan, and discussed the merits of a written constitution with Librarian Daniel Boorstin and Chief Justice Warren Burger. Charles also inspected Queen Victoria's letter of condolence to Mary Todd Lincoln after the President's assassination. The Princess visited a Straight drug rehabilitation centre in Springfield, Virginia, with Nancy Reagan and talked to addicts and former addicts. 'Will you feel a stronger person after you leave?' she asked one. Of another she enquired: 'Did you start getting on drugs in the first place because you wanted to escape the responsibility that life produces?' Reporters were frankly incredulous about this question and one later suggested: 'Maybe she was reading it from the back of her hand.' The couple then changed, he into naval uniform, she into a purple Bruce Oldfield dress, and set off in a fourteen-car motorcade to Arlington Cemetery. There, to a twenty-one-gun salute, Charles laid a wreath on the Tomb of the Unknowns, and they visited the memorial display room. On their return the crowds, hemmed in by police, applauded, whistled and yelled: 'Diana, we love you!!!' After another quick change, into evening clothes (she wore a Japanese-designed, one-shouldered, long-sleeved, silver-sparkly beaded dress which hugged her slender figure), the couple attended a gala dinner and reception at the National Gallery. There were 500 guests at the reception and 107 at the dinner. Those who enjoyed the full meal included a number of extremely rich benefactors of the gallery as well as celebrities like actress Brooke Shields ('I feel like tonight is definitely a dream come true'), cellist Yo Yo Ma ('I've heard Prince Charles plays the cello'), and gymnast Mary Lou Retton ('Oh my gosh! Such an honour! Really!').

On Tuesday the weather turned cloudy and the royal pair waved their farewells to Washington ('the merry waves of Windsor', quipped the press) and headed for the sunshine of Palm Beach, Florida. In this plush resort, a plutocrat's playground 'run by career dowagers of immense fortune and bejewelled hauteur', they briskly completed the final engagements on their American itinerary. But there were some embarrassing contretemps. One concerned seventy-one-year-old John W. Kluge, who had sold Metromedia to Rupert Murdoch for a reported two billion dollars and was co-chairman of the charity ball which the Prince and Princess were to attend. It was revealed that his young wife Pat had once posed for nude photographs in a British magazine called *Knave* and the Kluges found it instantly necessary to go to Europe for 'a vacation'. Mary Sanford, doyenne of Palm Beach society, also made her excuses and left – in a huff at discovering that she was not, as she had thought, organizing the ball. Various of Palm Beach's other bluebloods were equally miffed that the man who was in charge, the petroleum magnate Armand Hammer, was an outsider – and this in a community where antisemitism still prevails and non-residents have to carry identity cards. Furthermore, Hammer was proposing to charge $10,000 per double ticket (twice that for those who wanted to be photographed keeping company with the royals) for an alien charity, the United World College Fund. The likes of Joan Collins paid up and looked pleased. But grander names with older money were inclined to boycott the affair. Gregg Dodge, widow of the automobile manufacturer, announced that she would not attend, explaining (reasonably enough): 'That's the day I have my legs waxed.' Some of Palm Beach's élite even went so far as to throw a rival ball, tickets for which cost only five dollars less than for the royal one. It featured a comical menu including peasant's pot soup, 'poor man's caviare' and shepherd's pie (decorated with little Union Jacks).

If the Prince and Princess of Wales felt snubbed by any of this they did not show it. After all, even America's nearest equivalent to a royal family, the Kennedys, had been ostracized by Palm

Beach – they could only join the 'Jewish' country club. As it happened, the Kennedys, sole challengers for the US crown, Mickey and Minnie Mouse, were on hand from Disney World to welcome the royal couple when they arrived in the early afternoon for their first engagement. This was a polo match, prefaced by the usual razzmatazz, marching bands and gyrating cheerleaders from the Miami Dolphins. A polo priest prayed over the loudspeakers that the riders should stay in their saddles, while a television cameraman hoped *sotto voce* that the Prince would fall off and break a leg . . . 'Let it be *something*.' Nothing happened, except that Charles missed enough shots to make the spectators wince. But although his presence was described as 'mainly ornamental' and the other players seemed to treat him with kid gloves, Charles's team won and he received a silver and porcelain trophy and a kiss from the Princess. In any case, the sport scarcely mattered. It was clear that the 12,000-strong crowd had come to watch royalty not polo.

Crowds gathered again outside the Breakers Hotel to watch arrivals at the charity ball. Some guests just drove down the road from their $25 million houses, but the best-known names, Bob Hope, Eva Gabor, Merv Griffin, Gregory Peck, had flown in from all over the United States. What everyone had in common, though, was wealth; and the ladies, jewelled and spangled from head to toe, obviously regarded this as the moment to display it. As a journalist remarked, 'If you added up the cost of the gowns here it would be equal to the gross national product of three small African countries.' Joan Collins's diamonds alone were worth a king's, or at least a prince's, ransom. By now she had denied getting married for a fourth time in order to upstage the Princess: 'Ludicrous, ludicrous, ludicrous, absolutely ludicrous.' But she did start further speculation at the ball by wearing a black costume whose neckline plunged right off the deep end. The Princess of Wales, by contrast, in a chaste cerise panne gown, exhibited only her back. Charles did dance with la Collins, but no film star or fashion plate or glittering *femme fatale* could outshine Diana, whose royal aura was above the price of rubies. As one of the guests exclaimed when she arrived, 'I feel like history walked past me. She's a perfect Cinderella.' And, like Cinderella, after the ball she had to go home. So, the final banquet eaten, the concluding quips made, the valedictory thanks and handclasps given, 'the tired, probably overfed and over-fawned-upon royal couple' flew back to London.

That, at least, was *Time* magazine's somewhat astringent last word on their visit. Throughout it, indeed, there had been an ample flavouring of sour comments with the sweet, though only the latter were reported in Britain. There were a number of protests at the awe-struck 'lord- and lady-worshipping' that the tour had provoked. Even 'Miss Manners', columnist Judith Martin, was disgusted by the social jockeying and she insisted that free-born Americans should not fall into the obsequious transatlantic habit of curtsying to royalty. It was noted that hardly any black guests had been invited to the various royal functions. There was much criticism about the Prince's 'shameless sales pitch for the British heritage'. One columnist wrote: 'To be sure, when British royalty comes to the United States it always has something to sell, since in its present condition the British throne is reduced to little more than an agreeably housed and over-remunerated promotions office.' Many resented the amount of 'hype' accorded to the royal pair, and reckoned that their visit was 'inconsequential, a prime example of a media-created event'. Some were as much bemused as outraged by the attention given to the 'absurd collection of trivia and maudlin, boring gossip' which the visit had produced. 'Why we Americans should continue to be so obsessed with the comings and goings of an effete and parasitic monarchy, which we shed blood in 1776 to be rid of, will forever remain a mystery. . . . This is not to denigrate the civility or the quality of other British cultural institutions for which we have a deep and abiding respect. But after all is said, God bless the Republic.'

Of course, not all Americans are republicans. A few even indulged in a little royalist nostalgia during the visit. After Charles had called on him in the Library of Congress, for example, Dr Boorstin mused: 'What might the consequences have been if George Washington hadn't refused the throne here? We might have this thing every day in America, a prince and princess roaming around making people happy.' During his eight-minute sermon in Washington Cathedral, Bishop Walker wondered whether the American Revolution would come unravelled 'if the Prince said: "All is forgiven, come home."' This was an improbable speculation, even from a man of the cloth. But presumably such sentiments were uttered more out of politeness, or perhaps temporary infatuation with royalty, than out of any real desire to turn the clock back to the time of George III. Most citizens of the United States were inclined to endorse Huckleberry Finn's conclusion that 'all kings is mostly rapscallions, as fur as I can make out'. And one columnist said that had Emerson been in Washington for the royal visit he would surely have considered the lines in his 'Boston Hymn' a gross understatement:

> God said, I am tired of kings,
> I suffer them no more;
> Up to my ear the morning brings
> The outrage of the poor.

The revulsion against 'the state of terminal gaga into which we have collapsed while we are going berserk with the sheer ecstasy of it all' was doubtless chiefly felt by hard-bitten journalists, metropolitan sophisticates and disaffected intellectuals. Ordinary Americans, or many of them, were glad to indulge for a while in escapist fantasies about 'the royal heroic couplet', as *Time* dubbed them. But this was surely because Charles and Diana were real-life celebrities to eclipse even soap-opera queens, because they combined vivid human interest with rich Ruritanian spectacle. 'Why does the sight of the Waleses make Americans go dopey?' asked a Washington columnist. 'Because we love camp. In a town full of people with pomp-less power, it is a kick to see powerless pomp, like seeing a vice president in sash and sword.' To Washington, Charles and Diana were star players on tour in a stunning, but mercifully short-running, extravaganza. Americans could only visualize them as exotic, alien and temporary. They could barely grasp the British attitude towards royalty, described by the *Boston Globe*'s European correspondent Steven Erlanger as 'an astonishing devotion and a heartfelt sentimentality that can verge on the obsessive'. Michael Cole, the BBC's court correspondent, laboriously explained to Washington journalists: 'I don't want to give you a civics lecture, but you can't make the mistake of thinking that this is all just decoration and a fairy tale princess and our version of Camelot. Americans make that mistake, you see. And the monarchy is the living fabric and fibre of Britain.'

The fact is, though, that while republicanism is the gospel of an eccentric sect in Britain, royalism is the faith of a dwindling minority throughout the world. A poll taken in 1984 found that only 5 per cent of the British people thought they would be 'better off' without the monarchy, whereas 77 per cent thought they would be 'worse off'. But in global terms monarchs are threatened with extinction. The United States, like the vast majority of other nations, reckons that a crowned hereditary ruler, be he never so decorative, is a feudal anachronism. He (or she) is incompatible with democracy, the basic tenet of which is that each one shall count for one and no one for more than one. In Britain the monarchy may seem as secure as a rock, but the tide of the times is running strongly against it. For, as Philip Howard has written: 'In an age of democracy, it is hierarchic; in an age of egalitarianism, it is élitist; in an age of scepticism, it is mystical.'

He might have added that, in an age when freedom of information is increasingly deemed essential to the health of a body politic, it is hermetic. What Harold Laski called an 'organized silence', unparalleled outside the closed societies of the Eastern bloc, surrounds the British monarchy. As Walter Bagehot said, every power in a popular democracy ought to be known. 'A secret prerogative is an anomaly – perhaps the greatest of anomalies.' But monarchy is incompatible with truly open government; silence is essential to reverence. So lips are sealed in large matters; no one knows, for example, how much influence the sovereign wields today. And over small matters the passion for concealment sometimes takes pathological forms. When the Queen Mother was taken to hospital in 1982 with a 'foreign body' stuck in her throat, her official spokesman would not say what it was. And when journalists finally discovered that it was a fishbone, he refused to disclose the fact that the fish in question was a trout. When, in February 1986, British Rail lost the key to the door connecting the royal saloon with the dining car, and stewards were seen scuttling down the platform at Ely with silver salvers, the Palace refused to confirm that they were carrying the Queen's breakfast.

To the astonishment of Americans, British official secrecy is reinforced by social taboo. As Steven Erlanger wrote, 'The monarchy is Great Britain's most sacred cow, more unassailable now in a democratic age than in the days when sovereigns ruled as well as reigned. You may question almost anything in British life and be considered witty, but too vigorous a criticism of the

Royal Family or a loud preference for republicanism means instant pariahdom.' Over the last hundred years British loyalty to royalty has waxed just as orthodox religion, for which it may be a secular substitute, has waned. Like the Pope himself, the monarch has lost in power and gained in prestige. And those inclined to approach the throne without due reverence are liable to be visited with all sorts of reprisals. Malcolm Muggeridge was banned from appearing on the BBC and sent used pieces of lavatory paper through the post. Lord Altrincham was disowned by the *Observer*, a newspaper of impeccable liberal traditions, to which he contributed regularly. Almost thirty years later, little seems to have changed. The *Observer* commissioned me to write an outspoken article on the monarchy – it is the kernel of this book – and then declined to print it. It finally appeared in the *New Statesman*. In 1984, by even seeming to censure the Queen, Enoch Powell managed to erode his populist power base and to make himself even more of a parliamentary Ishmaelite than before. However desirable this effect, its cause raises a serious question: can Britain's national life be regarded as healthy when at its centre there exists an institution which it is blasphemy to criticize?

This in turn provokes other questions. Can Britain become a modern and progressive state when at its heart there exists a hereditary monarchy whose most crucial activities are secret and unaccountable, yet whose every public appearance is greeted with hysterical adulation? Is the royal family a symbol of the unity, stability and probity of the nation? Or does it symbolize a determinedly backward-looking Britain, a museum of quaint customs and antique attitudes, a repository of entrenched privilege and Victorian values, a caste-ridden, horse-riding, philistine nation, throttled by the old school tie? Has not the Crown always reinforced the archaic influences which retard Britain's advance? Has it not discouraged enlightened policies and rational judgement in favour of ritual, incantation and fantasy? Is the monarchy perhaps what John Osborne called it, the 'gold filling in a mouth full of decay'? Could it be just a matter of chance that the rise of kings and queens in popular esteem coincided precisely with the decline in Britain's global fortunes? Or does the change in public attitude merely reflect changes in the institution itself? Should there be more changes? Can an examination of the monarchy's often lurid past shed light on its opaque character today? Can Britain afford to keep up the royal family and keep out of step with the republics proliferating all over the world?

These are important questions, though writers about royalty, preferring to deal in simpering newspaper sycophancy or extreme literary unction, seldom pay much attention to them. This book attempts to give some straight answers. Yet just because there are so few chinks in the wall of secrecy which surrounds today's monarchy, the answers are largely to be sought and found in history. Like the student of evolution, the student of kingship cannot scrutinize his subject at first hand. In order to construct the present he has to delve into the past. He must unearth mouldering bones, piece together the fossil record and make inferences from the evidence which is available. Thus the early chapters of this book take a long look at the antecedents of Britain's sovereign institution and its evolution from Hanoverian ill fame to its present hallowed status. They examine the royal rose by reference to its roots, stem and prickles. This procedure has its difficulties. But because Britain has never undergone a fundamental revolution, and because of the continuity and traditionalism of the royal family – Prince Philip acknowledges that being 'old-fashioned' is their métier – it is surprisingly revealing. As the later chapters suggest, the modern régime in Britain bears a striking resemblance to the *ancien régime*.

Two

George III Should Never Have Occurred

During his Washington visit Prince Charles briefly devoted himself to the uphill task of persuading Americans that George III was after all rather a good king. His great-great-great-great-great-grandfather had received 'a bit of a raw deal in history', Charles maintained, describing hostile interpretations as 'propaganda'. 'I think slowly but surely people are realizing he wasn't such an ogre as they made out.' Surprisingly, the Prince's view got some support in the Library of Congress. Describing the residual royalism that existed in America after the War of Independence, the chief of the manuscripts division, Dr James Hutson, told him that there had been a move to invite George III's second son, the Bishop of Osnaburgh, to become king. 'The Prince liked that,' Dr Hutson said. Well might he. For the defection of the American colonies, generally thought to have been provoked by George III, was the most serious reverse England suffered during the eighteenth century. And it must long have been a pipe-dream of the House of Hanover, renamed the House of Windsor in 1917, to recover the United States to its royalist allegiance, even if only in the attenuated form of Commonwealth membership. Be that as it may, it is interesting that Prince Charles has chosen to try to restore the reputation of George III. For he was the last king of England to exercise significant executive power.

George III's reign thus provides an excellent starting-point from which to examine the modern monarchy. For by his time the idea and practice of absolute rule was defunct and the constitution was beginning to take its present shape. Despite Magna

Carta, parliament and the common law, monarchs had been tyrants when they wished to be before the seventeenth century. Henry VIII, for example, boasted that in his domain he was both Pope and Emperor, and a recent student of his reign has described the 'police-state atmosphere' he established. Queen Elizabeth, too, although more circumspect, thought it a 'monstrous' notion 'that the feet should direct the head'. But the execution of Charles I in 1649 effectively destroyed the possibility of royal despotism.

After the Cromwellian interregnum, Charles II's effort to restore royal power, on Louis XIV's model, was always tempered by his determination 'never to go on his travels again'. Thus control of the executive continued to slide away from him. But Charles was still able to effect a secret treaty with France against the wishes and interests of his people, to rule for his last few years without parliament, and to squander an inordinate amount of the national income on keeping up his mistresses. His brother James II spent less on *his* mistresses – who were so ugly that Charles suggested his confessor must have given them to him as penance. But during the moments snatched from his principal occupation – adultery – the Roman Catholic King swiftly managed to alienate most of his subjects. Before he had reigned three years, they evicted him from the throne in favour of his daughter Mary and her homosexual husband William of Orange. The Glorious Revolution and the various financial limitations imposed by parliament on James's successors, making them paid servants of the state, created a 'mixed' monarchy. John Locke, the philosopher of the revolution, asserted that the Crown's authority derived from the consent of the people, who had agreed to a 'social contract' by which their obedience was conditional on the government's acting in their interests and protecting their 'natural rights'. This theory did not favour democracy any more than it favoured republicanism. In fact, Locke provided a classic justification for limited monarchy and propertied oligarchy. But in doing so he was seen decisively to have demolished the notion of the divine right of kings.

The last of the Stuarts, Queen Anne, was also the last British sovereign to touch for the King's Evil or scrofula – a magic touch which failed to cure the young Samuel Johnson. She was also the last monarch to veto a bill passed by parliament. But Anne was less a queen than a pawn in the bitter party strife which dominated her reign. As for her consort, Prince George of Denmark, he was so lethargic – in every sphere but the pro-creative – that it was reckoned lucky he suffered from asthma, otherwise he would have been taken for dead and buried. Anne herself died and was buried – so dropsical was she that her coffin was almost square – having done virtually nothing to secure the Hanoverian Succession. But in 1714, as in 1688, the English were willing to override the principle of legitimacy because of their fear of Popery. This was the national paranoia of the time, the Augustan Red Scare, though doubtless, as Defoe said, many who cried out against Popery 'know not whether it be a man or a horse'. Still, the English preferred their Church to their king, and parliament firmly excluded the Jacobite Pretender in favour of unprepossessing German princelings with hardly a drop of Stuart blood in their veins.

Their claim to the throne being so tenuous, the first two Hanoverians were largely prepared to reign while the Whig oligarchy ruled. Certainly they were disinclined to risk their new crown by a vigorous exercise of their remaining prerogatives. These were quite considerable in theory. The sovereign was still regarded as the executive, the legislature being a check on the abuse of power. So the monarch could call and dissolve parliaments, appoint and dismiss ministers, and determine foreign policy. Perhaps even more important, the Crown possessed an immense influence through the many offices in its gift. The distribution of places and pensions was regarded by its defenders as essential to the practice of good government – it 'oiled the wheels of the constitution', in Macaulay's phrase. In particular, it prevented the House of Commons from using its control of the purse to monopolize power in the state. Critics complained not just that the patronage system was corrupt, but that it opened up the possibility of reviving the royal ascendancy. Tom Paine made the point with his usual force: 'Wherefore, though we have been wise enough to shut and lock the door against absolute monarchy, we have at the same time been foolish enough to put the Crown in possession of the key.'

Actually George I gave the key to Sir Robert Walpole. He did so, it is true, with much reluctance and after some delay. But Walpole made himself indispensable, dominating the Whig oligarchy, managing the House of Commons and securing the Protestant Succession. Unable to speak English, the King did not continue the practice of attending cabinet council meetings. He anyway preferred to go off to his home in Hanover whenever he could. At Herrenhausen he was his own master. An Elector in name but an autocrat in fact, he kept his unfaithful wife shut up in a castle for thirty-two years, until her death. And he had no need to indulge in the *noblesse oblige* which was expected in England: 'I must give five guineas to Lord Chetwynd's man,' he grumbled, 'for bringing me my own carp, out of my own canal, in my own park.' Cold, formal, surly, as well as parsimonious, with the full lips and bulging eyes which were to be prominent features of successive Hanoverians, George made no secret of the fact that he valued England merely as a counter in the game of continental politics. So little did he comprehend the English that he proposed to enclose and plough up St James's Park in order to grow turnips.

The English reacted to him in a predictably xenophobic fashion:

> Hither he brought the dear Illustrious House,
> That is himself, his pipe, close stool and louse,
> Two Turks, three whores, and half a dozen nurses,
> Five hundred Germans, all with empty purses.

Two of his least popular attendants were his mistress, the Baroness von Schulenberg, and his half-sister (also reputed to be his mistress), the Baroness von Kielmansegge. They were both influential, corrupt and rapacious – between them they obtained all Queen Anne's jewels from the King, so that at George II's coronation his Queen, Caroline, had to appear in borrowed gems. George I's bizarre sexual tastes are suggested by the nicknames of these two ladies: 'the Giraffe' and 'the Elephant'. Horace Walpole, Sir Robert's son, remembered being terrified as a child by the latter:

> Her enormous figure was as corpulent and ample as the Duchess was long and emaciated. Two fierce black eyes, large and rolling beneath two lofty arched eyebrows, two acres of cheeks spread with crimson, and an ocean of neck that overflowed and was not distinguished from the lower half of her body, and no part restrained by

stays – no wonder that a child dreaded such an ogress, and that the mob of London were highly diverted at the importation of so uncommon a seraglio.

So George I had his hands full – even when he was not engaged in his favourite hobby of cutting out paper figures. He was further preoccupied by an obsessive hatred for his son, whom he schemed to have deported to America. This kind of antipathy was a feature of Hanoverian life which extended over several generations. It is not altogether a surprising one, since the monarchs and their offspring could scarcely avoid finding much about each other to dislike. But the family's Oedipal complexities were important because heirs to the throne in the eighteenth century became the focus for the 'reversionary interest'. In other words, opposition politicians tended to adhere to each Prince of Wales in the hope of gaining office at his succession. They were usually disappointed. When his father died in 1727, George briefly appointed a favourite nonentity as chief minister, only to find that he could not do without Walpole. The King and Queen Caroline also found that they detested their first-born, Frederick, with even more pathological ferocity when he became Prince of Wales.

The Queen described him as 'the greatest ass and the greatest liar and the greatest canaille and the greatest beast in the whole world, and I heartily wish he were out of it'. The King, faced with the perennial Hanoverian difficulty of finding a suitable Protestant princess to marry his son, wrote: 'The Princess of Denmark he would not have. The Princesses of Prussia have a madman for their father, and I did not think engrafting my half-witted coxcomb upon a madwoman would mend the breed.' Eventually Frederick married Princess Augusta of Saxe-Gotha, making himself conspicuous at the wedding supper by winking at the servants and consuming large quantities of jelly, supposedly an aphrodisiac. His marriage soured relations with his parents still further. They would only give him half of the £100,000 annual allowance which he considered his due. And when, in 1737, he whisked his wife away from Hampton Court in the middle of the night rather than allow her to bear their first child under his parents' roof, they ostracized him. Accordingly, he established a rival court at Leicester House. But he did not live to reward his followers. His funeral, which occurred in 1751 at Henry VIII's Chapel, Windsor, was an unceremonious affair, without benefit of organ or anthem. George II admitted that he was glad his son was dead. The sentiment was evidently a general one, though a famous anonymous epitaph, quoted by Horace Walpole, extended it to encompass the entire dynasty.

> Here lies Fred
> Who was alive and is dead:
> Had it been his father,
> I had much rather;
> Had it been his brother,
> Still better than another;
> Had it been his sister
> No one would have missed her;
> Had it been the whole generation,
> Still better for the nation:
> But since 'tis only Fred,
> Who was alive and is dead, –
> There's no more to be said.

English aversion to the whole Hanoverian clan was understandable and George II returned it with interest, calling his subjects king-killers and republicans. Like many royal personages, George was brave to the point of foolhardiness; he had twice demonstrated his courage, if not his military skill, on the battlefield – at Oudenarde and Dettingen. But he was otherwise an unattractive figure. As Thackeray said, he was a 'dull little man with low tastes' – everyone knows of his allergy to 'bainting and boetry' – who invariably 'claimed and took the royal exemption from doing right which sovereigns assumed'. He appeared to think that his rank gave him *droit de seigneur* over any pretty woman who caught his gooseberry eye. George's court combined casual impropriety with rigid formality. Like all monarchs, he was imprisoned by etiquette and pinioned by protocol. True, his state could have been worse. Philip III of Spain is said to have died of a fever he contracted by sitting too near a hot brazier because the flunkey whose duty it was to remove it could not be found. Charles II of England had scorned ponderous European monarchs, who could 'do nothing but under some ridiculous form or other, and would not piss but another must hold the chamber pot'. But George II's court slavishly adhered to convention. The King, who had no intellectual interests save the familiar ones of his caste, uniforms and genealogies (and, to be fair to him, music), was made uneasy, often to the point of hysteria, unless engaged in a strict and unvarying routine. Lord Hervey gave a vivid description of the tedium of life at Hampton Court:

> No mill-horse ever went in a more constant track, or a more unchanging circle; so that by the assistance of an almanack for the day of the week, and a watch for the hour of the day, you may inform yourself fully, without any intelligence but your memory, of every transaction within the verge of the court. Walking, chaises, levees and audiences fill the morning. At night the king plays at commerce and backgammon, and the queen at quadrille, where the poor Lady Charlotte runs her usual nightly gauntlet, the queen pulling her hood, and the Princess Royal rapping her knuckles. The Duke of Grafton takes his nightly opiate of lottery, and sleeps as usual between the Princesses Amelia and Caroline. Lord Grantham strolls from one room to another (as Dryden said) and is forbid to speak; and stirs himself about as people stir a fire, not with any design but in hopes to make it burn brisker. At last the king gets up: the pool finishes; and everybody has their dismission. Their Majesties retire to Lady Charlotte and my Lord Lifford; my Lord Grantham to Lady Frances and Mr Clark: some to supper, some to bed; and thus the evening and the morning made the day.

The ornamental futility of the royal round gives some substance to the view, propounded by his son Frederick and the Leicester House opposition, that George II was 'a King in toils', a royal cipher, a monarch bound hand and foot by a gang of aristocrats. Actually George worked conscientiously, went into paroxysms of fury when he was thwarted, cursed 'that damned House of Commons', and sometimes succeeded in having his way with both measures and men. But at least three times he was publicly defeated over the constitution of a ministry. As that egregious time-server Bubb Dodington wrote, 'the King would sputter and make a bustle, but when [ministers] told him it must be done from necessity of his service, he must do it'. It seemed to many, including the future George III, that a new king must, in Dodington's words, 'rescue monarchy from the inveterate usurpation of oligarchy', must eradicate the corrupt factions which dominated Westminster, and must purify the entire political system. In 1760 the King's twenty-three-year-old grandson got his chance. On 25 October George II rose, as usual, at six in the morning, took his invariable cup of chocolate, and retired, as he regularly did, to his privy. A few moments later his German valet, hearing, as Horace Walpole put it, 'a noise louder than the royal wind', ran in and found the King lying on the floor, dead. Walpole's callous comment, incidentally, was not untypical of an age when monarchs were treated with a crude ribaldry which makes the television series *Spitting Image* look refined. Queen Caroline, for example, had faced death with remarkable courage; she begged the doctor to pause till she could stop laughing when his wig caught fire as he was bending over her to operate. Yet Pope's comment on her ruptured womb was vicious:

> Here lies, wrapt in forty thousand towels,
> The only proof that Caroline had bowels.

King George III was that rarity, a good king. This is not to say that kings are naturally bad. It is simply to suggest that vice stems as much from opportunity as from inclination and that, of all people, monarchs have traditionally had the most scope to practise it. (When Louis XV of France was advised by his doctors not to take aphrodisiacs he denied doing so, only to be told that the greatest aphrodisiac of all was variety.) George was brought up by his mother and his tutor, Lord Bute, to prize virtue. His early letters are so full of conscientious tributes to elevated principles that they would have done credit to a prim Victorian lady. George was a simple young man, hard-working, high-minded and genuinely religious. He was patriotic, glorying in the name of Britain and having no time for 'that horrid Electorate which has always liv'd upon the very vitals of this poor country'. In his personal habits he was orderly, frugal, charitable and decorous. Unlike his two predecessors and his two successors, he kept no mistresses, remaining 'resolutely faithful to a hideous queen'. He was stubbornly determined that his subjects should be as upright as their sovereign. In 1758 he had promised to 'attempt with vigour to restore religion and virtue when I mount the throne'. And on mounting it, two years later, he proclaimed

his resolve to 'punish all manner of vice, profaneness and immorality'. The reign of rectitude was at hand.

George III was, then, in Mrs Thatcher's phrase, a 'conviction
politician'. (It must be said, though, that he would probably have
regarded the expression as a contradiction in terms: he despised
politics as a form of chicanery and was involved with it only
faute de mieux.) Holding his views with kingly self-confidence
and armed with an invincible sense of his own righteousness,
George was obstinate to the point of pig-headedness. His motto
might have been: 'I know I am doing my duty and therefore can
never wish to retract.' Being as obtuse as he was inflexible,
George never considered that the convictions of others might
have been as valid as his own. His intransigence, like that of
Charles I and James II, amounted almost to an assumption of
royal infallibility. Having 'great command of his passions', he
would, it was noted, 'seldom do wrong except when he mistakes
wrong for right'. There was the rub. George's political percep-
tions were as limited as his political principles were rigid. The
historian Richard Pares has described him as 'the spiritual ancestor of Colonel Blimp'. Blinkered, outspoken, dogmatic,
reactionary, he was the *ancien régime* in stars and garters. The
King did not understand the body politic any more than his
doctors understood the royal body but, like them, he had one
invariable remedy – a purge. Anyone who stood in his way must
surely be part of the corruption which he was trying to eliminate.
Unfortunately, there is much truth in Thackeray's ironical
comment with reference to George III: 'It is by persons believing
themselves in the right that nine-tenths of the tyranny of this
world has been perpetrated.' Or, to paraphrase a celebrated
Victorian observation: bad men are bad, do bad and go to the
bad, but it is amazing the harm which a really good man can do.

It used to be said that George precipitated the ministerial chaos
which followed his accession – there were six changes of
government in ten years – because he was attempting to restore
the arbitrary rule of the Stuarts. Encouraged by reading Boling-
broke's *Patriot King*, by his mother who allegedly urged him
to 'be a king', and by his tutor, George was supposed to have
tried to subvert the constitution. This was not the case, though
there is perhaps more in the old myth than has sometimes been
admitted. It is true, for example, that Frederick, Prince of Wales,

in his political testament, had urged his son to 'retrieve the glory of the Throne'. But George interpreted this as encouragement to make the system work better, to destroy faction and to play his part in governing honestly in the interests of the entire nation. Because the British constitution is unwritten there can always be arguments about the propriety of this policy, for one precedent can be cited against another. In assuming more authority than the first two Hanoverians, in refusing to be governed by his ministers as they had been, George III was certainly doing nothing illegal. However, as Edmund Burke said, 'the discretionary powers of the Crown when abused can, without violating the letter of any law, operate against the spirit of the whole constitution.' Furthermore, although the King was entitled to appoint and dismiss ministers, he was foolish to do so without being guided by the will of parliament. As the Whig politician Henry Fox observed, 'If a King of England employs those people that the nation have a good opinion of, he will make a great figure; but if he chooses them through personal favour, it will never do and he will be unhappy.'

The charge against George III, then, is not that he acted unconstitutionally but that he acted ineptly. The replacement of the most famous and successful statesman of the age, William Pitt the Elder, by George's own tutor, Lord Bute, was his first and worst mistake. Bute, self-righteous and self-serving, was no politician. In fact, his sole qualification for office appeared to be his legs, the shapeliest at court – he was rumoured to be the lover of the King's mother. A more sinister count against him was his Scottishness. English xenophobia towards poor and parasitic north Britons was rampant. Pitt's reckless partisan, John Wilkes, went so far as to accuse the Caledonian 'favourite' of being responsible for the demise of 'Mr John Bull, a very worthy plain honest old gentleman of Saxon descent. He was choked by inadvertently swallowing a thistle which he had placed by way of ornament on top of his salad.' Bute could not stand his unpopularity – jackboots (a pun on his name) were burnt in the streets. So in 1763, despite royal pleas to stay, he went. For a couple of years he still exercised some secret influence on the King, a state of affairs which critics railed against into the 1770s. Doubtless Bute was chiefly hated because he was, in every sense, an outsider. But he did represent a principle inimical to the recognized interests of the nation: in office he was sustained solely by royal favour; out of office he was the 'minister behind the curtain'. He thus exercised power without responsibility – in Kipling's classic phrase, 'the prerogative of the harlot throughout the ages'.

In the priggish style with which George invariably addressed his tutor, he wrote: 'Though young I see but too much there are few, very few honest men in this world; as my Dear Friend has quitted Ministry I don't expect to meet with it there again; I shall therefore support those who will act for me and without regret change my tools whenever they act contrary to my service.' The King was as good as his word. Throughout the 1760s ministers followed one another in quick succession – Grenville, Rockingham, Chatham, Grafton – each proving unsatisfactory for one reason or another. That acidulous pamphleteer Junius commented pertinently that the idea 'of distributing the offices of state by rotation was gracious and benevolent in the extreme, though it has not produced the many salutary effects which were intended by it'. Equally pertinent was Edmund Burke's verdict that the increase in royal power stemmed from the failure of politicians to unite. There was no reversionary interest to amalgamate the opposition. Instead of strong, organized parties at Westminster, there was 'a tessellated pavement without cement'. Only a combination of politicians could 'teach the Court that it is in the interest of a prince to have but one administration, and that one composed of those who recommend themselves to their sovereign through the opinion of their country not through the obsequiousness of a favourite'.

In the event it was the King who managed to construct a stable ministry from the competing political groups. In 1770 he found in Lord North a competent and pliable chief minister who would do his bidding yet could handle the House of Commons. North made a convincing show in debate and proved even more convincing when pulling wires behind the scenes. Having the King's confidence, North could exploit the whole field of royal patronage. He kept his supporters happy with a plethora of offices, emoluments, sinecures and pensions. Burke was soon complaining that 'The power of the Crown, almost dead and rotten as Prerogative, has grown up anew, with much more strength, and far less odium, under the name of Influence.' However,

George's very success carried within it the seeds of failure. The fact that he was so clearly identified with North meant that when his government was defeated and discredited, the Crown was tarnished. One of the most humiliating rebuffs in royal history occurred in 1780 when all North's arts of management failed to secure the rejection of Dunning's famous Commons motion 'That the influence of the Crown has increased, is increasing, and ought to be diminished.'

This vote of censure stemmed largely from the fact that George III was heavily implicated in the disastrous policy of trying to coerce the American colonies. The King was not merely a dyed-in-the-wool conservative, he was the proponent of paternalistic ideas which were obsolete even in his own day. He regarded himself as the father of his people, a patriarch whose duty it was to chastise them if necessary. He equated American resistance to political authoritarianism and economic exploitation by the mother country with childish rebellion. It was on a par with the insubordinate radical stirrings of 'the middling and lesser sort of people' at home. Like most monarchs, George cherished the principle of hierarchy, with himself conveniently placed at the top. The duty of Americans, honorary members of the British lower orders, was to obey their superiors. Talk of liberty or equality or democracy, let alone of republicanism, smacked of sedition. When talk led to action the King had only one policy – force. 'The colonies must either submit or triumph,' he said. If 'any one branch of the Empire is allowed to cast off its dependency,' he maintained, 'the others will infallibly follow.'

North had sought conciliation but George insisted on confrontation. The result was not just defeat in the New World but the rise of a hostile coalition in the Old. Even after the British surrender at Yorktown the King was determined to continue. He would not listen to a remonstrance from the City of London which succinctly announced the result of the war: 'Your armies are captured. The wonted superiority of your navies is annihilated. Your dominions are lost.' But this conclusion was echoed in the Commons, where a tearful and demoralized North could barely hold his own. Charles James Fox declared that it was only 'the influence of the Crown in the two Houses of Parliament that enabled his Majesty's ministers to persevere against the voice of reason, the voice of truth, the voice of the people'.

George could not ignore *Fox Populi*, as the dissolute young politician liked to be called. Driven to the wall, the King spoke of abdication and summoned the royal yacht to take him back to Hanover.

Of course, it was not the monarch but the minister who had to go. George was for a time obliged to accept some unpalatable measures (such as modest reforms in the patronage system) and some even more unpalatable men (such as Fox, who tried to establish the Commons as the real agent of government). But by the end of 1783 he had found a satisfactory new chief minister, the young William Pitt. He protected his master from the royal *bête noire*, Fox, whose political sins were compounded in George III's eyes by his having supposedly corrupted the young Prince of Wales – nothing if not an eager pupil. And the King sustained Pitt against hostile majorities in the Commons until he could hold a general election. This he duly won, helped by the copious exercise of royal patronage – as Horace Walpole remarked: 'They are crying peerages about the streets in barrows.' The snag was that the sovereign and his prime servant became one another's prisoners. But George's freedom of manoeuvre was probably more restricted by his dependence on Pitt than vice versa. During Pitt's eighteen-year ministry there was a gradual decline in royal power. It was assisted by the King's increasing preference for living the life of a country gentleman at Windsor. Pitt conducted much of the royal business and he took complete control when, in 1788, the King succumbed to his first serious bout of madness.

Retrospective diagnoses are problematic but it seems that George was the victim of a rare disease called porphyria. The main evidence for this is that his urine (though not his blood) turned blue. Whatever the physical basis of his illness, however, contemporaries considered him insane and his behaviour was undoubtedly lunatic. Admittedly, even under normal circumstances the King's manner was odd. His mode of discourse, for example, consisted of incessant questions; but he did not listen to the answers, punctuating them instead by laughter, interruptions and staccato exclamations of 'What! What! What!' He often talked so fast that his speech became a gabble. His eyes goggling, his head nodding, his shoulders rolling and his thick lips slavering, the King progressed round the room repeating to one person what he had just been told by another. No wonder that Fanny Burney was frightened by her sovereign. Close observers noted that George's incoherence was degenerating into delirium. At different times he became melancholy, agitated, deluded, raving, indecent, violent. He talked for as much as nineteen hours at a stretch, spied Hanover through a telescope, wrote notes to Don Quixote, and allegedly shook hands with an oak tree in Windsor Park, mistaking it for the king of Prussia. The barbarous medical remedies of the day were duly applied: purging, bleeding, cupping (to draw out, through blisters, his 'gout in the head') and forcible restraint. There was some public sympathy for the 'good old king'. But the opposition prints were merciless:

> If blisters to the head applied
> Some little sense bestow,
> What pity 'tis they were not tried
> Some twenty years ago.

Still, even the lampoonists were not as callous as the King's own children: two of them, the Prince of Wales and the Duke of York, were said to have made a drunken show of mimicking their father's frenzied gestures and actions. Partly because the Prince was so unpopular, partly because the opposition was so rabid for office (it struck one observer as lamentable that the King was confined to a straitjacket while Edmund Burke was permitted to remain at large), Pitt managed to stave off a regency. And in 1789 the King gradually returned to his senses, his recuperation assisted by a spell at the seaside. When George bathed he was followed into the waves by a machine full of fiddlers playing 'God Save the King'. There was much jubilation at the royal recovery. But it was probably also a public expression of relief at having escaped, at least for a time, the rule of the Prince of Wales. Had that incarnation of dandified debauchery taken over his father's duties at a time when the whole of Europe was thrown into ferment by the French Revolution, the English monarchy might not have survived.

In fact, as the *ancien régime* began to collapse in France, patriotic satisfaction over George III's restoration to health was rivalled by a growth of reforming and republican sentiment in England. Britons of all political persuasions hailed the fall of the

Bastille as the blissful dawn of an age of liberty. Radicals were not content with the destruction of symbols of tyranny across the Channel. They saw kingdoms everywhere 'starting from sleep, breaking their fetters and claiming justice from their oppressors'. They aimed to revolutionize the corrupt and inequitable system of government at home and get rid of the 'wretched farce of royalty'. Tom Paine was their most eloquent champion. In pithy phrases he lambasted the prime apologist for conservatism, Edmund Burke, who had waxed sentimental about the beauty of Queen Marie Antoinette while ignoring the sufferings of the French people: 'Mr Burke pities the plumage but forgets the dying bird.' Paine argued that hereditary monarchs were not only inherently tyrannical, they were inherently absurd – as absurd as hereditary judges, or mathematicians, or poets. Selection by birth, instead of election on the basis of character and achievement, created sovereigns according to the whim of nature. One might be a Solomon, another a despot, another a traitor, another an idiot, another a rake, yet others 'collections of all the vices'. Monarchy was a 'puppet-show', Paine declared, 'the popery of government, a thing kept up to amuse the ignorant and quiet them into taxes'. It diminished the masses, who became an audience 'thrown into the background of the human picture'. It degraded the aristocratic supporting cast, whose fondness for titles 'marks a sort of foppery in the human character'. It turned the royal principals into master-fraudsters whose business was to impose upon the credulous. It made government a matter of mummery and artifice, whereas in a republic 'there is no place for mystery'. 'What is called the splendour of the throne,' Paine concluded, 'is no other than the corruption of the state.'

Paine's book, *The Rights of Man*, became a bestseller. Mindful of the part which Paine's pamphlet *Common Sense* had played in fostering the American Revolution, George III instituted proceedings against him and he was forced to flee the country. Meanwhile the French Revolution entered a more extreme phase, which provoked a conservative reaction in England. It was all too easy to equate reformers and republicans at home with Jacobins and regicides abroad. Some radicals gave countenance to such suspicions: Orator Thelwell, for example, blew the head off a pot of foaming porter and exclaimed: 'This is the way I would serve all kings.' As early as 1791 a 'Church and King' mob in Birmingham destroyed the houses of dissenters, including the famous laboratory of the Unitarian minister Dr Joseph Priestley. Doubtless remembering that his coronation oath obliged him to uphold the law, the King deplored the means, though he could not 'but feel better pleased that Priestley is the sufferer for the doctrines he and his party have instilled'. Soon the government was proceeding with its own policy of repression. It clamped down on reforming societies, prosecuted their leaders (unsuccessfully) for treason, suspended the Habeas Corpus Act, imposed censorship, restricted the holding of meetings, banned trade unions and so on. Vestiges of anti-monarchical feeling were occasionally made manifest. In 1795 a hungry mob threw stones and mud at George III's state coach, shouting: 'No War, No Pitt, No King!' In 1798 Charles James Fox proposed a toast to 'Our Sovereign's health – the Majesty of the People!' But it became extremely dangerous to hold radical opinions. A Scottish lawyer was sentenced to fourteen years' transportation for re-commending that people should read *The Rights of Man*. That book, in reality an exposition of ideas which had been gaining ground during the Enlightenment, became regarded in England as the gospel of sedition. As a young don at Oxford, John Henry Newman kept his copy locked in a desk drawer so that it would not contaminate undergraduate minds.

In George's eyes all opposition was factious, and he was the last man in the world to be swayed by it. Beset by a perilous war with France, with his subjects in distress, his allies in disarray and his navy mutinous, the King refused a compromise which might have brought tranquillity to the most troubled of his dominions – Ireland. Pitt hoped to prevent a repetition of the 1798 uprising by uniting that island to the rest of Britain and giving Roman Catholics the right to sit in parliament. The King sabotaged this dual policy, accepting the union but rejecting Catholic emancipation. He declared that it was inconsistent with his coronation oath. Caught between entrenched royal bigotry and incipient royal insanity, Pitt resigned. His successor, Henry Addington, rivals Lord Goderich and Lord Home for the dis-tinction of being the most insignificant premier in British history. George suffered two more serious bouts of madness, in 1801 and 1804. During the second one he had to be restrained from riding his horse into Weymouth church, and the Queen finally locked her door against him. Despite his evident incapacity George prevented Pitt from forming a broad-bottomed, national ministry in 1804 – he insisted on Fox's exclusion. And in 1807 the King took what was perhaps the most high-handed action of his reign. Agitated by the continuing prospect of some form of Catholic emancipation, he rid himself of the 'Ministry of All the Talents' and appointed an administration headed by Lord Portland. The new government duly won a general election, assisted by what George had once called the 'gold pills' of royal patronage and by the enlightened slogan, 'No Popery'. So, in the midst of the Napoleonic War, the fate of the British nation was determined by 'an old, mad, blind, despised and dying king'.

Actually, George lived until 1820. But, as Shelley's line indicates, the monarch's last decade was spent in a tragic, twilight world of dementia and senility. By the end of 1809, in the disrespectful words of George Canning, 'poor old Knobbs' was 'just as mad as ever he was in his life', and a Regency soon had to be established. The King did experience some lucid intervals, when he was pathetically aware of his own state. He once selected a complete concert programme of music concerned with madness and blindness. And he often spoke of himself as 'the late King'. However, natural human sympathy for the mad monarch should not be allowed to obscure his faults. Nor should the fact that his blackguard sons ('Princes, the dregs of their dull race, who flow/Through public scorn, mud from a muddy spring') were an even more glaring advertisement for republicanism than he was. Nor should the 'trumpery panegyrists' who praised George after his demise be permitted to distort the true picture. For, as Thackeray wrote,

> the part which pulpits play in the deaths of kings is the most ghastly of all ceremonial: the lying eulogies, the blinking of disagreeable truths, the sickening flatteries, the simulated grief, the falsehood and sycophancies – all uttered in the name of Heaven in our state churches: these monstrous threnodies have been sung from time immemorial over kings and queens, good, bad, wicked, licentious.

Even George's moral virtues cannot be allowed to eclipse his political vices. For it was his determination to do right which so often led him to persevere with such disastrously wrong policies.

The fact is, though, that George's fundamental defect was an unconquerable obscurantism. He himself owned that he hated novelties and was 'a great enemy of innovations'. He attached the utmost importance to ancient forms of protocol and observed 'the nicest distinctions of [social] inequality'. He bitterly opposed reform. He was contemptuous of the liberty of the subject and the rights of electors. He tried to prevent the reporting of parliamentary debates. He provoked and prolonged the American conflict. He supported the slave trade. He refused to conciliate the Irish. In the age of the French Revolution he sought to revive the obsolescent prerogatives of the English Crown. 'In a word,' concludes the historian Lecky, 'there is scarcely a field of politics in which the hand of the King may not be traced – sometimes in postponing inevitable measures of justice and reform, sometimes in sowing the seeds of enduring evil.' Narrow-minded, unimaginative, punctilious, indissolubly wedded to tradition, George was anachronism writ large. He was, in Walter Bagehot's phrase, a 'consecrated obstruction'. But his fault lay, surely, more in his position than in his personality. Immured in the clotted formality of court, George suffered from that ossification of the intellect to which princes are congenitally prone. A remote, feudal figure, surrounded by the genuflexions of toadies and the incense of flatterers, the King could have little notion of the real world, let alone of adapting himself to it. There was more than a grain of truth in the bitter remark which Junius addressed to his sovereign: 'It is the misfortune of your life . . . that you should never have been acquainted with the language of truth, until you heard it in the complaints of your people.'

Three

Prinny and Billy

George the First was always reckon'd
Vile – but viler George the Second;
And what mortal ever heard
Any good of George the Third?
When from earth the Fourth descended,
God be praised, the Georges ended.

Landor wrote too soon, of course. But he summed up the feelings of many of his countrymen, who then considered that the fourth King George was the worst of the breed. In fact, 'the First Gentleman of Europe' had his defenders. That staunch old Tory, Sir Walter Scott, his mind impregnated with notions of medieval chivalry, doted on the Prince Regent. Others praised his affectionate disposition, his transcendent charm and his great powers of mimicry – Beau Brummel said that he 'would have been the best comic actor in Europe'. Still others discovered in him an elegance of manner and a refinement of taste all too rare in his kind. The Prince larded his speech with classical quotations, and courtiers, aghast at his erudition, failed to notice that he had only two tags at his command, one from Homer and one from Virgil. The Prince was supposed to associate on equal terms with the great figures of his day, and appeared to encourage schemes for the promotion of science, literature and the arts. It took a writer like Thackeray, whose vision was unclouded by deference and who understood the follies of Vanity Fair better than any man, to expose the absurdity of such claims.

Fiddlesticks! French ballet-dancers, French cooks, horse-jockeys, buffoons, procurers, tailors, boxers, fencing-masters, china, jewel and gimcrack merchants – these were his real companions. At first he made pretence of having Burke, Pitt and Sheridan for his friends. But how could such men be serious before such an empty scapegrace as this lad? Fox might talk dice with him, and Sheridan wine; but what else had these men of genius in common with their tawdry young host of Carlton House? That fribble the leader of such men as Fox and Burke! That man's opinions about the constitution, the India Bill, justice to Catholics – about any question graver than the button for a waistcoat or the sauce for a partridge – worth anything!

No doubt the royal wastrel's character was largely attributable to his upbringing. Like many fathers, King George III had resented his son's growing maturity and he kept him in girls' frocks long after his contemporaries were dressing as boys. Even as an adult, when he gave more than ample proof of his hetero-sexual bent, there remained something epicene about the Prince. The Duchess of Devonshire thought that he looked 'like a woman in men's clothes'. Certainly he did not receive the rigorous masculine education of the day. True, he was beaten for moral faults such as lying. But the Prince's governor was said to have been 'perfectly satisfied that he had done his duty as long as he was unremitting in his exhortations to his royal pupil to turn out his toes'. The Prince's boldest initiative seems to have been playing more or less cruel practical jokes on his inferiors, an inveterate royal vice. The King did little but rail against the idle and trivial life his eldest son was leading as he grew into manhood. And though his younger siblings were fond of him, the respect in which the Prince of Wales was held by senior members of the royal family can be gauged by his uncle the Duke of Cumberland's nickname for him – a crude allusion to his title – Taffy.

Reacting against his father's abstemiousness, the young George soon learnt to wallow in extravagance. He placed an inordinate value on dress. Having nothing better to do, he spent endless time and money on clothes, constantly closeting himself with shoemakers and tailors, a dummy in every sense, for their wares. He loved to appear, exquisite in

a bottle-green and claret-coloured striped silk coat and breeches, and silver tissue waistcoat, very richly embroidered in silver . . . and coloured silks in curious devices and bouquets of flowers. The coat and waistcoat embroidered down the seams and spangled all over the body. The coat and cuffs the same as the waistcoat. The breeches were likewise covered in spangles. Diamond buttons to the coat, waistcoat and breeches, which with his brilliant diamond epaulette, and sword, made the whole dress form a most magnificent appearance.

The Prince took fashion seriously. He introduced high collars (perhaps to hide swollen glands in his throat). He invented a new shoe-buckle. He blubbered when that other arbiter of the *comme il faut*, Beau Brummel, disdained the cut of his coat. He bought clothes in bulk, ordering waistcoats by the dozen, boots by the score and gloves by the gross. After his death his wardrobes were found to be crammed with enough finery to equip a legion of fops. 'Every faculty of his soul, spirit, purse, and person' had been, in Carlyle's disapproving opinion, 'heroically consecrated to this one object, the wearing of clothes wisely and well'. Like all dandies, the Prince of Wales had made a 'willing sacrifice of the Immortal to the Perishable'.

The truth was that the Prince had no occupation and no inclination to devote himself to anything but trifles. But no trifles were more costly than his trifles. It was said that what the nation was expected to pay for his upkeep would itself have supported an army of five thousand men. He spent money, one MP complained, with 'that squanderous and lavish profusion, which . . . resembled more the pomp and magnificence of a Persian satrap, seated in the splendour of Oriental state, than the sober dignity of a British Prince'. Gambling, guzzling, drinking, womanizing, building, decorating and furnishing swelled his debts to astronomical proportions. By 1795 they amounted to six hundred thousand pounds – many millions at today's values and then as much as four per cent of the national budget. At a time when war and industrial revolution were bringing desperate hardship to so many of his compatriots, the Prince risked more money on the turn of a card at Brooks', or the result of a race at Newmarket, than artisan families could earn in a lifetime of drudgery. He adorned Clarence House so lavishly that its ornate opulence was condemned as vulgar. His gaudy seaside folly, the Brighton Pavilion, was decorated in the modish Chinese taste because 'there was such a cry against French things, etc. that he was afraid of his furniture being accused of Jacobinism'. In fact he probably did more to promote domestic radicalism than any man in England. As a loyalist paper, the *True Briton*, complained in 1796: 'We have long looked upon his conduct as favouring the cause of Jacobinism and democracy in this country more than all the speeches of Horne Tooke, or all the labours of the Corresponding Society.' Some conservatives did argue that 'in these times of democratic frenzy it was necessary to support the splendour of Courts and Princes'. But George III himself disagreed and few could be found to defend his most prodigal son.

The Prince barely tried to disguise the fact that profligacy was the business and pleasure of his life. He was 'a man visibly used up by dissipation'. According to the Grand Duchess of Oldenburg: 'His much boasted affability is the most licentious, I may even say obscene, strain I have ever listened to.' The Duke of Wellington, too, was much less struck by the Prince's graceful airs and his lavish generosity than by his reckless impropriety: 'By God, you never saw such a fellow in your life as he is . . . he speaks and swears so like old Falstaff, that damn me if I was not ashamed to walk into a room with him.' Respectable women were ashamed to stay in a room with him. Declaring (like many others) that 'I really believe his father's malady extends to him, only takes another turn,' Lady Blessington, who was a grandmother well advanced in years, described the Prince's attempt to seduce her. He 'threw himself on his knees, and clasping me round, kissed my neck before I was aware of what he was doing. I screamed with vexation and fright: he continued, sometimes struggling with me, sometimes sobbing and crying . . . that immense, grotesque figure flouncing half on the couch, half on the ground.' Lady Blessington found his method of wooing as much comical as distasteful, and she was especially struck by the absurdity of his trying to simulate sickness in order to arouse her pity.

This was a technique which the Prince employed during his most celebrated infatuation, with Mrs Fitzherbert, when he actually went so far as to stab himself with a pen-knife. But despite this and other frantic importunities, she remained sadly unaccommodating. In fact, she refused to gratify his passion unless he married her. This he was strictly prohibited from doing, first by the Act of Settlement (1701), which forbade English monarchs to wed Roman Catholics, and secondly by the Royal Marriages Act (1772), which prevented any member of the royal family from marrying without the sovereign's consent.

So the Prince kept his nuptials secret, mendaciously assuring his friend Fox that they had never taken place so that the Whig chief could issue an authoritative denial in parliament. Such was the Prince's devotion to Mrs Fitzherbert that it actually seemed as if she might reform him. For a while his whoring and swearing and carousing ceased. But, as Sheridan said, the Prince of Wales was 'too much every lady's man to be the man of any lady'. Nor could George keep away from his drunken cronies – they frightened his new wife so much that she hid from them under a sofa. She must have been even more terrified when her husband rode his horse up the staircase of her house and left it in the garret – two blacksmiths were required to bring the animal down.

The Prince's style of life naturally increased his indebtedness, and by 1794 he faced a crisis. He owed so much that he was in danger of being refused fresh credit. Royalty's traditional resort in this situation was to obtain a new establishment from parliament by getting married. This the Prince did, ignoring his alliance with Mrs Fitzherbert which, whatever its legal status, was certainly valid in the eyes of the Church.

The royal bigamy was embarrassing enough, but it could be plausibly denied and effectively concealed. What soon became all too apparent, however, was that his new wife, Caroline of Brunswick, chosen sight unseen because she was almost the only possible Protestant Princess, was repulsive to him. She was, so to speak, heaven's revenge on the Prince. For she was as dissolute as he was – cartoonists delighted to represent them as equals in licentiousness, the pot and the kettle, Nero and Octavia. Of course, the Princess's conduct then seemed more shocking because the sexual double standard was generally accepted.* But what appalled the Prince himself was his consort's evident coarseness. He was a refined rake. She was a vulgar trollop. He was fastidious, whereas her character was said to be 'exceedingly loose' even by the standards of Brunswick, 'where they were not at that period very nice about female delicacy'. Lord Malmesbury, who brought her over to England, had to admonish her not only about the gross impropriety of her language but also about the unclean smell of her underclothes. When the Prince first met her he tottered backwards, gasping to Malmesbury: 'Harris, I am not well. Pray get me a glass of brandy.'

* See p. 181.

The Prince drank several glasses on his wedding day and, according to the Princess, he spent their wedding night in the fireplace, where he had fallen in a state of insensibility. In the morning, however, he recovered sufficiently to give her proof of his virility (for the only time, it seems) if not of his affection. Nine months later, in January 1796, she bore a daughter, Princess Charlotte (who died in 1817). Well before his official wife was brought to bed the Prince regarded her as a 'fiend'. He declared that he 'would rather see toads and vipers crawling over my victuals than sit at the same table with her'. For her part, the Princess despised him as an effeminate popinjay. '[I] ought to be the man and *he* the woman to wear the petticoats. . . . He understands how a shoe should be made or a coat cut, or a dinner dressed, and would make an excellent tailor, or shoemaker, or hairdresser, but nothing else.' Soon after the birth of their only child they agreed to separate.

Over the next few years Caroline's conduct was so rash and indiscreet that contemporaries thought she must be insane. Her house was 'all glitter and glare and trick . . . tinsel and trumpery . . . altogether like a bad dream', and she went in for 'low nonsense and sometimes even gross ribaldry'. Lady Hester Stanhope thought the Princess 'a downright whore . . . she danced about exposing herself like an opera girl'. There were strong rumours that she had given birth to at least one child. This, of course, had serious dynastic implications. As Lord Thurlow told the Prince, 'Sir, if you were a common man, she might sleep with the Devil; I should say let her alone and hold your tongue. But the Prince of Wales has no right to risk his daughter's crown and his brother's claims.' So in 1806 a parliamentary Commission of Enquiry was set up to conduct what became known as 'the Delicate Investigation'. It heard many allegations of improper conduct, including a footman's testimony that the Princess was 'very fond of fucking'. But it uncovered no actual proof of adultery. Even so George III found it necessary to reprimand the Princess and exclude her from court. It was an indication of the Prince's astonishing unpopularity that, as a result of this apparent persecution, his sluttish wife should have become a royal heroine while he himself, for once relatively innocent, was reviled.

Any stick was good enough to beat the Prince with, the people evidently thought. For he and his brothers were lumped together in the public estimation as, to quote the Duke of Wellington's celebrated comment, 'the damnedest millstone about the necks of any government that can be imagined'. Wellington went on to say that the royal dukes 'have insulted – *personally* insulted – two thirds of the gentlemen of England'. They had scandalized everyone else by yielding, in Philip Ziegler's phrase, 'a crop of vices to fill every circle in Dante's Inferno'. The Duke of York⋆ had to resign from the army in disgrace when it was revealed that officers had paid bribes to his mistress, of which he had perhaps taken a share, to obtain promotions. The Duke of Kent was forced to retire from his governorship of Gibraltar when his martinet methods provoked the garrison to mutiny. The Duke of Cumberland is the best remembered of Queen Victoria's 'wicked uncles'. Indeed, with his horribly scarred face (he lost an eye at the battle of Tournai) and his viciously reactionary opinions, he seemed to epitomize the breed. Cumberland was rumoured not only to have had an incestuous affair with his sister, but to have cut his valet's throat in order to prevent his blackmailing him about their homosexual relationship. In fact, the valet may have tried to murder Cumberland. But the Duke's evil reputation was so widely established that the Duchess of Kent slept in the same room as her daughter, Princess Victoria, to stop Cumberland murdering her and stealing the throne.

Damned by his association with such brothers, the Prince of Wales scaled new heights of unpopularity when he became Regent in 1811. Instead of bringing the Whig friends of his opposition days into power, the Prince embraced his old enemies, the Tories. The Whigs were too inclined to prate about the Glorious Revolution and to oppose Crown influence, and the Regent was only prepared to offer them places in a coalition government, which they rejected. The Tories were traditionally the royalist party. In 1804, for example, Lord Chancellor Eldon (a man so reactionary that he wore his wig in bed even though it gave him a headache to do so) explained to parliament why he, a

---

⋆ Also bearing the title of Bishop of Osnaburgh, he it was whom loyal Americans had considered making their king after the War of Independence, though his real claim to fame lies in his having marched his ten thousand men to the top of the hill and marched them down again – a prototypical royal military achievement.

member of Addington's government, had used his influence to get
Addington turned out of office: 'To do my duty to His Majesty
is to do my duty to the country.' The Tories accepted, in fact, a
kind of diluted version of the divine right of kings. Being now a
quasi-king, the Regent found that this suited him very well. Certainly he needed all the support he could get. For as the Napoleonic Wars reached their climax and economic hardship became
even more widespread, royal excesses became less defensible. Of
the junket to celebrate the inauguration of the Regency the poet
Shelley wrote sourly: 'It is said that this entertainment will cost
£120,000. Nor will it be the last bauble which the nation must
buy to amuse this overgrown bantling of Regency.' The Prince
was now often hissed in the street. In April 1812 even a smart
Pall Mall crowd greeted him in 'dead silence', without 'one single
token of applause'.

Of course, flatterers were also thick upon the ground and the
Regent liked to wallow in their attentions. This seventeen-stone
sybarite, his face waxy from greasepaint and unguents, his cheeks
covered in thick brown whiskers, some of them artificial, his
belly stuffed into well-corseted pantaloons, was particularly fond
of being complimented on the attractions of his person. Reacting
against popular abuse and the contempt of the poets – Charles
Lamb called him 'the Prince of Whales', Byron a 'double tyrant'
and Coleridge 'a blackguard king' – the Tory *Morning Post* duly
obliged. 'You are the *glory of the People* – you are the *Maecenas*
of the Age – wherever you appear you *conquer all hearts*, wipe
away tears, excite *desire and love* and win *beauty* towards you –
you breathe *eloquence*, you inspire the Graces – you are an *Adonis*
in loveliness.' This grotesque adulation was duly punctured by
Leigh Hunt who, in *The Examiner*, described the Adonis as 'a
corpulent gentleman of fifty . . . a violator of his word, a libertine
over head and ears in debt and disgrace, the companion of de-
mireps, a man who has just closed half a century without one
single claim on the gratitude of his country or the respect of
posterity'. Perhaps because this slap was so stingingly accurate,
Leigh Hunt was prosecuted, fined and imprisoned for two years.
The punishment merely provoked a further outburst of invective.
Shelley described the Regent as a 'crowned coward and villain'
who demanded money 'for supplying the Augean stable . . . with
filth which no second Hercules could cleanse'.

After Napoleon's final defeat the London crowds cheered the Russian Tsar, not the English Regent. Postwar distress was so acute that the Prince's lavish victory celebrations were deemed singularly inappropriate. Prinny, as the Regent was called, increasingly tended to take personal credit for having won the war. Indeed, such were his powers of self-deception that he actually gave circumstantial accounts to his intimates of his own heroic exploits on the battlefield. Indulging in ever more reckless expenditure, the Regent basked in the victorious glow of Waterloo while his wretched subjects were sabred by dragoons at Peterloo. As one lady wrote in 1817: 'At present we have a starving population, an overwhelming debt, impoverished landholders, bankrupt and needy traders; but we have fine balls at the Regent's.'* The only person in Europe who was more extravagant than the Regent was Princess Caroline. Bribed by him to stay abroad at an annual rate of £50,000, she scandalized the continent by her escapades – a topless ball in Geneva, half-naked gambollings and indecent pictures in Italy, an illicit relationship with her chamberlain, Pergami, on the Mediterranean. Well before her return to England in 1820, when Prinny became King, Caroline was the subject of obscene jokes. It was said that in Algiers 'she was happy as the Dey was long'. And Henry Brougham, Caroline's advocate at her trial, reckoned that 'she was pure *in-no-sense*'.

The 'trial' was actually an inquiry into Caroline's conduct, provoked by the new King who was determined to divorce her. Against the advice of his government, who feared that the public washing of dirty linen, his as well as hers, would harm the nation's morals and might even provoke revolution, the King insisted on bringing in a Bill of Pains and Penalties. Its purpose was to deprive his wife of her title as Queen and dissolve her marriage to him. As the House of Lords proceeded to hear the evidence, ministers' worst forebodings seemed likely to be realized. Caroline was hailed raucously in the streets. Even the

---

* Royal biographers are generally so awe-struck by the mystique of monarchy that they engage in that curious species of deference, retrospective syco-phancy. Thus, in his anxiety to defend the Regent, Roger Fulford whimsically invokes today's 'economic wizards, who would hail the Prince as one who really understood finance because he appreciated that personal extravagance was the proper weapon with which to combat post-war depression'.

military appeared to be on her side – it was said that 'the extinguisher is taking fire'. The newspapers were in full cry, scurrility knew no bounds, and *The Times*, by taking Caroline's side, doubled its circulation. The cartoonists revelled in the salacious details. Cruikshank, who had been paid £100 not to portray the King in an 'immoral situation', represented him instead as a water scorpion, 'an offensive insect' living 'in stagnant waters', sallying forth 'in search of a companion of the other sex and soon [siring] an useless generation'. The Lords finally voted for the Pains and Penalties but by such a small majority that it was clear the bill would be defeated in the Commons, especially as Brougham was holding much of his evidence about the King's sexual exploits in reserve. So the government announced that the bill would be withdrawn. There were wild rejoicings throughout the country. London, from which Prinny had sensibly banished himself, was illuminated on three successive nights, the mob smashing darkened windows. There was much talk about the 'rebellious, licentious, disgraceful and revolutionary spirit' of the people. The fact that they were investing so much hysteria in a half-mad harridan indicates that the modern monarchy had reached its nadir.

Inevitably there was a reaction, partly caused by the coronation, which worked its usual magic. Admittedly it was anything but the immaculate ceremony of later days. The King, who was said to look 'more like an elephant than a man', seemed not so much impressive as laughable. Smothered in satin and diamonds, with a nine-yard train of crimson velvet ornamented with gold stars and a large black Spanish hat decorated with ostrich feathers and a heron's plume, he provoked Leigh Hunt's 'Coronation Soliloquy', a sweet revenge:

> Yes, my hat, Sirs,
> Think of that, Sirs,
> > Vast and plumed and Spain-like,
> See my big
> Grand robes; my wig,
> > Young, yet lion-mane like.
> Glory! Glory!
> I'm not hoary;
> > Age it can't come o'er me;

Mad caps, grave caps, gazing on the grand man,
All alike adore me.

The dignity of the occasion was not enhanced by the fact that
the King arrived late and behaved badly at the most solemn
moments, taking sal volatile and ogling the ladies. After the
service, peers and courtiers rushed to get out of the Abbey and
into Westminster Hall for the banquet, where prize-fighters were
employed to keep order.

Such a coronation, with its mixture of elevated ritual and low
farce, might well have stimulated the sort of sentiments expressed
by John Wade, the radical Utilitarian author of the *Black Book*
(1820): 'Pageantry and show, the parade of crowns and coronets,
of gold keys, sticks, white wands and black rods; of ermine and
lawn, maces and wigs; are ridiculous when men become enlightened, when they have learned that the real object of
government is to confer the greatest happiness on the people at
the least expense.' However, the fact is that, flawed though it
was, the coronation provoked a genuine outburst of loyalty to
the throne. Queen Caroline was jeered when she unsuccessfully
sought entry to the Abbey, whereas the King was everywhere
cheered. Sir Walter Scott, though not an unbiased witness, reflected the revulsion against that 'Bedlam Bitch of a Queen' and
recorded that 'never monarch received a more general welcome
from his subjects'.

Soon afterwards the Queen died, and the King largely
withdrew from the public gaze. He did, it is true, make several
tours of his dominions, visiting Ireland, Hanover and Scotland,
and behaving, in Lord Dudley's view, less like a monarch than
'like a popular candidate come down upon an electioneering trip'.
But George IV was increasingly sensitive to the ridicule which
his obese person attracted – his Stuart tartan kilt had provoked
particular ribaldry, especially when he bowed – and he preferred
to remain in seclusion. For the most part he stayed at Royal
Lodge, Windsor, where he indulged in a tearful romance with
his last mistress, the bored, bloated and rapacious Lady
Conyngham. Together they went for drives in his phaeton, fished
on the lake at Virginia Water to the strains of his band, and ate
enormous meals. He took snuff from her shoulder and continued
to lavish fantastic sums on clothes and building (including the

bogus Gothic embellishments to Windsor Castle). He also dabbled in religion. Much of his time he spent in bed, nursing his ailments and imbibing large doses of laudanum 'to calm the irritation which the use of spirits [huge potations of cherry brandy] occasions'. Sometimes he roused himself to take part in ceremonies – in 1822, for example, he opened parliament. But what with his 'indescribable oglings', his 'heavy robes, his crown slipping down on to his nose, his great train making his fat neck look still fatter – everything conspired', according to Princess Lieven, 'to heighten the comic effect'.

No sooner had Prinny embarked on the royal business as Regent than he discovered that 'playing at king is no sinecure'. In practice he treated it as such. He lazed, procrastinated and did not concern himself overmuch with politics at all. In 1827 he was far more interested in the arrival of a beautiful giraffe for his menagerie than whether Lord Goderich would become his new prime minister. Thus a significant amount of the power which his father had exercised slid imperceptibly away from the monarchy between 1810 and 1830. The sovereign could not be ignored, of course, especially as he was quite capable of laying down the law to members of his government. But, as Canning said, 'Ministers have to endure without answering back the epigrams by which a King seeks to avenge himself for his impotence.' George IV had to accept Canning, a liberal Tory whom he initially disliked, thus implicitly acknowledging the growing power and cohesion of Lord Liverpool's party. The King had to bow to his ministers' decision to recognize the new South American republics in 1824 (though he refused to read a statement to that effect, saying that he had lost his false teeth) and to introduce Roman Catholic emancipation in 1829. He did not submit gracefully. Wellington once expostulated that the King was 'the worst man he ever fell in with in his whole life, the most selfish, the most false, the most ill-natured, the most entirely without one redeeming quality'. But this was the opinion of a splenetic moment. Wellington's more considered judgement was that his sovereign was 'the most extraordinary compound of talent, wit, buffoonery, obstinacy and good feeling – in short a medley of the most opposite qualities, with a great preponderance of good – that I ever saw in any character in my life'.

This more flattering verdict, though not altogether unjust, was too complimentary in the end. For, like all prime ministers, Wellington took the task of protecting royal reputations seriously. When George IV, by then an enormous 'feather-bed' of a man, expired in 1830, Wellington was moved to discover a locket on a black ribbon round the dead King's neck containing a portrait set in diamonds of Mrs Fitzherbert. But he personally burned George's letters to her, saying that 'the publication would be mischievous, as the Prince by marrying a Catholic had by law forfeited the crown'. Wellington also warned Lady Conyngham, who departed from Windsor with a vast baggage-train full of booty, that she resembled Madame du Barry, whose extravagance had helped to precipitate the French Revolution.

An adamantine Tory like the Duke of Wellington might feel a twinge of sorrow at the King's demise, but Englishmen generally did not. All Windsor got drunk. London rejoiced. There were no signs of mourning anywhere. At the royal lying-in-state the crowds bandied 'rude and indecent jokes' around the two-ton coffin and behaved more as though they were 'hastening to a raree-show, than to a chamber of death'. Instead of attending chapel the Naval Knights of Windsor engaged in a public-house brawl, using their wooden legs as clubs. *The Times* appeared edged in black but its obituary was merciless. 'There never was an individual less regretted by his fellow-creatures than this deceased King. What eye has wept for him? What heart has heaved one sob of unmercenary sorrow? ... If George IV ever had a friend – a devoted friend in any rank of life – we protest that the name of him or her never reached us.' George's funeral was aptly described as a ceremony of 'tinsel magnificence'. Most of the congregation chattered and joked throughout, including the new King, William IV, who left before the service ended.

Echoing Charles II's comment on James II, George IV had expressed complete contempt for his brother William: 'Look at that idiot! They will remember me, if ever he is in my place.' His scorn was not unjustified. From his youth up William had been a boorish, bawdy and sometimes brutal character. He had early been sent into the navy, which only succeeded in coarsening his moral fibre. As a midshipman he was arrested in Gibraltar for engaging in a drunken brawl. And although he behaved with characteristic Hanoverian courage at the battle of Cape St Vincent and even won the admiration of Horatio Nelson – or so the ambitious little hero said – William proved completely unamenable to discipline. For a time he was exiled in Hanover, whence he wrote to the Prince of Wales: 'Oh, for England and the pretty girls of Westminster, at least to such as would not clap or pox me every time I fucked.' Eventually, thanks to his stubborn insubordination, William was beached for good. To his intense chagrin he was given no command during the Napoleonic Wars. And this despite his stoutly conservative views – he described the French Revolution as a 'pernicious and fallacious system of equality and universal liberty' which 'must be checked'.

William was made Duke of Clarence in 1789 and, to his horror, George III faced the prospect of having yet another son wasting his substance on riotous living. William was certainly an uncouth, ill-tempered and foul-mouthed fellow. He gloated over his father's madness. He delighted in crude practical jokes, though he was too dim to understand the humour of the clown Grimaldi who so convulsed the Prince of Wales that his stays hurt. William described those who wanted to abolish the slave trade, including Wilberforce, as 'fanatics or hypocrites'. He liked to get others drunk while remaining sober himself. He invited intimacy and then snubbed those who responded to his overtures. Yet, as a radical journalist wrote, the Duke of Clarence was 'not so deeply immersed in vicious destructive folly' as his brothers. Although William lived with, and to some extent off, a generous actress called Mrs Jordan, he remained faithful to her for twenty-five years and he doted on his ten ungrateful bastards. Of course, royal sexual indulgence is always supremely titillating and *The Times* allowed its imagination to run amok: Mrs Jordan 'had been admitted into the secrets of harems and palaces, seen their full exhibition of nude beauty and costly dissoluteness; the whole interior pomp of royal pleasure, the tribes of mutes and idiots, sultans and eunuchs, slavish passion and lordly debility'. William's far from exotic domestic idyll scarcely merited this. But his mode of dismissing Mrs Jordan, when his debts forced him to marry Princess Adelaide of Saxe-Meiningen, deserved the most outspoken censure. Without even a quarrel he abruptly abandoned his mistress, who died abroad soon afterwards in a state of destitution.

Everything in William's career suggested that he would be an overbearing king. He had, for example, quickly been forced to resign from his position of Lord High Admiral after an intolerable assertion of what should have been largely ornamental powers. But, initially at least, he was so delighted, at the age of sixty-four, to have become a figure of such consequence that he manifested an almost universal affability. For some time he had been gargling two gallons of water a day to ensure that no germ came between him and the throne. Now, Princess Lieven considered, 'the proverb "Happy as a King"' had been specially invented for him. The monarch's red-thatched face, 'like a frog's head carved on a coconut', beamed with pleasure at his subjects. Unlike his brother, William was not afraid to mingle with them in the street. He would nod and smile and doff his hat in acknowledgement of their bows, giving every indication that he was entirely relaxed. Some thought he was too relaxed, especially when he spat out of the window of his coach. Washington Irving remarked that 'His Majesty has an easy and natural way of wiping his nose with the back of his forefinger, which, I fancy, is a relic of his middy habits.'

William's oddities turned out to be a form of self-assertion. The *Morning Post* expostulated: 'Can anything be more indecent than the entry of a sovereign into his capital with one bastard riding before him, and another by the side of his carriage? The impudence and rapacity of the FitzJordans is unexampled even in the annals of Versailles and Madrid.' In contrast, again, to his brother, William loathed ostentatious ritual. Having, too, an understandable aversion to being kissed by bishops, he wanted to dispense altogether with the coronation. But he finally agreed to take part in a cheap, abbreviated ceremony which was known as the 'half-crownation'. The King's indiscretions increasingly became the subject of adverse comment. He publicly called the French 'the natural enemies of England'. He threatened to kick the president of the Royal Academy downstairs for exhibiting the portrait of a naval captain whom the King disliked. The diarist Charles Greville reckoned that the new monarch was 'a mountebank bidding fair to be a maniac'.

William's ministers quickly came to a similar conclusion and Wellington complained that he had to write long answers to the King's letters 'respectfully telling him what an old fool he was'. At first, though, it seemed as if the monarch was not going to exercise his vestigial powers to any great extent. He appeared willing to support his new Whig government and to respond positively to the growing movement for parliamentary reform. He seemed to take heed of the various factors which suggested that it would be wise to make concessions, notably the 1830 Revolution in France, the spectacle of seasick Bourbons who had learnt nothing and forgotten nothing arriving at English ports, and the Queen's fear that she would not do well in the role of Marie Antoinette. (The King ignored his wife's suggestion that he should run away to Hanover and form a coalition of European powers to impose autocracy on Britain.) Thus he refused to advocate 'the Rights of the Sovereign', something which so impressed his recent biographer, Philip Ziegler, that he described William as Britain's first truly constitutional monarch.

This is not a convincing characterization of a monarch who proved so prone to thwart, betray and dismiss his ministers. William soon turned against the Whigs' reform proposals. Extending the franchise, he concluded, was a step along the road to universal suffrage ('one of the wild projects which have sprung from revolutionary speculation') and even the secret ballot ('a practice which would ... abolish the influence of fear and shame'). This King, like all kings, was 'desirous of maintaining the established order of things'. So in 1832 he reneged on his promise to create more peers in order to get the Reform Bill through the House of Lords. He told the Whig leader, Lord Grey, that he principally looked to the upper house 'for the support of the Monarchy, and for the exertion of due vigour in resisting popular clamour' – a perennial royal opinion.

Fearful of the violent clamour which he himself had aroused, the King capitulated. He had, in fact, no choice, for after Grey's resignation Wellington had been unable to form a ministry. The Reform Act altered little, being, as Felix Holt said, 'nothing but swearing in special constables to keep the aristocrats safe in their monopoly'. But in 1832 the sovereign's last major prerogative, the right to choose his ministers, was restricted. For, as Sir Robert Peel said, 'How could he make a partial change in the Administration in times of public excitement with any prospect that the Ministers of his choice ... would be returned to Parliament?' The King was uncomfortable with an administration which looked to popular support rather than royal patronage. As

Brougham remarked, William was 'panting for the quiet of a Tory Ministry, the natural favourite of all kings'. He was also annoyed by the failure of the Whigs' lackadaisical new leader, Lord Melbourne, to coerce the unruly Irish. When the houses of parliament were burnt down in 1834, the King prodded the smouldering ruins with his stick, as though intent on completing the work of destruction. There was perhaps an element of symbolism, too, in his attempt to establish parliament in Buckingham Palace.

Certainly William thought that the Whigs were becoming too radical and in 1834, although they still had a majority in the Commons, he found an excuse to dismiss them. Peel's Tory administration was in a hopeless position and he could only justify it in terms of loyalty to royalty. 'I could not reconcile it to my feelings, or indeed to my sense of duty, to subject the King and the Monarchy to the humiliation, by my refusal of office, of inviting [back] his dismissed servants.' It was said that Peel had every virtue except resignation. But royal influence was now a shadow of its former self and, not being able to win a majority in the country or in the Commons, Peel did have to resign in 1835. There was some question of whether William might have to follow suit. He remarked: 'I feel my crown tottering on my head.' But Melbourne, who found being prime minister a 'damned bore', was no republican, though he resented the royal harangues to which he was exposed – 'a mass of muddle and impropriety' – and thought the King 'all but crazy'.

William himself was haunted by his father's madness and there were times when he seemed unable to control himself. Admittedly, he had his troubles. He was tormented by his ten implacable bastards. He was plagued by ill health. He found it difficult to pardon the Whigs for his humiliating defeat and sometimes threatened to have his ministers impeached. He was also infuriated by the Duchess of Kent who, as the mother of his heir presumptive, Princess Victoria, behaved in a singularly presumptuous fashion. At a large banquet which they all attended in 1836 the King spoke out with characteristic vehemence. He expressed the hope that his 'life may be spared for nine months longer' so that Victoria would be of age to inherit the throne without a regency, her mother being 'surrounded by evil advisers and . . . incompetent to act with propriety in the station in which she would be placed'.

William got his wish. Indeed, by ordering his doctors to 'try if you cannot tinker me up to last out', Sailor Bill even fulfilled his ambition to see one final Trafalgar Day. He died with dignity in 1837, but his funeral was as disreputable as George IV's had been. Greville found it a 'wretched mockery' and thought the plain obsequies of a common soldier 'more impressive, more decent, more affecting than all this pomp with pasteboard crown, and heralds scampering about, while idleness and indifference were gazing and gossiping round about the royal remains'. William IV's obituary in *The Times* was almost as devastating as his eldest brother's: 'His late Majesty, though at times a jovial and, for a king, an honest man, was a weak, ignorant, commonplace sort of person.' It was clear that the monarchy could hardly fall much lower in public esteem.

Four

Windsor Wonderland

Queen Victoria's three predecessors had been, in the words of Edward VII's biographer Sir Sidney Lee, 'an imbecile, a profligate and a buffoon'. She was none of these things and during her reign the monarchy, despite some alarming ups and downs, established itself in the affections of the people. A major reason for this was the Queen's Victorianism. She embraced respectability, that secular form of salvation so dear to the Evangelicals who, since Wesley's time, had been creating Britain in their own image. A new word was coined to describe the Queen's rigid adherence to the proprieties – Balmorality. Victoria thoroughly disapproved of her 'wicked uncles', which did not stop her teasing piquant details of their lives from her complaisant prime minister, Lord Melbourne. He took rather an indulgent view of them – 'they were such jolly fellows, Ma'am.' But Melbourne's views were old-fashioned and eccentric. He would not go to church 'for fear of hearing something very extraordinary'; he thought one should take note of good character only where 'lowly persons' were concerned; and he remarked of the more rigorous standards of the Victorian court: 'This damned morality will ruin everything.' The Queen disagreed. She believed that King William had been too lax and approachable, and that what the country now wanted was more sovereign strictness. She was full of high seriousness, telling herself that 'Very few have more real good will and more real desire to do what is fit and right than I have.' Unfortunately, like George III, she tended to think that she alone knew what was right. And she did not hesitate to pronounce with regal self-confidence on the subject. As a girl her 'great admiration' had been Louis XIV. As a woman she increasingly came to resemble the Red

Queen in *Alice*, being outspoken, capricious, obstinate and bigoted.

At first, of course, the new Queen was greeted with enthusiasm. Young, graceful, cordial, dignified, frank, and all the more vulnerable because brought up under unhappy circumstances, she was a delightful contrast to her old uncles. True, her coronation was in the ancient, chaotic tradition. Only two peers, both of whom had taken part in theatricals, knew how to put on their robes. According to the young Benjamin Disraeli, Lord Melbourne held the sword of state like a butcher. The clergy lost their place in the service, Victoria herself did not know what to do, the Archbishop of Canterbury hurt her by jamming the ring onto the wrong finger, two train-bearers talked throughout, and the aged Lord Rolle delighted punsters by rolling down the steps of the throne. Harriet Martineau commented acidly that the service had erred by endowing the Queen with divinity and God with royalty. But such criticism has never seemed to worry the British people. And the Queen's subsequent formality, not to mention the exclusion of her troublesome mother, the Duchess of Kent, from all public business, gained her widespread approval. To be sure, the diminutive figure of the monarch could sometimes be seen on the dance floor at three o'clock in the morning. But the Queen recognized that 'in my station I unfortunately cannot valse and gallop'. Moreover the court was pleasingly dull, 'so dull', Greville thought, 'that it is a marvel how anybody can like such a life'. He described its inhabitants as deaf, stupid, vulgar bores. He also recorded a conversation with the Queen to prove his contention that she was neither clever nor amusing, and to illustrate the 'trivial, laboured and wearisome amenities of the Royal circle'. It surely epitomizes regal small talk for the ages.

Q. – Have you been riding today, Mr Greville?

G. – No, Madam, I have not.

Q. – It was a fine day.

G. – Yes, Ma'am, a very fine day.

Q. – It was rather cold.

G. – (*like Polonius*) – It *was* rather cold, Madam.

Q. – Your sister, Lady Frances Egerton, rides, I think, does she not?

G. – She does ride sometimes, Madam.

(*A pause, when I took the lead though adhering to the same topic.*)

G. – Has Your Majesty been riding today?

Q. – (*with animation*) – Oh, yes, a very long ride.

G. – Has Your Majesty got a nice horse?

Q. – Oh, a very nice horse.

And with a bow on his part and a smile on hers she proceeded round the room.

The Queen's honeymoon with her subjects was short-lived. Inexperienced, imperious and, as Greville said, 'blinded by her partialities', she foolishly became involved in a scandal. She supported allegations that her mother's unmarried lady-in-waiting, Lady Flora Hastings, was pregnant when in fact she was suffering from a tumour which killed her. The Queen was hissed at Ascot, a form of disrespect that she thought should be prohibited by law, and a man shouted, 'Mrs Melbourne'. Her partiality for the Whig prime minister next engaged the Queen in what became known as 'the Bedchamber Crisis'. In 1839 Melbourne lost control of the Commons and resigned, so that the monarch reluctantly had to call on Peel to form a government. But she then refused his request to dismiss some of the Whig ladies in her household. Without this mark of royal confidence Peel declined to proceed, and Melbourne returned. Even the Whig leader was doubtful about the propriety of the Queen's action and it was the last time a British sovereign prevented the formation of a ministry which commanded support in the Commons. Some believed that the royal intransigence was a sign that Victoria was going mad, like George III. Others were convinced that she had damaged the Crown. Wellington thought 'the monarchy is in danger' and Lord Ashley considered that any repetition of such political favouritism would 'destroy the position of the Queen'. Greville commented: 'It is a high trial of our institutions when the caprice of a girl of nineteen can overturn a great Ministerial combination.' He opined that 'making the private gratification of the Queen paramount to the highest public considerations' was a strange constitutional doctrine and noted the 'most revolting virulence and indecency of press attacks on the Crown'.

The attacks increased when the Queen married Prince Albert

of Saxe-Coburg-Gotha – the Coburgs being, as Bismarck irreverently remarked, the 'stud-farm of Europe'. As everyone
knows, Victoria had fallen passionately in love with the Prince.
She filled her journals with glowing tributes to his beauty, commented artlessly on his elegant white pantaloons with *'nothing
under them'*, and gushed incessantly of her adoration for him: 'My
dearest Albert put on my stockings for me. I went in and saw him
shave; a great delight for me.' The public did not share her affection
and greeted Albert with predictable xenophobia. People bawled
anti-German songs in the street. Butchers' shops displayed enormous sausages, a satirical comment on German eating habits.
Halfpenny broadsheets were sold containing rhymes like this:

> He comes to take 'for better or for worse'
> England's fat Queen and England's fatter purse.

Further comments, in an un-Victorian strain of obscenity, were
made about the royal wedding night: one visualized Albert going
in at Bushy, passing through Virginia Water, entering Maiden-
head and leaving Staines behind.

Shy and reserved, Albert always attracted criticism. Although
he showed that he could hunt and turned shooting into the mass
slaughter of game birds, the Consort held aloof from English
society. He seemed a princely prig – one, moreover, who was
intent on making his royal mark on British politics. Actually
Albert had rather a pawky sense of humour and he was as full of
good intentions as his wife, though without her alloy of selfishness and stupidity. But popular fears were not entirely ground-
less. Albert tried to use Lord Palmerston's seduction of one of
the Queen's ladies in 1837 as a reason for dismissing him in
1850. And he told Lord John Russell that the sovereign had
'an immense moral responsibility upon his shoulders with regard
to his Government and the duty to watch and *control* it'. There
was at least a grain of truth in Disraeli's characteristically florid
pronouncement that if the Prince Consort had lived he would
have introduced England to the benefits of absolute rule.

Melbourne wrongly said that Prince Albert was 'indolent' and
remarked that 'it would be better if he was more so, for in his
position we want no activity'. Albert could not resist interfering,
however. As he shrewdly observed, princes were bound to have
'political opinions' and a monarch was 'necessarily a politician'.

His first endeavour was to try to wean his wife away from Melbourne. In this he was successful, though when Peel took office, after winning the 1841 general election, the first occasion on which the people chose the prime minister for the sovereign, Queen Victoria for some time carried on a clandestine correspondence with his defeated rival. But by 1846 she had become fully reconciled to Peel and convinced that the monarchy was only safe in Tory hands. As Gladstone wrote: 'The Prince is very strongly Conservative in his politics and his influence with the Queen is overruling; through him she has become so attached to Conservative ideas that she could hardly endure the idea of the opposite Party as her ministers.' The wheel had turned full circle. In 1839, as Greville wrote, Victoria had 'made herself the Queen of a party' – the Whig party. By 1846 she had made herself the Conservative Queen. But once again royal partisanship backfired. For by supporting Peel in his endeavour to repeal the Corn Laws, the Queen, and still more the Prince, helped to precipitate a split in Tory ranks which virtually kept the party out of power for two decades. And during that period the Whigs, led by radicals like Lord John Russell and swashbucklers like Lord Palmerston, were disinclined to pay serious attention to royal wishes. Albert's confidant Baron Stockmar went so far as to assure the Prince in 1854 that 'Our Whigs are nothing but partly conscious, partly unconscious, Republicans who stand in the same relation to the throne as a wolf does to lambs.'

Oddly enough, Queen Victoria liked to call herself a Liberal, but her prejudices were invincibly Conservative. She sympathized with the poor but opposed Lord Ashley's Ten Hours Bill because it would deprive industry of seven weeks' child-power each year. She pitied the starving Irish but when they agitated her response was that of George III to the Americans: all she could talk about was 'insubordination'. In almost every sphere she opposed reform. She tried to prevent Cardwell from modernizing the army. She opposed civil service examinations on the grounds that they would exclude gentlemen. She condemned the 'mad wicked folly of "Women's Rights"'. She considered it a grave defect in the constitution that radical governments could attain power 'merely on account of the number of votes'. Like Lady Bracknell, who was surely modelled on her, the Queen thought education was carried too far: it 'ruined the health of the higher classes uselessly and rendered the working classes unfitted for good servants and labourers'. She was given to charity but she detested the Chartists. In foreign policy she preferred to support reactionary régimes. In 1848 she told Russell: 'I maintain that Revolutions are always bad. . . . Obedience to the laws & to the Sovereign is obedience to a higher power, divinely instituted for the good of the *people*, not of the Sovereign, who has equally duties & obligations.'

In the 'year of revolutions' the Queen was understandably alarmed that the foreign contagion would spread to Britain. Radical papers contrasted the royal luxury in which she lived with the pauperism of English cities, something the Queen preferred not to see – she liked the slums to be swathed in bunting when she visited them and she would have the blinds of her railway saloon drawn down when passing through particularly blighted areas. Peel himself advised her to placate public opinion by living without ostentation. On 6 March 1848 a crowd smashed the lamps outside Buckingham Palace. Its leader shouted: 'Vive la république!' and when he tried to shake hands with one of the sentries he was arrested. Taking the government's advice, the royal family retreated to their residence at Osborne, on the Isle of Wight, before the planned Chartist march from Kennington to Westminster. The Queen even spoke of bringing up her children for '*whatever station* they may be placed in – *high or low*'. But the march was a fiasco. Although the Chartists agreed that the rights of property were the wrongs of the poor, there was not a strong republican, let alone revolutionary, spirit in this heterogeneous movement. The Chartist mayor of Birmingham went so far as to tell Prince Albert that 'he would vouch for the devoted loyalty [to the monarchy] of the whole Chartist body.'

This was an exaggerated claim. Albert's unpopularity, great in the 1840s, became greater still in the early 1850s, largely because he appeared bent on thwarting Palmerston's aggressive initiatives in foreign policy. Early in 1854 joyous crowds actually gathered outside the Tower of London in response to a rumour that he had been arrested for treason and was about to be imprisoned there. Newspaper attacks on him before the outbreak of the Crimean War were particularly vicious – he was pilloried as the German 'Prince Prime Minister'. Albert became obsessed by the irresponsibility of the press, damning even William Howard

Russell's dispatches from the front as those of a 'miserable scribbler'. However, as a rule wars foster an intense loyalty to the Crown and the royal couple duly became the focus of rabid patriotic sentiment during the struggle with Russia. The Queen's evident belligerence was much appreciated, as was her sympathy for the wounded. She gave selected men dinner in the Servants' Hall and presented common soldiers with medals – which only cynics could dismiss as 'half a crown and a pennyworth of ugly ribbon'.

The monarchy also benefited, in the late 1850s, from the fact that the royal family was, to paraphrase Bagehot, a 'brilliant edition' of a revered Victorian institution. Such a family 'sweeten[ed] politics by the seasonable addition of nice and pretty events'. It seemed to provide a model of respectable domesticity for the entire nation. If Albert was not quite the Victorian patriarch of legend, he was far from being, as a modern apologist has suggested, the liberal modern father. His children were often 'whipped'. Their nursery was freezing in winter. The frugality of their diet (much boiled beef and carrots, and semolina pudding) astonished the maids. For untruthfully claiming that she had been given permission to wear her pink bonnet, Vicky, the eldest child, was 'imprisoned with tied hands'. But if these details would not have offended contemporaries, they would have been shocked by Victoria's hysterical outbursts against the husband she had proposed to but whom she had promised to obey – his infuriating response was to write her reasoned memoranda, designed to prevent the recurrence of George III's malady.

Luckily, too, the public was not privy to the Queen's frantic complaints about her eldest son and heir, Bertie (the future Edward VII), whom she regarded as a caricature of herself with all her faults exaggerated. Again and again she railed against his juvenile tantrums, his inveterate idleness, his chronic dullness, his low tastes, his fondness for trivia, and his 'wretched mediocrity'. Though an affectionate youth, Bertie possessed little intellect, less principle and no sense but clothes sense. Yet, much to his parents' chagrin, the Prince of Wales was becoming a popular figure. The Queen could not understand it. 'Handsome I cannot think him, with that painfully small head, those immense features and total want of chin.' And when he married Princess Alexandra of Denmark, a lady with the 'smallest head' she had ever seen, Queen Victoria wondered whether to call back the phrenologist who had examined Bertie's boyish bumps in an effort to find out whether he had inherited the family weakness. Certainly, the Queen considered, it would be 'great misfortune' if the couple had children and she prayed that Bertie 'may never succeed me' – off with his head.

If she did not go quite that far, the great Victorian matriarch was certainly inclined to blame Bertie for bringing her domestic bliss to an end, which led in due course to the throne's being plunged into discredit. For in 1861 the Prince Consort became quite distraught – heart-broken, the Queen said – over the news that his son had become sexually embroiled with an actress called Nellie Clifden. Visualizing paternity suits and publicity, he excitedly rebuked the Prince of Wales: 'she will be able to give before a greedy multitude disgusting details of your profligacy for the sake of convincing the Jury, yourself examined by a railing indecent attorney and hooted and yelled at by a Lawless Mob! Oh horrible prospect . . .' Ill and exhausted by overwork, the Prince Consort travelled to Cambridge in order to remonstrate further with his son, which he did during a long walk in the rain. Albert's resistance to the typhoid which he had already contracted was fatally weakened. He had time to do one signal service for his adopted country – toning down a dispatch which might have provoked war with the northern states of America – before, on 14 December, he died.

By nature the Queen was disposed towards a morbid melancholia and her life now became an epic of grief. She was prostrated by 'paroxysms of despair and yearning'. Daily, when she tried to bury her sorrow in work, and nightly, when she slept with Albert's old red dressing-gown, she herself longed to die. She could not set eyes on her eldest son without shuddering. She felt 'a rending asunder of heart and body and soul'. She filled her letters with bitter lamentations. She kept Albert's room exactly as it had been at the time of his death – every day servants laid out his clothes and brought in hot shaving water. The Queen wrapped Windsor, which she described as a 'living grave', in miles of black crêpe. And Windsor station now had to be cleared of passengers when she travelled by train. For in her bereavement she retired almost entirely from her subjects' gaze.

Efforts by her ministers to bring Queen Victoria back into

public life made her ill – she and others feared for her reason. It seemed as though she proposed to stay in seclusion for ever, and the sympathy which her loss at first generated gradually turned into irritation and then antipathy. Widowhood was one thing, purdah another. In 1864 a notice was pinned to the railings of Buckingham Palace: 'These commanding premises to be let or sold, in consequence of the late occupant's declining business.' A royal equerry complained to Gladstone that 'There is only one great capital where the sovereign is unrepresented, and that capital is London.' Criticism turned into ribaldry as it was rumoured that the Queen was comforting herself in the arms of her uncouth and overbearing Scottish servant, John Brown. The Queen was popularly known as Mrs Brown and police reports reaching Gladstone said that she was referred to in 'terms that would befit a brothel'. Brown did, it is true, sometimes address her with rough affection as 'wumman', but he almost certainly took no more intimate liberties. Nevertheless his incongruous eminence provoked *Punch* to issue, in 1866, a mock Court Circular from Balmoral: 'Mr John Brown walked on the slopes. He subsequently partook of a haggis. In the evening, Mr John Brown was pleased to listen to a bag-pipe. Mr John Brown retired early.'

A more serious indictment of the Queen's position was issued a year later, when Walter Bagehot published his classic, *The British Constitution*. Today Bagehot is often regarded as the Victorian version of his plummy modern editor, the Conservative MP Norman St John Stevas, friend and defender of royalty and pillar of the Establishment. In fact, Bagehot's was an incisive and astringent intelligence, and he was reckoned by Queen Victoria (who disapproved of her grandson George's reading him) to be a dangerous radical. This was not surprising in view of his strictures on the Queen herself. He said that she had 'done almost as much to injure the monarchy by her long retirement from public life as the most unworthy of her predecessors did by his profligacy and frivolity'. Furthermore, Bagehot had no high opinion of royalty in general. A king tended to be an ordinary man of restricted capacity, he thought. 'His education will be that of one who has never had to struggle; who has always felt that he has nothing to gain; who has had the first dignity given him; who has never seen common life as in truth it is.' Bagehot clearly feared that the 'unemployed youth' of the 'retired widow' – that is to say Queen Victoria's son Edward – would be an even worse king than this royal stereotype. Perhaps if such a 'pleasure-loving lounger' were idle he would do no harm. But Bagehot found it 'easy to imagine, upon a constitutional throne, an active and meddling fool, who never acts when he should, who warns his Ministers against their judicious measures. It is easy to imagine that such a king should be the tool of others; that mistresses should corrupt him; that the atmosphere of a bad court should be used to degrade free government.'

Bagehot did not even believe that monarchy was the best form of government. It was possible to dispense with its trappings in the United States, for example, where universal (male) suffrage, widespread education and improved living standards enabled the people to elect a fair legislature. In England, however, where the 'bovine stupidity' of the masses was all too apparent, circumstances made a monarchy essential. Paradoxically, though, ever since 1832 England had been a republic, according to Bagehot, but a *disguised* republic. In other words, the essential business of the state was carried out by the elected government and the monarchy was simply a convenient fiction whose purpose was to dupe the people. Its function was to cast a spell over them, to win their allegiance both by investing authority with a human face and by making itself the focus of a cult. It was 'to be the visible symbol of unity to those still so imperfectly educated as to need a symbol'. Of course, Bagehot said, the monarchy could only be such a symbol if it were genuinely impartial and above such political activities as would cause enmity and desecration. Accordingly, he uttered his most famous dictum: the Crown had only 'the right to be consulted, the right to encourage, the right to warn'. He also said that although the sovereign should be 'commonly hidden like a mystery', she should also be 'sometimes paraded like a pageant'. Since Albert's death the Queen had disappeared from view and the court was 'in a state of suspended animation'. 'To be invisible was to be forgotten,' Bagehot insisted. His book, which became the Bible of British constitutional monarchy, was a plea for the sovereign to appear, clothed in the habiliments of majesty.

Strange to say, the republican movement, which reached its apogee in the early 1870s, was also stimulated by too little rather than too much monarchy. The Queen's seclusion made it an easy matter to attack her for dereliction of duty. This was an important charge levelled against her by the radical Charles Bradlaugh, who was hailed at home as 'the brains and soul of English republicanism' and in the United States as 'the Future President of England'. He complained that 'Parliament is usually opened and closed by commission – a robe on an empty throne, and a speech read by a deputy, satisfying the Sovereign's loyal subjects.' Bradlaugh's assault would have been strengthened had he known that Gladstone's attempt to persuade the Queen to stay in London while parliament was sitting in 1871 caused her finally to decide that she detested him. The Liberal prime minister wrote that 'the repellent power which she so well knows how to use' had been put into action against him and he declared that her royal obstinacy had been his most 'sickening' experience in forty years of public life. '*Worse* things may be imagined, but smaller and meaner causes for the decay of Thrones cannot be conceived.'

Napoleon III's throne had decayed in a moment and it was easy to visualize Victoria's going the same way after 1870. Bradlaugh reckoned that 'four or five years of political education' would be enough to end monarchy, together with the corrupt system of privilege of which it was the pivot. His optimism was reinforced by the founding of a new journal, the *Republican*, in 1870, and by the publication of articles hostile to the monarchy elsewhere. In *Fraser's Magazine*, for example, 'A Working Man' claimed that, far from being loyal worker bees adoring the Queen Bee, as the press constantly averred, members of the labouring class were, in ninety-nine cases out of a hundred, republicans inspired by 'hatred and contempt for royalty'. He described how his fellows were sickened by the 'simulated ecstasy, slavish tone and meaningless unmanly drivelling of the daily papers' about the royal family. 'Men – decent, steady artisans ... speaking amid applauding circles of shop-mates, wished that "the whole tribe of Royalty were under the sod," while women, mothers themselves, prayed that its women might be made unfruitful, so that the race of royal paupers might not be increased.' Many loyal to the Crown agreed with his strictures on the heavy expenditure needed to maintain a sovereign who was doing nothing to earn her keep. Bradlaugh estimated, for example, that in thirty-two years Queen Victoria had cost the nation £12,320,000, as against a figure of only £160,000 for the American presidency.

This criticism was taken up in a very effective and popular pamphlet, entitled *What Does She Do With It?*, written by Lord Macaulay's nephew and biographer, G. O. Trevelyan, in 1871. Trevelyan (writing under the pseudonym Solomon Temple) stated that he was a loyal friend of the monarchy at a time when the current of the English mind had set 'towards Republicanism'. He expressed concern that since 1861 the annual payment of £385,000 had been far in excess of royal needs because court ceremonial had been so diminished. People 'do not like to pay for Royal State and not to have it,' he observed. Worse still, public money had obviously 'been applied in creating a private fortune for the Queen'. Trevelyan cited evidence of her growing opulence, her lavish presents, the increased size of her estates, the fact that her horses were housed at a cost 'that would have built a comfortable cottage for more than one labouring family'. (He might also have drawn attention to her parsimoniousness, exemplified by her freezing palaces and the newspaper squares in her lavatories.) Of course, like everyone else, Trevelyan could only guess at the extent of the Queen's wealth. 'In the absence of authentic information,' he declared, 'it must not be a matter of wonder that statements which are probably great exaggerations should find belief.' He considered that 'the people of England have a right to be informed'. 'Let there be no mystery', for secrets breed 'suspicion and disaffection between the Queen and the people'. Trevelyan concluded by asserting that the monarch's possession of a large private fortune was 'unconstitutional and most objectionable'. Royal hoarding divided the sovereign from the Crown and it could be seen as 'the secret preparation of a raft on which the captain may leave the ship'.

This was a telling indictment. But it is worth making the point that the efflorescence of republicanism, brief though it was, drew strength from much deeper roots. They burrowed back into egalitarian soil that was well cultivated by medievals, who asked:

> When Adam delved and Eve span
> Who was then the gentleman?

The provenance of Bradlaugh's republicanism is well illustrated in his execrable version of the Marseillaise:

Has England forgotten Cromwell's teaching?
Is Hampden's poured-out blood all in vain?
Shall the land which saw a king's impeaching
Now be bound by a Brunswick chain?
Our sires veil their faces in shame
For the sons who disgrace their name,
Who bow to a crowned thing,
To a puppet they call a King.
To arms! Republicans!
Strike now for Liberty!

Though tenuous, England's republican tradition could boast better poets and nobler ornaments. There was Shelley: 'Oh, that the free would stamp/The impious name of king into the dust.' There was Thackeray, who wrote in 1855: 'The days are over in England of that strange religion of king-worship, when priests flattered princes in the Temple of God; when servility was held to be another duty; when beauty and youth tried eagerly for royal favour; and woman's shame was held to be no disgrace.' And in 1872 there was Frederic Harrison, the arch-Positivist, who, at the request of the *Fortnightly Review*'s editor, John Morley, delivered one of the heaviest broadsides ever fired against the British monarchy.

Harrison regarded the institution as a 'venerable fetish', a piece of 'sublime hocus'. It resembled the Roman Lectisternium, the Senate's parading of the old images in order to solve its current problems, or the savage's beating of gongs and tom-toms as sovereign cures for an eclipse. In a state whose principle was merit, not privilege, there should be no place for an 'hereditary grand master of ceremonies'. Harrison resented the suggestion that 'our dogedom' was essential as a focus of loyalty. The Americans were patriotic without a monarch and the Spaniards were faction-ridden with one. Loyalty was owed to the nation as a whole. It was not to be narrowed down to allegiance to a dynasty, whose head was now an 'irreproachable lady' but might just as well be a 'debauched booby'. In any case, 'rallying round the throne means intriguing for cards to a court ball, waving a handkerchief in a grand stand, or a holiday and extra beer'. In fact, people would be made equally happy by other forms of entertainment. 'We see millions roused out of their vacant and dismal lives by a boat-race or a horse-race, though they do not know the difference between a row-lock and a fetlock.' The argument, worthy of Falstaff, that the masses needed pageants 'might be a plea for the Lord Mayor's Show or the revival of tournaments, but hardly for making the entire constitution culminate in pasteboard'. A society which 'still maintains a purely sinecure monarchy consecrates dignity without responsibility, wealth without toil, display for its own sake'. It was no wonder, Harrison concluded, that as 'the ceremonial Majesty of the throne grows daily more alien to our self-respect, the practical majesty of the nation becomes a more present force'.

Harrison's view was sustained at the beginning of the 1870s by the formation of over fifty republican clubs in large towns, by the spread of republican prints, and by the holding of mass rallies. In September 1870 red caps of liberty were raised on poles in Trafalgar Square and orators hailed the coming of the republic. The movement was given a further boost in 1870 when the Prince of Wales was subpoenaed as a witness in Sir Charles Mordaunt's divorce case. He was exonerated from any 'criminal connexion' with Lady Mordaunt, largely, it seems, because of the English convention that adultery does not take place at tea-time; but his mother wailed: 'The animal side of our nature is to me – too dreadful.' Now ambitious politicians seemed intent on jumping aboard the republican bandwagon. Joseph Chamberlain, then a radical, pronounced: 'I do not feel any great horror at the idea of the possible establishment of a republic in our country. I am quite certain that sooner or later it will come.' Another leading parliamentary radical, Sir Charles Dilke, declared: 'If you can show me a fair chance that a republic here will be free from the political corruption which hangs about the monarchy, I say, for my part – and I believe that the middle classes in general will say – let it come.' This was scarcely a call to the barricades, and Dilke did not intend it to be such, for he regarded the monarchy as being just a centre of waste, privilege and inefficiency in national life. However, his assault crystallized republican feeling. The Queen herself, remembering that she had met Dilke when he was a small boy and stroked his head, merely 'supposed she must have rubbed the brains the wrong way'. But her private secretary, Sir Henry Ponsonby, reckoned that only the English spirit of chivalry was now sustaining Her Majesty. If she had been a man 'they would simply have turned him off the throne'.

Of course, there was a reaction. Dilke was vehemently attacked, *The Times*, in particular, condemning him for 'recklessness bordering on criminality'. And his republican campaign, if it could be so dignified, was nipped in the bud by a singular event. At the end of 1871 the Prince of Wales caught typhoid and for over a month he was so ill that everyone despaired of his life. The country waited anxiously for news and Alfred Austin wrote the famous lines which proved how eminently qualified he was for the office of Poet Laureate:

> Across the wires, the electric message came:
> He is no better; he is much the same.

During that time, as Roy Jenkins has written, 'the Prince accomplished more for the popularity of his house than during the whole of his previous thirty years of life'. There was a spontaneous outburst of sympathy for the royal family, assisted by speculation that the Prince was destined to die of the same disease and at the same time of the year as his father. *Reynolds's Newspaper* might denounce 'the great epidemic of typhoid loyalty' but it spread throughout the country and infected all classes of people. Loyalists rioted when Dilke rose to speak and his attempt to set up an inquiry into the royal finances was defeated by 276 votes to 2 in the Commons. Dilke soon withdrew from the fray and eventually recanted. Queen Victoria concluded that the monarchy would 'last her time', though she made no plans for the future of her dynasty. But, of course, in political terms British republicanism has been a dead duck ever since.

It did not, indeed, expire overnight and ever since lone figures have sought to revive it. Furthermore, sporadic attacks on the monarchy continued, many of them inspired by sympathy for the Paris Commune. As late as 1879 the House of Commons actually debated the dangerous growth of royal power. In the 1880s there were outbreaks of republicanism, hissings and refusals to stand during the national anthem. *The Times* demanded that the widow of Windsor should 'show herself to the present generation which knows her not'. When the Queen visited the East End of London in 1887 to open the People's Palace she was assailed by 'a horrid noise', '*quite* new' to her ears, '"booing" she believes it is called'. In the 1890s Henry Labouchere, the proprietor of *Truth*, suggested that Buckingham Palace should be converted into a home for fallen women. Other newspapers could joke that there was nothing between the Prince of Wales and Lillie Langtry, 'not even a sheet'. But scurrility about royalty was becoming much less common towards the end of the Victorian age. Organizations like the Republican League petered out amid faddist and sectarian squabbles. Radicals and Socialists looked elsewhere for reforming targets, acknowledging that the republican struggle was hopeless. Bradlaugh said that 'Monarchy has been truly described as a government for children: Republicanism is for men.' But privately he despaired of the nation's ever growing up.

Actually the nation was developing in other ways, many of which were helping to consolidate the monarchy's position. First of all, the age of imperialism had dawned. Disraeli, who helped to conjure it up, did his best to associate imperialism with royalism, and Conservatism with both. In this endeavour he had a very apt pupil in the Queen herself. She was a born nationalist and she needed little encouragement to become an ardent jingoist. She was, to be sure, horrified to learn, when Disraeli annexed the Fiji Islands in 1874, that cannibals were being allowed into the Empire. But he had no difficulty in persuading her that 'these Fijians are all Methodists'. Henceforth Victoria became infatuated with England's colonizing 'mission' and she referred to Disraeli's imperial policy as 'our' policy. She was correspondingly furious with Gladstone for condemning imperialism as 'territorial aggrandisement, backed by military display'. When she persuaded Disraeli to promote her to Empress of India in 1876, on the grounds that the subcontinent 'ought to belong to me', Gladstone was still more withering. He dismissed the new title as 'theatrical folly and bombast'. The Grand Old Man might expostulate but Disraeli's imperial vision was an alluring one, especially at a time when new nations, Britain's rivals (and increasingly successful ones) in the search for power and prestige, markets and raw materials, were also looking for 'a place in the sun'. During the last decades of the nineteenth century, Crown and Empire were intimately associated and loyalty to one stiffened loyalty to the other.

Both brands of loyalty were strengthened by the growth of

pageantry which took place between about 1875 and 1914. This was, to quote the historian David Cannadine, the heyday of 'invented tradition'. Old ceremonies were staged with novel splendour and punctilio. New rituals were created to enhance the dignity of the Crown and to mobilize popular devotion. The first major innovation was the celebration of Queen Victoria's Golden Jubilee in 1887. She was extremely reluctant to emerge from her seclusion even for this, and steadfastly refused to swap her widow's bonnet for a crown when she did so. But the festivities proved an astounding success, not only in Britain but throughout the Empire. In India, for example, the event was marked by spectacular illuminations, by countless memorials and by universal rejoicing. It was all encouraged, admittedly, by the government, which remitted taxes and distributed largesse to the poor in an effort to blot out, with the royal occasion, horrid memories of the Mutiny, whose thirtieth anniversary it also was. In Calcutta the Viceroy explained that 'through the mysterious decrees of Providence the British nation had been called to undertake the supreme government of this mighty Empire', and he paid tribute to its ruler – 'a more beloved sovereign the world has never seen.' At home there were similar flourishes, processions, thanksgiving services, feasts, solemn acts of obeisance. On 31 December the Queen wrote in her journal: 'Never, never can I forget this brilliant year, so full of the marvellous kindness, loyalty, and devotion of so many millions, which I really could hardly have expected.' Less lyrically, the Archbishop of Canterbury concluded: 'Everyone feels that the Socialist movement has had a check.'

Ten years later, at the Diamond Jubilee, latent British insecurities, as expressed in Kipling's *Recessional*, were forgotten in an orgy of imperial drum-beating. It was supervised, ironically enough, by the former republican, now colonial secretary, Joseph Chamberlain. He had never been a fire-eating republican like Bradlaugh, it is true. Indeed, he had welcomed the Prince of Wales to his bailiwick of Birmingham with extravagant civility, asserting that 'a man might be a gentleman as well as a Republican'. But now he had become the champion of aggressive imperialism, the prophet of the gospel that 'trade follows the flag'. Referring to his family's small-arms factory, *Punch* quipped: 'The more the empire expands, the more the Chamberlains contract.' Never was so much flag-wagging done as in 1897. At the Spithead Jubilee review the Queen inspected three lines of ships (including more than fifty battleships) stretching over seven miles. She passed through a London which had never mounted a more glittering spectacle, the streets decorated and illuminated, St Paul's lit up by searchlights, 50,000 troops from all over the Empire on parade, the largest force ever assembled in the capital. In her journal the Queen wrote: 'The crowds were quite indescribable, and their enthusiasm truly marvellous and deeply touching. The cheering was quite deafening, and every face seemed to be filled with real joy.'

It would be easy to dismiss all this as a tribal rite, on a par with Indians sacrificing goats before statues of the Great White Queen, or inhabitants of remoter districts of the British Isles rubbing her image on gold coins to ward off sickness. But the rejoicing stemmed, at least in part, from a rational assumption that homage was due to the Queen as a constitutional monarch in the sense that Bagehot prescribed. People were convinced that she was a genuinely national symbol, above party, politically neutral. Of course, they could not ascertain how much power, if any, she exercised. This was a mystery hidden even from the élite. As the legal historian F. W. Maitland noted in 1888: 'Few indeed are the people who really know how much or how little the Queen's own wishes affect the course of government.' He added that if, Lord Salisbury being prime minister, 'Gladstone insisted on constantly having the Queen's ear ... our Constitution would soon be topsy-turvy.' That it was not topsy-turvy, as we know, was largely due to the restraint of Gladstone himself. For although the growth of organized parties and the expansion of the electorate since 1867 had left the Crown with very little power, the Queen had continued to behave, in the Grand Old Man's view, less like George III than like James II. As late as 1880 Gladstone said that he 'would never be surprised to see her turn the Government out, after the manner of her uncles.'

That would have been impossible. But the Queen interfered constantly. She still had considerable influence, especially over appointments. For example, she delayed Dilke's entry into the cabinet for three years and excluded 'that horrible lying Labouchere' altogether. She badgered her ministers unmercifully. Gladstone exclaimed that 'The Queen alone is enough to kill any man.' Salisbury found her more difficult to deal with than the prime ministership and the Foreign Office (though not than Lord Randolph Churchill). Her nagging helped to cause Lord Rosebery's breakdown in health. On his deathbed even the unctuous Disraeli refused a final visit from the Queen: 'No, it is better not. She'd only ask me to take a message to Albert.' Worse than this harrying was the Queen's perpetual intriguing, which was directed with special virulence against Gladstone. This did not just stem from her personal preferences, though, as everyone knows, Disraeli treated the Queen like a woman and laid on his faery flattery with a trowel, whereas Gladstone treated her as a department of state and addressed her like a public meeting. But Queen Victoria also disapproved of the Grand Old Man's opinions.

He was unsound on the monarchy. The fawning Disraeli announced that 'The principles of the English Constitution do not contemplate the absence of personal influence on the part of the sovereign.' The implacable Gladstone retorted: 'It would be an evil and perilous day for the monarchy were any prospective possessor of the crown to assume or claim for himself a preponderating, or even independent, power in any one department of state.' Naturally the idea of a 'democratic monarchy' was anathema to Queen Victoria. Gladstone was also unsound on the national interest. After he won the election of 1880 the Queen declared that she would 'sooner abdicate than send for or have any communication with that half-mad firebrand who would soon ruin everything and be a Dictator'. She asked the defeated Disraeli (by then Lord Beaconsfield) 'what he advised me to do for the real good of the country, which we both agreed was inseparable from my own'. Above all, Gladstone was unsound on Ireland. The Queen wanted coercion and she did everything possible to sink Gladstone's policy of Home Rule, including acting in collusion with the Tories and secretly sending Salisbury copies of her most important correspondence with Gladstone.

In 1892 the Queen dreaded having to entrust the empire to that 'poor but really wicked old G.O.M.'. In the Court Circular she announced Salisbury's resignation 'with regret' and privately raged about her new prime minister, 'a deluded old fanatic', 'an old, wild, incomprehensible man of eighty-two and a half'. He in turn compared their meeting at Osborne to that which took place between Marie Antoinette and her executioner. When, two years later, Gladstone resigned for good, she expressed neither thanks nor regrets. She displayed once again what Lady Ponsonby called 'the cold egotism which seems to chill you in all royalties'. Yet Gladstone had done more than anyone to ward off republicanism by trying to establish constitutional monarchy as Bagehot had defined it. He had treated the Queen with respect but had not permitted her to exercise any real power. His habit was to begin cabinet meetings by reading out the Queen's hectoring letters and then to push them aside with the words: 'And now, gentlemen, to business.' In life he had been eminently discreet about the Queen's indiscretions (such as her rebuking him in an uncoded telegram after the death of General Gordon). Lady Ponsonby feared that, if provoked too much, 'Gladstone will show his teeth about Royalty altogether, and I wouldn't answer for its lasting long after that.' Yet even in death, by putting an embargo on the royal revelations in his correspondence, he did his best to protect Victoria.

A greater force even than the Grand Old Man also established itself as the Queen's defender towards the end of the nineteenth century. This was the popular press, which had grown up as a result of improved technology, cheap paper and increasing affluence and literacy. The old, largely Liberal, provincial newspapers had seen it as their function to educate the middle class. Most had been hostile to the Crown – Queen Victoria had tried to persuade Palmerston that journalists were not to be received in polite society. The new, mainly Conservative, national press aimed to entertain a mass audience. And it quickly discovered that nothing was better for the circulation than royalty. Nothing pleased the advertisers more – 'SOLDIERS OF THE QUEEN KNOW THE VALUE OF BOVRIL'. Nothing had greater continuing 'human interest'. So the popular press became the trumpet of royalty. Whether dealing in anodyne gossip ('The Prince of Wales is known as Tum-Tum to his friends because of his graceful rotundity of person'), or in pictures (thanks to better techniques of photographic reproduction the new ceremonies could be conveyed with new immediacy), or in straight reporting, or in editorial comment, Fleet Street did its best to create a sacrosanct monarchy.

A few journalists resisted the royalist tide. In 1888 T. P.

O'Connor spitefully reported that the Queen's Jubilee gift of
£70,000 to the Nurses for the Poor, 'over which so many of our
contemporaries have gushed', was only bestowed after 'fierce
pressure from wiser heads' – she had wanted 'to spend the money
on a necklace for Princess Beatrice'. And O'Connor was not alone
in flaying the Prince of Wales during the Tranby Croft baccarat
scandal in 1891, when it emerged that Edward habitually played
this illegal gambling game. Remarking that the Prince had
'succeeded in establishing over social London a despotism the
completeness of which nobody outside society can fully appreciate', O'Connor complained that 'Servility to royalty has reached
such a pitch in England that it is a degradation to the country
and marks us out among all the peoples of the world as a nation
of snobs, toadies and tuft-hunters.' There were, too, so many
'radical attacks in low papers and scurrilous ones' during 1891
that the Admiralty was afraid to promote the Queen's sailor
grandsons, Eddy and George.

In general, though, the national press boomed royalty in order to
boom itself, beginning a symbiotic relationship which, though
sometimes uneasy, has suited both ever since. During the Tranby
Croft case newspapers did not reveal that the Prince of Wales
actually played baccarat in a private room behind the court. At
Queen Victoria's Diamond Jubilee Alfred Harmsworth, later Lord
Northcliffe, brought out a special edition of his recently founded
newspaper the *Daily Mail*, full of purple prose printed in golden
ink. During the next reign Northcliffe 'quintupled' the space he
devoted to royalty. He summed up his view of the relationship
between Fleet Street and Buckingham Palace in a letter to the
King's private secretary: 'The editors of newspapers are really
very glad to receive any hint as to what or what not to publish.
Sometimes, when His Majesty is at Marienbad or Biarritz, we shall
be very glad to be told what to print and what to omit.' No one
knew better than the Napoleon of Fleet Street that 'the power of
the press is not as great as the power of suppress.'

Perhaps even more important than the salutes and subterfuges
of the Beefeater press in stimulating unprecedented veneration
for the monarchy was the Queen's longevity. Old age conferred
respectability and every year the Queen remained alive after
about 1875 increased the devotion of her subjects. H. G. Wells's
mother must have been typical:

She followed the life of Victoria, her acts and utterances, her goings forth and her lyings in, her great sorrow and her other bereavements, with a passionate loyalty. The Queen, also a small woman, was in fact my mother's compensatory personality, her imaginative consolation for all the restrictions and hardships that her sex, her diminutive size, her motherhood and all the endless difficulties of life, imposed on her.

Wells himself, incidentally, heard altogether too much about the Queen. He came to the conclusion that the monarchy was 'a profoundly corrupting influence on our national life, imposing an intricate snobbishness on our dominant class, upon our religious, educational ... and combatant services generally'. He also thought that Queen Victoria 'was like a great paper-weight that for half a century sat upon men's minds' and that only when she died could ideas blow about again.

Such sentiments were unusual. John Galsworthy, in *The Forsyte Saga*, came nearer to expressing the general feeling at her death. 'There it was – the bier of the Queen, coffin of the Age slowly passing! And as it went by there came a mourning groan from all the long line of those who watched, a sound such as Soames had never heard, so unconscious, primitive, deep and wild. . . . Tribute of the Age to its own death.' Or, as Sir Shane Leslie said, 'It seemed as though the keystone had fallen out of the arch of heaven.' Unlike William IV's funeral, Queen Victoria's was a model of solemn dignity. Only one thing went wrong. At Windsor the horses broke their harness and the gun-carriage had to be pulled by sailors. But this innovation proved to be so popular that it became an instant tradition, one of the many modern inventions which today masquerade as part of Britain's ancient heritage of pageantry. Still, there is no denying the authenticity of the public grief, the genuine feeling of loss, at the old Queen's death. As Henry James remarked, 'We all feel motherless today. We are to have no more little mysterious Victoria, but instead fat vulgar dreadful Edward.'

Five

Edward the Caresser

Edward VII's extravagant worldliness certainly damned him in the eyes of sophisticated people. Even the poet of Empire, Rudyard Kipling, dismissed him as 'a corpulent voluptuary'. To someone like Beatrice Webb, a Fabian snob, the new King's 'lack of intellectual refinement and moral distinction' was an affront. 'One sighs to think that this unutterably commonplace person should set the tone of London "society",' she wrote. 'There is something comic in the great British nation, with its infinite variety of talents, having this undistinguished and limited-minded German bourgeois to be its social sovereign.' The fact is, however, that, for all his faults, Edward raised the monarchy to new heights of popular esteem. He did so because of his vulgarity, not in spite of it. After forty years of discreet royal seclusion, he provided the public with a glittering royal show. Above all things the new King loved to dress up and to put himself on display. When playing the star role in some colourful pageant he comported himself with magnificent dignity and style. He revived court splendour as it had not been since the days of George IV, perhaps even of Charles II. He invested monarchy with his own vitality and provided it with the essential ingredient which it had lacked for so long – glamour. At a time when domestic divisions and foreign rivalries were causing deep anxiety in Britain, and when the gilt of imperialism was, in George Dangerfield's words, 'tarnished with Boer blood', King Edward VII became a symbol of national pride and a focus of national unity.

The monarchy was perhaps the grandest of grand illusions but Edward himself was by no means a complete sham. Admittedly, after the Tranby Croft baccarat scandal he did announce that he had a 'horror of gambling'. But in general he thought hypocrisy beneath him. It was well known that the king of the castle was also a man of the world. Of course, his lifelong addiction to pleasure could scarcely have been disguised even had there not been the occasional public scandal. But it was patently obvious that he liked wine, women and song, that he was fond of shooting and sailing and smoking and racing. To some extent all this even enhanced his appeal. He was, after all, only demonstrating how much he had in common with the nobility and the working class, who were, as Lord Randolph Churchill memorably remarked, 'united in the indissoluble bonds of a common immorality'. Even members of the great middle class took it as a matter of course that the King should treat his social indulgences as some kind of divinely ordained duty.

They might have been shocked, as Queen Victoria was, by his suggestion that the date of Dean Stanley's funeral should be changed so as not to clash with Goodwood. They were certainly outraged by his refusal to interrupt his holiday in 1908, when the new prime minister, Asquith, had to go to Biarritz in order to kiss hands. And they would have been more so had they known that the King told Asquith's predecessor, the dying Campbell-Bannerman, that it would be personally inconvenient if he resigned while the monarch was abroad. But few thought the royal round – as fixed as the stars in their courses – odd or inappropriate. In January and February his traditional shooting was interrupted, when he became King, by the need to open parliament. In the early spring he went abroad, among other things to take 'the cure' – modern equivalent of the Roman vomitorium – for his gourmandizing. At the beginning of May he returned for the London season. In June he went to Windsor for Ascot, followed by other race-meetings. Yachting at Cowes followed, then shooting in Scotland. Finally he returned to Sandringham for his birthday (9 November) and Christmas. For Victorians the essence of gentlemanliness was dignified indolence, and only mavericks like Margot Asquith were moved to sarcasm by this routine. She remarked that the King 'devotes what time he does not spend upon sport and pleasure ungrudgingly to duty'.

Naturally, Edward's intimates were painfully aware of the private lapses concealed by his public performance. Ponsonby said that secretaries had to 'catch snap answers from him as he goes out shooting etc. Then he runs off to Trouville where of course business is impossible.' However, Edward was protected from the consequences of his idleness just as he was protected from the consequences of his indiscretions. When in 1871 a blackmailer threatened to publish incriminating letters he had written to Giulia Barucci, self-styled 'greatest whore in the world', his private secretary Francis Knollys came to the rescue and purchased them. High society as a whole remained tight-lipped about Edward's adulterous liaisons with patrician ladies. Occasionally his assumption of *droit de seigneur* so infuriated aristocrats that he was threatened with exposure. When, during the course of a complicated squabble over a woman, Lord Randolph Churchill tried to blackmail him with some other letters, saying: 'I have the crown of England in my pocket,' Edward actually challenged him to a duel, a challenge which was contemptuously refused. During a similarly heated affair, Lord Charles Beresford called the Prince a blackguard and a coward, yet by menacing him with publicity Lord Charles made Edward apologize to him. But in general there was a conspiracy of silence about the royal vices, loyally supported by the press. When the Prince's troubles did become public knowledge, the Establishment closed ranks. He gratefully remembered, for example, how 'Mr Gladstone, who was then Prime Minister, took all the *indirect* means in his power (and *successfully*) to prevent anything being brought out in the course of the [Mordaunt] Trial that could be injurious to the Prince, or the Crown.' On that occasion, Queen Victoria confided to her eldest daughter: 'The Monarchy almost is in danger if he is lowered and despised.' Instead, everything was done throughout his life to project Edward as a worthy prince and a worthy king.

Yet it is clear that from his youth up Edward was palpably unworthy. In particular he was incorrigibly idle, stupid and overbearing. His father said that he had never met such 'a thorough and cunning lazybones' in his life. Albert also observed that his son's 'intellect is of no more use than a pistol packed in the bottom of a trunk in the robber-infested Apennines'. Actually the Prince had a retentive memory for trivia, genealogies or guest-lists, and he was quick to spot sartorial solecisms or to put his inferiors right about niceties of etiquette. But as a child he had been described as not 'normally intelligent' and he had found learning almost impossible. As an adult he despised 'brainy' people and seldom opened a book. Indeed, he would probably have agreed with his great-uncle, King William, who said: 'I know no person so perfectly disagreeable and even dangerous as an author.' The Prince thought in clichés and talked in platitudes. He took no interest in culture and remained all his life a consummate philistine. In Egypt, for example, he preferred to shoot crocodiles or even lizards – anything that moved – rather than look at 'tumbledown' old temples. Brought up at a court where, as Lord Granville noted, a *bon mot* caused less amusement than getting your thumb shut in the door, and where practical jokes were so much the rage that the Princess of Pless once mistook an earthquake for a prankster under her bed, Edward had no chance of developing a sense of humour. He had a sense of fun, and his idea of fun was to squirt waiters with soda siphons. Sometimes he found it more amusing to inflict pain than humiliation, and his governess thought he lacked all sense of right and wrong. As a child he beat his tutor with sticks; as a young man he rapped his valet on the nose. He never achieved much self-control. His juvenile rages were so violent that they were described as 'fits' and his mature bellow terrified all who heard it.

Edward's frenetic pursuit of diversion was less a matter of social duty than of psychic necessity. So few interior resources did he possess and so easily was he bored and irritated (the drumming of his podgy fingers was the danger sign) that he needed constant distraction. Work could not provide it, for although he sat on one or two commissions (where he spent much of his time doodling Union Jacks) he found that business threw out his social life. Anyway, his mother permitted him no major role except a decorative one. In this she was sensible. For he had no marked political ability and was inclined to talk what ministers called 'royal twaddle'. He was also resoundingly indiscreet: he often made undiplomatic remarks about Prussia and he once passed a confidential note from Sir Henry Ponsonby round a dinner table. However, having excluded him from any serious responsibility, the Queen should not have been surprised that he became a confirmed royal playboy. In fact, she complained bitterly about his frivolity and extravagance, and said that he spent his whole life in a 'whirl of amusements'.

In order to find a proper outlet for his sexual energies, the Prince was married off as soon as possible to the beautiful but empty-headed Princess Alexandra. But although he performed his conjugal duties conscientiously, Edward could not settle down to domestic life. Queen Victoria protested that he and the Princess were 'nothing but puppets, running about for show all day and all night'. Sometimes, when his wife was pregnant, for example, the Prince ignored her altogether. Then he ran about all day in the *haut monde*, where, during the time he could spare from gaudy entertainments and twelve-course meals, he engaged with society belles on sofas, so earning his nickname, Edward the Caresser. And he ran about all night with raffish friends, frequenting bowling alleys, casinos, cockpits, billiard rooms where pornographic pictures were shown, and brothels. Though acknowledging that her eldest son did possess 'good and amiable qualities', the Queen lamented: 'Oh, how different poor foolish Bertie is to adored papa.' More prosaically, that puritan among muck-raking journalists, W. T. Stead, concluded that the Prince of Wales was a 'wastrel and whoremonger'.

Queen Victoria warned her son that the country could never bear to have another George IV as Prince of Wales. In this she may or may not have been right. But Edward managed to disguise the fact that he was as much of a royal roué as his great-uncle by paying elaborate homage to the proprieties. So pathologically restless that he could not endure a complete church service, he regularly appeared in his pew at Sandringham in time to hear the sermon, pulling out his watch to ensure that it did not last longer than ten minutes, joining loudly in the final hymn. Flushed with impatience, he forced himself to sit through endless levees and rituals of all sorts. He was invariably genial in public and in private he never permitted the slightest criticism of existing institutions. He paid fanatical attention to correctness of dress and decoration, etiquette and ceremonial, precedence and protocol.

Sometimes his obsessiveness gave offence, as when he insisted that King Kalakaua of Hawaii should take precedence over the Crown Prince of Germany. With trenchant logic Edward declared: 'Either the brute is a king or else he is an ordinary black nigger, and if he is not a king, why is he here?' Edward also caused adverse comment by opening social doors to riches as well as rank. John Buchan, for example, deplored 'the vulgarity and the worship of wealth' which appeared with the next century. But both as prince and king, Edward loved luxury and he was happy to associate with grocers and brewers provided their entertainments were sufficiently lavish. He shocked many of his countrymen even more by his willingness to consort with affluent Jews. Sir Ernest Cassel, in particular, was graciously permitted to assist with the royal finances. One quid pro quo was that, as King, Edward used his influence with his cousin Tsar Nicholas II to promote a Russian loan from which Cassel (and perhaps the King himself) stood to make a large profit. Of course, this was a secret known only to a few, though it enabled the Kaiser to sneer at his uncle Edward, whom he considered as nothing but 'a jobber in stocks and shares'. The fact is that Cassel's friendship not only enabled Edward to pay for his sybaritic style of life, it also assisted him to fulfil the crucial Victorian duty of keeping up appearances.

Sometimes, of course, sharp-eyed contemporaries saw through the royal flummery. Royal nuptials usually stimulate huge outbursts of loyalty, but Edward's splendid marriage in 1863 outraged many, who thought it distracted attention from the 'crisis of national agony' caused by unemployment. *Reynolds's Newspaper* thought that Coventry ribbon makers and Spital-fields weavers should more appropriately be producing funeral shrouds rather than wedding favours. 'What in the name of all that is reasonable,' it expostulated, 'is the use of a Prince of Wales – or for that matter, of a constitutional monarch – but to conjure the money of simpletons from their own into the pockets of publicans, courtiers, prostitutes, place men, and other political vermin who batten and thrive on the follies and calamities of the human race?' It was also generally recognized that Edward's tour of India in 1875 was a pleasure jaunt. Even Ponsonby acknow-ledged that 'The object of his mission is amusement.' 'Yes,' said Lord Salisbury, 'And to kill tigers.' *Reynolds's Newspaper* was even more forthright: the Prince was only interested in 'pig-sticking and women', while working men were being robbed to pay for the spree. The cry was taken up by Bradlaugh and his friends. At demonstrations all over the country orators asked why the Prince would keep the gifts he received from the Indian maharajas, while British taxpayers had to foot the bill for his presents to them. The Prince was unabashed. He demanded huge sums of money and a detachment of life guards so that he could progress in imperial state. Eventually the prime minister persuaded him that such ostentation would be imprudent; and the government of India was prevailed upon to contribute an extra £100,000, even though famine was rife in the subcontinent.

Actually the tour was a triumphant success. Edward adored being the central figure in a picturesque series of durbars, receptions, banquets, processions, ceremonies, addresses, investitures and reviews, though the Queen became wearied by the 'constant repetition of elephants – trappings – jewels – illuminations and fireworks'. The English Prince impressed the Indian princes by his majestic bearing and by his enthusiasm for sport. Edward, assisted in the hunt by 1,200 elephants and 10,000 troops, was delighted with his large bag of tigers. He also enjoyed the disgusting gladiatorial animal fights which were staged for him. Everywhere except in Lucknow the natives, who apparently assumed that he would do something to improve their lot, greeted their future Emperor with enthusiasm. The British community was somewhat less euphoric. The Prince disapproved of their condescending attitude towards the Indians, especially those of princely rank. And for all his devotion to protocol Edward made it distressingly plain that he preferred canoodling with voluptuous young maidens to doing his duty by the stringy memsahibs who, according to seniority, merited his attention. Doubtless Princess Alexandra's suspicions on that score had contributed to her anguish at being left behind in England – Disraeli thought she was going to commit suttee.

The Prince of Wales returned home with a huge treasure trove of gifts, which he got permission to import without paying duty. But this did not help him with his heavy day-to-day expenses. Money, or rather insufficient money, has always been the Achilles' heel of monarchy, and the cost of Edward's upkeep both as prince and king was a perennial source of friction between himself and his government and people. It was made worse because, as Knollys delicately put it, Edward did not possess the 'qualities' of a philanthropist – whereas he did possess a large amount of slum property in Lambeth. In 1900 he admitted, while opening a new housing estate in Bethnal Green, that conditions in his own property were a disgrace to a Christian country. But, with remarkable insouciance, he explained that he was unable to do anything about it because the accommodation was let in small lots on long leases. In view of his professed, and doubtless sincere, concern for improving social conditions, it seemed incongruous that he should continue to make insatiable demands on the public purse while making no effort to live within his income. Yet in general governments brassed up without too much demur. And, as king, Edward actually managed to induce the Treasury to pay his expenses for entertaining foreign sovereigns not only when they were making official visits but on purely private visits as well.

Not all politicians were so obliging. Labouchere opposed increases in grants for the royal family. When the Prince of Wales sarcastically enquired whether he was expected to drown his children like puppy dogs, Labouchere retorted: 'No sir, but Your Royal Highness should live within your income.' * However, for all his public assaults, 'Labby' privately assured the Prince that he was loyal at heart. And he told Knollys that 'there is not the slightest anti-monarchical feeling among the Rads'. Sidney Webb confirmed this view, informing the Prince of Wales in 1897 that the Socialist movement felt a profound affection for the royal family. This was not entirely true. A few Socialists blamed monarchical sentiment for keeping their movement in bourgeois thraldom. But these subversives, men like Keir Hardie, only proved the rule enunciated by Jimmy Thomas in 1920: 'No question of Republicanism as a serious proposition ever found place in Labour discussions.' As it happened, Edward regarded Socialists as being beyond the pale. In his view they were revolutionaries who threatened to destroy the very fabric of a society in which the monarchy was at once the cornerstone and the apex. However, he was willing to patronize suitably deferential Labour MPs, men like Henry Broadhurst, who was delighted to spend a weekend at Sandringham even though he had to eat dinner in his bedroom because he could not afford evening clothes. Edward was also prepared to befriend republicans, if only to persuade them of the error of their ways. He once reproached Gambetta for being a republican: the French-

---

* Commenting on this exchange, Kenneth Rose, the accomplished biographer of George V, betrays a curious sense of values: 'Weighed against the Prince's paternal concern, the radical voice of reason fails to convince.' Rose does not mention that until recently allowances were being paid to Edward VII's bastards from a special royal fund.

man replied that he considered it logical for Edward to be a royalist.

Since nearly all Edward's public utterances were written by his private secretary and couched in the emollient, not to say banal, patois which has become the hallmark of royalty, his subjects could form no real appreciation of his views. He was, in fact, the instinctive foe of progress in almost all its forms. He opposed it in the navy, describing Jackie Fisher's scheme of promotion by merit as socialistic – the incensed admiral inveighed against the 'gimcracks and gewgaws of snobbery'. Edward opposed progress in the army, trying to preserve the traditional red coats at the expense of that 'hideous khaki'. He was a reactionary about the Empire. Despite a professed disapproval of race prejudice, he attempted to prevent the appointment of Indians to the Viceroy's Council. He was a rabid enemy of Home Rule for Ireland, though he did not want it known lest people should ask his opinion about other matters. He applauded the Jameson Raid – a Victorian Bay of Pigs and a prelude to the conflict in South Africa. During the Boer War he wanted to give Kitchener a 'free hand' and he deplored Campbell-Bannerman's all too justified criticism of British 'methods of barbarism'.

At home Edward also believed in the smack of firm government, telling his mother in 1869: 'The more the Government allow the lower classes to get the upper hand, the more the democratic feeling of the present day will increase.' He thought left-wing demonstrations and 'peaceful picketing' should be banned. In some areas, to be sure, he was open to reform and he approved of the gradual extension of the franchise. But by the end of his reign fewer than sixty per cent of adult males had got the vote and, needless to say, the King disapproved of votes for women and thought the Suffragettes pernicious. When the Liberal landslide occurred in 1906, Edward resisted the introduction of radical men and radical measures, and he deplored the fact that the House of Commons was no longer 'an assemblage of "gentlemen"'. He was delighted when the government received a 'wholesome *snub*', one of many, from the Tory-dominated House of Lords. And he was dismayed by Lloyd George's 'People's Budget', which aimed to tax the luxuries of the rich in order to provide the necessities of the poor. The King protested with particular vigour about the Welsh chancellor's attacks on selfish landowners, notably his famous animadversions against the peers – he compared the aristocracy to cheese, the older it is the higher it becomes, and said that 'a fully-equipped Duke costs as much to keep up as two dreadnoughts'. In short, as Sir Charles Dilke said, Edward was 'a strong Conservative and a still stronger JINGO'.

However, Dilke continued, the Prince of Wales was 'a good deal under the influence of the last person who talks to him'. Gladstone agreed. Noting Edward's 'real good nature and sympathy', the Liberal leader reckoned him better fitted to be sovereign than his mother because he was open to argument and would not dictate or domineer. Even so, the Grand Old Man recognized all too well that the Prince had a 'total want of political judgement, either inherited or acquired'. He had never been able to grasp details. He hated paper work. He considered a June general election 'a most untoward event in the middle of the London Season!' Accordingly, not even Tory politicians were willing to treat him as much more than a rubber stamp. His determination not to become a 'mere signing machine' was overridden. Ministers were appointed and dismissed, territory was ceded, and 'Crown' appointments (such as bishops) were made without reference to him. Arthur Balfour, who could barely repress a shudder of aversion at Edward's low brow and gross tastes, continued Gladstone's policy of restricting royal access to cabinet papers. Ministers thus presented monarchs with decisions rather than discussions, limiting the royal prerogative still further. Queen Victoria had complained that Gladstone had kept her 'completely in the dark'. Francis Knollys, on King Edward's behalf, protested that Campbell-Bannerman, though more personally congenial to his sovereign (they had a common interest in food) than the supercilious Balfour, was making 'an absolute fool' of him. The prime minister's reports of cabinet business were so perfunctory as to be almost useless and the King was being 'treated as an absolute puppet'.

Actually Edward did receive a good deal of political information from unofficial sources, especially from that ubiquitous *éminence grise* Lord Esher. Esher was so intimate with the King that Edward was suspected of having caught appendicitis from him shortly before the coronation. He was also a friend of ministers. But he refused several high public offices,

including the Viceroyship of India in 1908, on the grounds that
'I should be throwing away the substance of power for the
shadow.' Esher thus enjoyed power without responsibility and,
being a supreme embodiment of discretion, he became a founder
member of the Establishment.* An urbane courtier, he in-
gratiated himself with Liberals as well as Tories, though some of
the former were worried that so much influence should be
wielded by someone who had no official status. He had an un-
rivalled knack of polite wire-pulling and a penchant for high-
minded intrigue, all in what he took to be the national interest,
worthy of Sir Humphrey Appleby in *Yes, Minister*. Existing, as
Harold Laski put it, in a constant state of genuflexion, he also
flattered the King, giving him an altogether inflated impression
of his capacities. If anything, he said, Edward's authority was
'greater and more openly acknowledged' than his mother's.

This was not the case. King Edward could never be ignored.
He exercised a good deal of influence, especially in military and
diplomatic matters, and as a social arbiter. But he had very little
power. It is often said that he was responsible for ending Britain's
'splendid isolation' and achieving the Entente Cordiale with
France. It may be true that the King's ebullient Francophilia,
displayed to great advantage during his visit to Paris in 1903,
helped to reconcile England's traditional enemy (though not the
English people) to the Entente. With the sort of hyperbole which
kings attract and reward, Sir Charles Petrie has declared that
this was 'among the greatest personal triumphs in the history of
the British Royal Family'. It was, at any rate, his finest hour in a
life singularly devoid of real achievement. But Balfour's cool
comment puts this little Edwardian eminence in its correct perspective: the King 'never made an important suggestion of any
sort on larger questions of policy'.

It is true that on smaller questions in the field of foreign affairs
Edward did have considerable nuisance value. His refusal to
confer the Order of the Garter on the Shah of Persia in 1902
caused considerable embarrassment. So did his indiscreet espousal of the entente with Tsarist Russia in 1908 and his resentment of its unpopularity, which he interpreted as a personal
slight. So did his reference, during a speech in Naples in 1909,

* See p. 168.

to an Anglo-Italian 'alliance' which did not exist. But the greatest difficulties occurred over 'William the Sudden' of Germany. He was the son of Edward's sympathetic sister Vicky, who had found court life at Potsdam an even more sinister form of existence than at Windsor – the feet swelled from interminable standing and the conversation consisted of 'cross little remarks about nothing'. The English King so disliked his nephew, and the relationship between the two countries could be so easily affected by their personal rivalry, that the Foreign Office was always worried about the possibility of a rupture.

If Edward was a caricature of his mother, William was a caricature of his uncle. Indeed, with his coarse tastes, his bombastic manner, his volatile moods, his passion for uniforms, his brutal practical jokes (which had driven a junior officer to suicide), his personal barber (who daily gave the royal moustaches their soldierly erection), and his assumption that by moving from place to place he was getting somewhere, the Kaiser might be regarded as a burlesque on the whole notion of monarchy. Actually, he was a more sinister figure. He once remarked, after hearing about the vagaries of the British legislative system: 'Thank God I am a tyrant.' But it was not just in his contempt for the 'pig-sty' of parliament that the Emperor of the Second Reich was a frightening adumbration of the Führer of the Third. They had much else in common: the ranting monologues, the worship of power, the virulent antisemitism and willingness to kill off lesser breeds, the obscure sexual make-up, the mystical faith in Germany's world mission. Doubtless Edward found all this offensive. But he was even more offended by the fact that William was letting down the royal side. He was a comic-opera king.

His Impulsive Majesty gave way to ridiculous whims, pushed himself forward in the most grotesque fashion. The Viennese said that he insisted on being the stag at every hunt, the bride at every wedding, and the corpse at every funeral. Vain yet charming, egotistical yet warm-hearted, violent yet sentimental, strutting yet unbalanced, William had inherited a crown when he was only fit to wear cap and bells. Edward called him the 'most brilliant failure in history' and tried to preserve good relations between them. But the English King was jealous of his nephew, who inherited his throne first and was periodically cheered in the streets of London. He was exasperated by William's innuendos about his own lack of military experience – Edward was sensitive to taunts that although he wore a field marshal's uniform the closest he had got to war was taking part in the Battle of Flowers at Cannes. He resented the fact that his nephew had come to Cowes with a bigger and faster yacht than his own. Not being able to win any more, he withdrew from racing altogether. The King showed no talent for diplomacy *vis-à-vis* the Kaiser. Not only did he give vent to criticisms which reached his nephew's ears, in 1901 he actually handed him a series of confidential notes which the Foreign Office had prepared to guide the King in his discussions on Anglo-German differences. Despite this *faux pas* Edward tried to maintain his authority in the sphere of foreign policy. It was not surprising that the permanent under-secretary of state for foreign affairs, Eyre Crowe, went around muttering that the King 'must be taught that he is a pawn in the game'.

King or pawn – his people never knew. All they saw was a genial, courtly figure who, although only five foot seven, looked every inch a king. He sounded like a king too; his talk was booming, bonhomous and, except when he was undergoing the rigours of digestion, incessant. Even when he went incognito his majesty was apparent, and those who ignored it were rudely put in their place. Usually, though, even in mufti, the King put on an elaborate show of courtesy, raising his hat right off his head in acknowledgement of his subjects' bows. His popularity as a sportsman knew no bounds. He was especially delighted in 1909 when his horse Minoru won the Derby and the crowd (including even the policemen) roared in patriotic ecstasy: 'Good old Teddy! Teddy boy! Hurrah! Hurrah!' (His golfing would have drawn fewer plaudits – before he lost patience with the game Edward had every bunker he landed in moved.) Generally, though, his affability was quite unforced – he was such a doting paterfamilias that he encouraged his grandchildren to call him Kingy and race slices of buttered toast down the seams of his trousers.

In his ceremonial role, enhanced by the pomp and circum-stance of Elgar, King Edward was superb. The coronation was a spectacle of unprecedented magnificence, and only those in the know joked about the 'King's Loose Box' at Westminster Abbey. It was filled with what were euphemistically described as his 'special friends', including a white-clad Sarah Bernhardt. Nor did the newspapers mention that Edward's last *maîtresse sans titre*, Mrs George Keppel, accompanied him to Biarritz, hovered around him during his final illness and was permitted by Queen Alexandra to bid him farewell on his deathbed. Mrs Keppel's bonds of sympathy with the King had been gluttony and avarice as well as sex, but perhaps the Queen was in a magnanimous mood. For, as she triumphantly exclaimed, when showing Lord Esher her husband's corpse, 'Now at least I know where he is . . .'

Occurring at the beginning of the London season, on 6 May 1910, the King's death was a most untoward event. Everyone and everything was at once swathed in mourning. Edward was the first sovereign to lie in state at St Stephen's Hall, Westminster, something he himself had planned so that his subjects could more easily pay him their final homage – over a quarter of a million people filed silently past his catafalque. Edward had also planned his state funeral, an immense pageant, larger even than Queen Victoria's and much better arranged. Grief, too, was perhaps even more unconfined than at his mother's death. Once again, and possibly with greater emotion, the London prostitutes wore black. A ballad sold in the streets expressed the general feeling:

> A King he was from head to sole,
> Loved by his people one and all.

But what caught the public imagination most about the funeral was not the nine kings, the scarlet and gold cavalcade of princes, the hundreds of distinguished mourners (including Theodore Roosevelt), the gorgeous uniforms of the various regiments, the tolling bells, the minute guns, or the black horses with their nodding plumes, but King Edward's fox-terrier. His name was Caesar and he was led by a Highland servant immediately after the gun-carriage. Actually Caesar caused a problem with the Kaiser, who complained that he had done many things in his life but he had never been obliged to yield precedence to a dog.

People talked about the King's death as a terrible catastrophe and his obituaries painted his sepulchre pure white. The diarist Wilfred Scawen Blunt hoped that the country would soon 'return to comparative sanity, for at present it is in a delirium. He might

have been a Solon and a Francis of Assisi combined if the charac-
ters drawn of him were true. In no print has there been the
smallest allusion to his pleasant little weaknesses. . . . Yet all the
bishops and priests, Catholic, Protestant, and Non-Conformist,
join in giving him a glorious place in heaven.' Even *The Times*,
which on his accession had solemnly refused to pretend that there
was nothing in Edward's career to regret, now printed a flatulent
eulogy. Only one dissentient voice was heard, that of Sir Sidney
Lee. In due course he penned a surprisingly candid portrait of
King Edward for the *Dictionary of National Biography*. True,
the royal foibles were dignified by the swelling orotundity of the
prose. But Lee did acknowledge, among other things, that the
King 'lacked the intellectual ability of a thinker'. This shamefully
iconoclastic remark caused deep offence in the royal family and
hysterical indignation elsewhere. Balfour, who had told Lee that
both he and Lord Salisbury had 'had a very poor opinion of the
King's intellectual capacity', was now obliged to expend pearls
of ingenuity in shuffling off the blame.

It has been suggested that the astonishing hostility which Lee's
essay provoked was due to a fear of Socialism. As Vita Sackville-
West wrote, 'now that the King is dead I expect it will get worse'.
Perhaps this is so. But it is also clear that since the time when
monarchs became chiefly ceremonial figures their vices have been
systematically muffled in silence or cloaked in euphemism, while
their virtues have been displayed like the Crown Jewels.*
Writers, in particular, have willingly suspended disbelief and put
their critical faculties into cold storage. Journalists have become
heralds and biographers have transformed themselves into
hagiographers. As long ago as 1872 Frederic Harrison noticed
that the Crown was sapping 'the fibres of the intellectual world'.
He attacked 'our Royal Literary Funds, our Royal Associations,
our infinite Royal Shoe-blacking and Platter-licking Societies'.
He continued: 'Artist, critic, singer are transfigured into loftier
forms, and make a truly royal chorus singing one hymn – "It
were better to be a door-keeper in the house of my king than a
citizen in the republic of letters."'

The trend was pronounced in the published lives of Queen
Victoria, even Lytton Strachey's, which play down her arro-

* See Chapter 11.

gance, selfishness and, above all, her artless shallowness. This emerges quite plainly in her letters and journals. Here she remarks about the Highlands being full of Highlanders, there that Burns's poetry is 'so poetical', somewhere else that Cetewayo is 'very black'. The very fact that Edward's pleasant little weaknesses were more pronounced than his mother's seems to have made his literary subjects more eager to conceal them, disguise them or explain them away. In life the taboo on printed criticism was seldom breached except when there was an open scandal and Edward's *amour propre* was burnished by the idolatry of society. Long after his death the obsequiousness has scarcely abated. Even Sir Philip Magnus, in his excellent biography, is reluctant to call a jade a jade – he tends to refer to Edward's mistresses as his 'intimate friends'. What is especially strange is that the 1980s, a more candid era which affects to despise Victorian hypocrisy and Edwardian humbug, is in some respects even more mealy-mouthed than they were. Thus, for example, when announcing Prince Andrew's engagement, the BBC employs a courtier's code to describe his earlier sexual adventures, saying that his fondness for 'social life' is an 'open secret'. King Edward is still the victim of such sycophantic cant. In *The Concise Dictionary of National Biography*, published in 1982, Lee's essay is both summarized and distorted in the direction of flattery. The King's controversial lack of intellectual ability is omitted. His philanthropy, his liking for dumb animals and his courage squeeze out his obsession with punctilio, his fondness for his possessions and his addiction to 'the theatre's more frivolous phases'. Perhaps no one should be surprised that in the Valhalla of the Establishment royalty continues to enjoy its own special privileges. For British monarchs are beginning to resemble Roman emperors who, when they died, became gods. In life, certainly, as that dedicated royalist Sir Osbert Sitwell noted, twentieth-century British sovereigns are surrounded by a faint but unmistakable 'odour of ex-officio immortality'.

Six

Father Figurehead

King George V created the modern constitutional monarchy. He read Bagehot. He kept the Crown studiously neutral in politics. He came to terms with democracy. As Harold Nicolson, his biographer, said, 'The ordinary citizens learnt to regard King George both as the father of his people and as the reflection and magnification of their own collective virtues.' He synthesized the strengths of his two predecessors, respectability and pageantry, setting an example of personal rectitude and ceremonial splendour which is followed today. This, at least, is the standard view of his achievement. It would perhaps be more accurate to say that between 1910 and 1936 the monarchy took on its present character because the King lacked the intelligence and the strength to prevent it. George had prejudices rather than opinions, and he scarcely bothered to hide the fact that they were strongly conservative. But to the distress of Tories and the delight of left-wingers, he was unable to exert significant pressure on events. Thus the diarist 'Chips' Channon lamented that the King 'is so uninspiring and does nothing to stem the swelling Socialist tide. A man with more personality and charm could achieve much, and become a rallying point.' Lloyd George, by contrast, rejoiced that although the King was 'a very jolly chap', 'there's not much in his head'. The Welsh Wizard could run rings round the English monarch and he once admitted to having treated him 'abominably'. Balfour once asked Lloyd George: 'Whatever would you do if you had a ruler with brains?'

In George's defence it must be said that he was considerably brighter than his elder brother 'Eddy', Prince Albert Victor. The two boys, born respectively in 1864 and 1865, were brought up together and their tutor, the Rev. John Dalton, was struck by the 'abnormally dormant condition' of Eddy's 'mental powers'. He was a puny, vacuous creature, who seemed to be interested in nothing but practical jokes and uniforms. Less backward, George was made of sterner stuff. Since Eddy was thought to need his brother's moral support, they spent not only their childhood but most of their adolescence together. Despite Queen Victoria's strictures on the suitability of the senior service as a school for delicately nurtured princes – 'a most distasteful profession ... the worst for morals and everything that can be imagined' – they were enrolled as naval cadets. Life afloat taught George the virtues of discipline and, as a younger son, he seemed destined to make the sea his career.

Eddy, however, had to be educated for kingship. So he proceeded to Cambridge, even though, as one of his crammers declared, he 'hardly knows the meaning of the words "to read"'. His academic venture was as brief as the military one which followed it. Eddy became a dandified, moustachioed cavalry officer, earning the nickname 'Collars and Cuffs' because of the efforts he made to disguise his swan neck and simian arms. His behaviour was so peculiar that his general damned him as a 'lunatic' and there was talk of having him 'committed'. Some people suspected that he was Jack the Ripper. Others heard more plausible tales that the police had found him during a raid on a homosexual brothel in Cleveland Street, where he was known as 'Victoria'. The royal family's response to the threat of scandal was to give Eddy a new title, the dukedom of Clarence, and get him betrothed to the sensible Princess May of Teck. She was a minor royalty – a mere Serene Highness – who had been flattened into submission by her enormous, ebullient mother, Princess Mary Adelaide, herself a grand-daughter of King George III. The Tecks were anxious to see their daughter rise in wealth and status, and they sharply overrode May's doubts about marrying Eddy. Her mother snapped: 'If I can put up with your father for twenty-five years, you can handle the Heir Presumptive of Great Britain.' In the event, she was spared the ordeal. For in January 1892, before the wedding could take place, Eddy died of pneumonia. Even today rumours persist that he was poisoned because of the damage his succession would have done to the institution of monarchy. Certainly he was unfit to occupy the throne. Like more recent members of his family – Edward VIII and Princess

Margaret, in their different ways – Eddy constitutes a dire warning about the perils of the hereditary system.

So, stricken with grief and painfully aware that he was quite untrained for the regal office, George faced the prospect of one day succeeding to the throne. He felt altogether inadequate. He was agonizingly shy. His lack of education was palpable. So were his intellectual limitations: he wrote more slowly than anyone Lord Esher had ever seen and his idea of mental exercise was to pore over his stamp collection. So far was he from being a highbrow that, quite late in life, he confused the word with 'eyebrow'. He had a slight lisp and was so ashamed of his knock knees that he would make his own children wear splints to correct the defect. Although anything but mollycoddled in the navy, the Prince had remained surprisingly immature, as evidenced by his homesick letters to 'darling Motherdear', all signed 'your loving little Georgie'. He did, it is true, acquire a couple of mistresses, one in Southsea, the other in St John's Wood, whom he described as 'a ripper'. He also had a little flirtation with his cousin Marie, who was thought suitable and later became Queen of Romania. George was almost pathetically anxious to please his elders and betters. For her part, Queen Victoria decided that May of Teck was the stuff of which crowned heads are made and that she was as qualified to stiffen the sinews of one heir to the throne as another. Having no significant affections to transfer, May was agreeable. And George was willing. So, after a decent interval of mourning for Eddy, the match was, in every sense, arranged. George was instructed by his sister to 'take May out into the garden to look at the frogs in the pond'. There he popped the question and she accepted.

The newspapers did their best to represent this flagrantly dynastic transaction as a fairy-tale romance. But they received no help from the frogs and little from the principals. George and May were as formal and inhibited with each other as they were with others. They were stiff, bloodless figures, almost regal marionettes. They did not hold hands, let alone whisper, cuddle and kiss. As a court lady recorded: 'There is not even any pretence of love-making. May is radiant at her position and abundantly satisfied, but placid and cold as always; the Duke of York [as George had become] apparently nonchalant and indifferent.' The couple seemed to have little in common except royalty. She liked travel and antiques, the latter often acquired by a sovereign scrounging that amounted almost to kleptomania – before her visits, staff at Asprey's, the Bond Street jewellers, were instructed to lock away valuable trinkets because of her habit of pocketing them. By contrast, George had no cultural interests, agreed with his grandmother that Turner was 'mad', and got his main pleasure from killing animals – he was a superb shot. Neither had much imagination, but May enjoyed reading as much as she hated music. George read little except the occasional thriller – 'awful rubbish', as his wife tactfully informed one of his favourite authors, John Buchan. Although he had the royal 'treasure of the Nibelung' to choose from, George filled his modest house on the Sandringham estate, York Cottage, with reproductions from the Royal Academy and furniture from Maples.

Yet this ill-assorted pair grew genuinely fond of one another. George was a fearsome domestic despot and May a slavishly obedient wife – she even allowed him to dictate her clothes, which remained staidly old-fashioned. In the realm of ideas, too, May never challenged him. George's clever aunt Vicky wrote: 'All her thoughts, views and ideas appear to me to be rather banal, commonplace and conventional.' Yet 'George's dragon' possessed real strength of character and he depended on her so much that he felt ill if they were separated. The French called the full-busted May 'Soutien-Georges' – meaning George's support and a pun on *soutien-gorge* (brassière). An Englishman would describe them as 'George the Fifth and Mary the Four-Fifths'.* The singularly unemotional nature of their partnership was perhaps typified by May's remark when her husband first went down in a submarine: 'I shall be very disappointed if George doesn't come up again.'

As parents George and May were equally dispassionate. One contemporary described her as 'no mother at all'. George, obsessed by punctilio, behaved like a martinet and treated his offspring like errant midshipmen. May found it impossible to hug and kiss her infants, consigning them instead to the care of an insanely vicious nanny (who was eventually dismissed). The future King George VI apparently developed his stammer be-

* Her name was Mary, but until she became Queen she was known as May.

cause he was forced to struggle against the vice of being left-handed. Secretly May doted on her handsome eldest son, who was always called David in the family. But she did not show affection and seemed surprised when he did: 'I really believe he begins to like me at last, he is most civil to me.' Lack of parental love must have played its part in the future King Edward VIII's sacrificing the throne for a woman whom his mother called 'an adventuress'.

In society the Yorks were almost equally unbending. She retreated behind a glacial formality, never travelled without an enormous retinue of servants and laid down minute instructions about protocol. Though she enjoyed risqué stories, May seldom laughed, believing that her laugh was vulgar and made her look like a horse. He was described by Queen Marie of Romania as a 'real tyrant & stickler at form like his father, but without his father's renowned ease of manner'. However, among friends George could relax to some extent, though perhaps his booming loquacity was partly due to nerves. In 1895 the author Augustus Hare met the Duke of York at a grand house party. George was

> very unaffected and pleasant, really a very nice prince, and quite good-looking. He never fails to be punctual to the moment – a grand quality in a prince, and due, probably, to naval discipline. He talks a great deal, and talks well, but in reality princes have no chance – no chance at all – conversationally, as no one ever contradicts them however much they disagree; no subjects are aired but those which they choose for themselves, and the merest commonplaces from royal lips are listened to as though they were oracles.

Actually, George 'hated all insincerity and flattery', as Lord Esher noted. But in due course he got 'so accustomed to people agreeing with him that he resented the candid friend business'. Esher concluded wrly: 'Kings never like opposition or remonstrance, even the best of them.' Certainly by the time he became Prince of Wales, George was used to laying down the law and not particularly worried, or perhaps not aware, when others found his prejudices offensive. About ten years after Hare penned his comments, another author, Edmund Gosse, took a somewhat more jaundiced view of George: 'an overgrown schoolboy, loud and stupid, losing no opportunity of abusing the [Liberal] government'.

This was fair comment. When George inherited the throne in 1910, he could only be described as dim and reactionary. A satirical poet, unimpressed by the mystique of monarchy, celebrated the new reign with verses which ended alternately, 'The King is duller than the Queen' and 'The Queen is duller than the King'. Lloyd George, a particular *bête noire* of the monarch's, was revolted by the political air which pervaded the court:

> The whole atmosphere reeks of Toryism. I can breathe it and it depresses and sickens me. Everybody very civil to me as they would be to a dangerous wild animal. . . . The King is hostile to the bone to all who are working to lift the workmen out of the mire. So is the Queen. They talk exactly as the late King and Kaiser talked to me if you remember about the old Railway strike. 'What do they want striking?' 'They are very well paid', etc.

Certainly, in the two major political crises which blew up at the beginning of George's reign – Peers *v.* People and Home Rule for Ireland – he evinced a firm inclination to support the forces of reaction.

After they won the first general election of 1910 and passed Lloyd George's budget, the Liberals mounted a determined attack on the House of Lords, that hospital for Tory incurables and crucial buttress of the throne. Deeply resenting this, George encouraged the contending parties to reach a compromise at the constitutional conference held during the summer and autumn of 1910. In doing so he neglected Asquith's warning that 'it is not the function of a Constitutional Sovereign to act as arbiter or mediator between rival parties or policies. Still less, to take advice from the leaders of both sides, with a view to forming a conclusion of his own.' Inevitably, the conference failed. Now, it was clear, the hereditary assembly would have to be prevented by law from stultifying the purposes of the democratic one. Before he acquired a fresh mandate from the people, Asquith required a solid pledge from the King. Asquith wanted him to promise that he would, if necessary, create enough peers to ensure the passing of the Parliament Act, which would curb the Lords' powers. Though trying to preserve a façade of neutrality, George was most reluctant to give this guarantee because, as he told Ponsonby, he was being advised 'by the party whose views he does not support'.

In the last resort, however, he had no alternative. This did not stop him inveighing against Asquith's behaviour and asserting that he was 'not quite a gentleman' – a slur which Churchill disloyally passed on to the prime minister. Actually, in keeping the guarantees secret, Asquith saved the King much embarrassment. Throughout, the Liberal leader acted with a discretion that was perhaps too scrupulous. He insisted on the fundamental point that the Crown could only take ministerial advice, otherwise it would become 'the football of contending factions'. But he found dealing with his voluble and obscurantist sovereign a struggle. He likened going to see the King to having a tooth pulled, and he concluded patronizingly that George was 'a nice little man with a good heart and tries hard to be just and open minded. It is a pity he was not better educated.' His wife Margot was even less reverential about royalties: 'To them, clever men are "prigs"; clever women are "too advanced"; Liberals are "Socialists"; the uninteresting "pleasant"; the interesting "intriguers"; and the dreamer "mad".'

The King's attempt to arbitrate over the vexed question of Home Rule was also doomed. Admittedly, in view of the intransigence of Ulster where, as Churchill said, 'medieval hatreds and barbarous passions' raged, there was even less room for compromise. But George was hampered by the fact that his natural allies, the Tories, were flirting with treason in their determination to maintain the union. Balfour's successor as Conservative leader, Bonar Law, openly announced that he was willing to proceed to all extremes over the issue. Nor did he modify his language for royalty. Law said that now George was involved in the political struggle, he would either have to accept Home Rule or dismiss his ministers, 'and in either case, half your subjects will think you have acted against them'. George flushed and Law afterwards remarked: 'I think I have given the King the worst five minutes he has had for a long time.' Lord Esher went a step further than Law. In view of the danger of civil war, he positively advised the King to dismiss Asquith and appoint an impartial figure like Lord Rosebery, who would then hold a general election. The press got wind of rumours that the King was being influenced by 'Court hangers-on'. Of course, this was denied, and George smartly scotched Esher's irresponsible plan. However, the King did tell Asquith in February

1914 that the time '*would* come' when he 'should feel it his duty to do what in his own judgement was best for the people generally'. The surprised premier 'earnestly trusted' that the King would neither refuse his assent to the Home Rule Bill, such a thing not having been done since Queen Anne's reign, nor dismiss his ministers. George temporized. Then he pressed for a 'settlement by consent', which sounded suspiciously like a capitulation to the Ulster 'loyalists'. At any rate, the King complained to one Liberal minister, Lewis Harcourt, that if he signed the bill he would be hissed in the streets of Belfast. Harcourt retorted that if he didn't sign he'd be hissed in the streets of London. 'Damned impertinent,' growled the King.

Of course the Irish issue was swallowed up by Armageddon. But before that the King had done much to establish himself in the affections of all his subjects, notably through his dignified performance of splendid ceremonial. He found it a trial, as Max Beerbohm suggested in this account of the state opening of parliament in 1914: 'The little king with the great diamond crown that covered his eyebrows, and with the eyes that showed so tragically much of effort, of the will to please – the will to impress – the will to be all that he isn't and that his Papa *was* (or seems to him to have been) . . . such a piteous, good, feeble, heroic little figure.' Nevertheless, royal ritual obviously stimulated mass loyalty at a time of serious industrial strife. George was as hostile to Socialism as his father had been and, like him, wanted to outlaw peaceful pickets. He was inclined to interpret big strikes as incipient revolution and to talk about locking up union leaders and sending in troops who 'should be given a free hand'. Naturally he sympathized with the poor, but his idea of ameliorating their lot was to tour depressed areas – he was particularly delighted by the welcome he received in Keir Hardie's South Wales constituency. As a means of keeping the people happy he clearly had less faith in bread than in circuses. Oddly enough, he had an ally in Lloyd George. For his own cynical purposes, the Wizard conjured up the Investiture of Edward, Prince of Wales, at Caernarvon in 1911. There was no record of any such Welsh pageant having been held before. Nor was there a precedent for the Prince to be dressed in satin breeches and a mantle and surcoat of purple velvet edged with ermine. This 'preposterous rig' would, he feared, make him a laughing-stock among his naval chums.

The King himself, who thought David looked 'so nice', was touched by the Investiture. Later in the year, he was moved to tears by the demonstration of Indian loyalty which occurred at the Delhi Durbar – a spontaneous outburst which this magnificent spectacle was carefully calculated to provoke. (It must be said that George wept easily – at the sight of a dead garden bird, for example, despite the fact that he shot thousands of pheasants every year.) Decked out in the full coronation fig, and wearing a heavy new crown, which cost the people of India £60,000 (and which George took back to England with him), the King, accompanied by the Queen, who was dripping with diamonds, processed from the durbar camp, which covered twenty-five square miles and housed 300,000 people. They were escorted by a glittering cavalcade and saluted by 101 guns. At the specially prepared amphitheatre they entered the durbar hall, a tented pavilion with a golden cupola. Preceded by Indian attendants carrying peacock fans, yak-tails and gilt maces, flanked by picturesque dignitaries, their heavy purple trains carried by ten Indian pages of distinguished family, the King and Queen took their places on solid silver thrones raised on a high dais. After speeches and boons, the couple received the obeisance of the Indian princes. Dressed in their most sumptuous outfits and following one another in strict order of precedence, they paid homage and made fabulous offerings. The Nizam of Hyderabad's gift was a necklace of rubies, each one the size of a pigeon's egg; the Maharaja of Panna gave an umbrella, twelve inches in diameter, made out of a single emerald. No wonder the King put his trust in princes. He urged that those of India should be 'treated with greater tact and sympathy', more 'as equals' and less 'as schoolboys'. They might be feudal autocrats, they might be intelligent or insane, enlightened or corrupt. But their kind of paternalism met the needs of the British and of their own people – so, at least, George thought. And as if to show that royal irresponsibility knows no boundaries, he himself proceeded to neglect some of his official duties in pursuit of sport. His bag amounted to twenty-one tigers, eight rhinoceroses and one bear. The Viceroy complained about the King's 'craze for shooting': 'His perspective of what is proper is almost destroyed.'

In general, however, just as the King was neurotically punctual, he was a self-conscious model of propriety. He felt that the monarchy should be above reproach. When he came to the throne, for example, he quickly raised the very low wages of estate workers at Sandringham because he feared a scandal. Similarly, he paid £64,000 to prevent his father's compromising letters to the Countess of Warwick, a socialite turned Socialist, being published abroad. Like Edward VII, George did not like to hear criticisms of what was established, and he took great exception to Churchill's remark that there were 'idlers and wastrels at both ends of the social scale'. In private George was surprisingly tolerant of sexual peccadilloes, provided they were not homosexual – 'I thought people like that shot themselves.' Though he religiously read a chapter of the Bible every night (and found 'some very queer things in it'), propriety loomed larger in his world view than morality. His standards of etiquette were so strict and so archaic that people still had to ask permission to appear at court in spectacles. The autocrat of the breakfast table hid the mess made by his pet parrot, Charlotte, underneath the mustard pot.

However, George's blimpish prejudices and overflowing garrulity sometimes led him into imprudence. He did not always heed the counsel of Lord Rosebery, who told him in 1910 that 'every word of a King is treasured in this country as if it were God's'. This was not just because a monarch was regarded as a magical being but because, living permanently at the centre of affairs, he might be supposed to know more than others. George would have certainly done well to curb his tongue in talking to Prince Henry of Prussia on the eve of the Great War. For, by expressing the hope that England would remain neutral, the King encouraged the Kaiser's bellicosity. George was even less guarded on military matters, about which, thanks to his shipboard training, he could claim some expertise. Unhappily, he was a naval as well as a political conservative and he threw his weight against Admiral Fisher's necessary reforms before the war. As First Lord of the Admiralty, Winston Churchill was withering about the cheap and silly drivel spouted by the King on naval matters. Churchill had never heard such stupidity and his First Sea Lord, Prince Louis of Battenberg, agreed that the King knew nothing of naval strategy. Curiously, though, George's instinct that the erratic Fisher would be a disastrous successor to Battenberg, when anti-German hysteria drove him from office in October 1914, proved absolutely right. The ancient admiral reciprocated royal hostility in full, nicknaming the King and Queen 'Futile and Fertile'. Actually, Queen Mary's war work was less fertile than futile. She found it almost impossible to unbend sufficiently to commiserate with soldiers wounded in the trenches. And she arranged an orgy of knitting among the aristocracy which had the effect of increasing unemployment in the clothing industry.

Still, there is no doubt that the royal couple did become the paramount focus for patriotism during the First World War. The King could not carry off grand ceremonial occasions with the aplomb of his father. He was simply not an inspiring figure: inspecting the Grenadier Guards in France he looked, according to Raymond Asquith, 'as glum and dyspeptic as ever'. But George and Mary compensated for their dullness by transcendent worthiness. The frugal life they imposed on themselves was often cited as an example to the nation. So was the King's gesture of taking the pledge, part of Lloyd George's campaign to stop the war effort from being impeded by the demon drink. Of course, this somewhat naïve exercise (not imitated by its Welsh instigator) also attracted ridicule. This would have been more widespread if it had been known that, even after the medicinal potations which he had been permitted when seriously injured in a riding accident in 1915, the King continued to indulge in secret tipples.

An even more carefully guarded state secret was the fact that throughout the war George exerted all the influence at his command on the side of the 'Brasshats' and against the 'Frocks'. In other words, he supported the generals, especially Sir Douglas Haig and Sir William Robertson, against the elected representatives of the people, especially Lloyd George. Unfortunately, if George was little of a sailor, he was much less of a soldier, which did not stop him explaining to generals how they had conducted their campaigns or complaining that the normally laconic Kitchener talked so much he could not get a word in edgeways. Even his favourite commander, Haig, who had married one of the Queen's ladies-in-waiting, recognized that he had little grasp of war. Haig wrote: 'The King seemed anxious, but he did not give one the impression that he fully realized the grave issues both for our country as well as for his own House.'

The King only had one military axiom, which he expounded to Bonar Law in 1916: 'The politicians should leave the conduct of the war to experts.' Perhaps this axiom is never true, but during the First World War it was tragically erroneous. The experts delayed the introduction of convoys at sea, and on land they masterminded bloody slogging matches like the Somme and Passchendaele. By and large the politicians were more imaginative, and men like Lloyd George and Churchill possessed genius.

Thus the various royal interventions were sadly misguided, not to say unconstitutional. In March 1917, for example, Haig recorded in his diary: 'The King ... stated that he would "support me through thick and thin", but I must be careful not to resign because Lloyd George would then appeal to the country for support and would probably come back with a great majority. ... The King's position would then be very difficult.' Lloyd George's own position was difficult because the Liberals still owed nominal allegiance to Asquith, whom he had superseded in 1916. He was thus a prime minister without a party and, had he not possessed such superlative political gifts, the royal intrigues might have caused him more than inconvenience. Indeed, one of his first mistakes, made perhaps in an attempt to conciliate the sovereign, was to bow to his pressure and appoint Sir Edward Carson as First Lord of the Admiralty. But, as the King was all too aware, the premier could always go to the country if he were pressed too hard. He threatened to do so when George tried to insist on Robertson's being retained as Chief of the Imperial General Staff in 1918. The King might have called his bluff, but the monarchy itself would have been at stake and he was not prepared to risk it. Nor could he do much but fulminate about Lloyd George's 'assumption of autocratic powers' in response to the premier's other tactics. These were to leave the sovereign's letters unanswered, to starve him of information, to present him with *faits accomplis*, and occasionally to show him the iron fist. Thus in 1918 the King's private secretary, Lord Stamfordham, protested about the fact that his master had learned of General Trenchard's resignation as Chief of the Air Staff from the newspapers. An angry Lloyd George sent Stamfordham away 'with a flea in his ear, telling him that the King was encouraging mutiny by taking up the cause of ... officers ... whom the Government had decided to get rid of'.

Insulated from the excesses of popular chauvinism, the King had at first hoped that the belligerents would fight 'like gentlemen'. He had even hoped to remain on terms of personal friendship with German and Austrian princelings, many of whom, of course, were his relations. By 1917, however, when a German victory looked quite possible, George lost his nerve. Russia was knocked out of the war and his cousin, Tsar Nicholas II, and his family were imprisoned. At home H. G. Wells wrote to *The Times* asserting that the moment had come 'to rid ourselves of the ancient trappings of throne and sceptre'. He also disparaged the court as 'alien and uninspiring'. The King exclaimed indignantly: 'I may be uninspiring but I'm damned if I'm an alien.' Needless to say, his Teutonic ancestry was testified to in a thousand genealogies. Moreover his dynasty, Hanoverian, and his surname, Saxe-Coburg, were indisputably German. Rumours that he must therefore be pro-German abounded. When the King first heard them he 'started and grew pale'. So, like many of his subjects who were trying to conceal their German origins, the King changed his family name – to Windsor. An even more craven capitulation to contemporary hysteria was the withdrawal, at the King's insistence, of the government's offer of asylum to the Tsar and his family. Crowns and thrones were trembling and so was George V. Perhaps his father had been right to introduce him as 'the future last King of England'. To obviate this disaster, Lord Stamfordham was instructed to tell Arthur Balfour, who was foreign secretary in 1917, that 'the residence in this country of the ex-Emperor and Empress would be strongly resented by the public, and would undoubtedly compromise the position of the King and Queen'. Thus the ancient House of Romanov perished in order that the newborn House of Windsor should survive.

Later, apparently, Queen Mary was anguished by their failure to help the Tsar. But although George gave vent to a lot of what Asquith called 'man-in-the-bus nonsense' about the murderous Bolsheviks, there is no record that he ever expressed contrition for helping to block what was probably his cousin's only escape route. Still, his moral cowardice made political sense. For the less George was associated in the public mind with foreign autocrats, indeed with aliens of almost any description, the better. Before the war ended George would inform Franklin D.

Roosevelt: 'You know, I have a number of relations in Germany, but I can tell you frankly that in all my life, I have never seen a German gentleman.'

In 1918 the King's advisers were making a deliberate effort to improve what would later be called his 'image'. A press secretary was appointed. It was even suggested that some of the old-fashioned court practices should be abandoned, such as ladies' wearing trains and feathers. Clive Wigram, the assistant private secretary, wanted 'people of all classes' to come to Buckingham Palace, saying that 'the barriers have to be broken down if the Monarchy is to live'. Curiously enough, at almost the same time an older courtier, Sir Frederick Ponsonby, was giving precisely the opposite advice to the King's eldest son: 'I think there is a risk in your making yourself accessible. . . . The Monarchy must always retain an element of mystery. A Prince should not show himself too much. The Monarchy must remain on a pedestal.' The task of modern British sovereigns is, of course, to reconcile these irreconcilables, to combine the mythopoeic and the prosaic, to persuade democracy that the ginger-bread coach contains just folks, that the gloved hand retains the common touch. Being a rigid traditionalist, George V accepted Ponsonby's counsel rather than Wigram's. Even the Great War was not permitted seriously to disrupt royal routine. In February 1918 Lord Esher described Buckingham Palace as a Rip Van Winkle world, where nothing had changed for years. It consisted of a life made up of nothings, yet it was a busy scene, with constant telephonings about trivialities, perpetual discussions about protocol and costume. Still, it was evidently what the people wanted. When the armistice was signed, on 11 November 1918, crowds surged round Buckingham Palace in an ecstasy of mafficking.

In the frenetic postwar world King George represented solid prewar standards. He still wore a frock-coat, had his trousers creased at the side, put on the same collar stud he had been using for fifty years. He began his diary each day with a meticulous weather report and conducted his life with such precision that he seemed automated by some internal alarm clock. He deplored the new fashions, the short skirts and painted nails, the nightclubs and jazz, the cocktails and immoral weekends, films like *Battleship Potemkin*, which featured a naval mutiny, the all-round sloppiness. Much more did he lament the spread of democracy throughout the Empire and the spread of Socialism at home. But now he increasingly curbed and concealed his political prejudices. He had had a fright in 1917. He had another one in 1918 when, as the Prince of Wales wrote to him, 'a regular epidemic of revolutions & abdications' made it 'a hard & critical time for the remaining monarchies'. The King's advisers told him that his own position was now not as secure as it had been in 1914. On 4 November 1918 Lord Esher warned that 'The monarchy and its cost will have to be justified in the future in the eyes of a war-torn and hungry proletariat, endowed with a huge preponderance of voting power.' Early in 1919 Bonar Law found the King 'in a funk ... talking about the ... danger of revolution'.

It was now clear that Bolshevism was a contagion that could cross frontiers at the drop of a crown. Its ideology had evidently permeated the ranks of Labour. At a meeting in the Albert Hall immediately after the war, Bob Williams, secretary of the Transport Workers Union, announced: 'I hope to see the Red Flag flying over Buckingham Palace.' A couple of years later, on the third anniversary of the Russian Revolution, at a Communist meeting (also held at the Albert Hall) the King's name was hissed. Admittedly, at the Labour Party conference in 1923 delegates overwhelmingly rejected (by 3,694,000 to 386,000 votes) a motion that 'The Royal Family is no longer necessary as part of the British Constitution.' Even so, the rise of Labour was disquieting – Lloyd George himself was preferable. But the King took the only sensible course, which was to disguise his opposition to it. As the Tory Party chairman J. C. C. Davidson wrote, George V was 'an absolutely dyed-in-the-wool conservative. . . . He was very right-wing and he knew where his friends really lay, and that the Conservative Party was the King's Party and a radical party was not. But he managed to persuade the Labour Party that he was entirely neutral. That must have required a great deal of self-discipline.'

Perhaps so, but the King was manfully assisted by the Labour Party itself. To some extent this was a matter of political calculation: the monarchy was popular and there was no sense in alienating voters by attacking it. In any case, Labour was committed to gradualism. Those Fabian ideologues, Sidney and Beatrice Webb, concluded that the monarchy was a 'useful anachronism'. Compromises with the past were necessary. One compromise that Sidney did reject, however, was over knee-breeches, which enraged the King. He was only mollified when Jimmy Thomas, with whom George enjoyed a roguish relationship, explained that Sidney could not oblige him because Beatrice wore the knee-breeches. All the same, there was a lot of good old-fashioned snobbery in the Labour Party. Some Socialists could even be heard rhapsodizing over the 'mysteries of royalty' and the 'poetry of kingship'. As late as George VI's reign, Harold Nicolson noted in his diary that Herbert Morrison 'spoke of the King as Goebbels might have spoken about Hitler. I admit the King does his job well. But why should Morrison speak as if he were a phenomenon?' In George V's reign no one was more intoxicated by the romance of royalty, or more Heepishly humble in its presence, than Ramsay MacDonald. Formerly a fire-eating radical who had spoken of importing Bolshevism to Britain, the Labour leader now found his highest felicity in succumbing to the titled embrace.

When Stanley Baldwin led the Tories to defeat in the general election of 1923, the King must have shared Balfour's view that it would be a national catastrophe if Labour, which now had 191 MPs to 258 Conservatives and 158 Liberals, took office. So, probably in the hope that a Liberal–Tory coalition could be formed, the King persuaded Baldwin not to resign until he was defeated in the Commons. In the absence of a written constitution, it was unclear whether this was a misuse of the royal prerogative. Five years later, though, the monarch decided that the verdict of the poll was more important than the verdict of parliament, and should be implemented at once. The reason given for this was that by 1929 the franchise had been extended, but the King was scarcely one to attach undue importance to the 'flapper vote'. The fact is that for all his quarter-deck breeziness he was sensitive to criticism. After the election of 1923 he was accused of having tried to frustrate the will of the people. The King complained bitterly to MacDonald that, at a meeting in the East End, his Labour lieutenant George Lansbury had pointedly recalled the fate which had befallen Charles I. (The threat was particularly incongruous because Lansbury was a prominent pacifist whose *Daily Herald* contained even more royal coverage than its Fleet Street competitors.)

MacDonald could not have been more conciliatory. When the Liberals refused to cooperate with the Tories and a Labour government became inevitable, he promised to introduce 'no extreme legislation or . . . violent administrative changes'. He would not 'play . . . up the Clyde division' (i.e. his left wing), and he did not include Lansbury in his ministry. Once Labour was in power the only problem seemed to be what to do about court dress. There were compromises on both sides and Labour ministers presented themselves in blue, gold-braided tail-coats and white knee-breeches with sword. Some Labour MPs scorned their leaders for participating in a 'medieval circus' and surrendering to the 'swell mob'. But the King was much reassured. He found MacDonald 'quite straight'. For his part, the prime minister found the King 'considerate, cordially correct, human and friendly'. In February 1924 George wrote to 'Motherdear' about his new servants: 'They have different ideas to ours as they are all socialists, but they ought to be given a chance & ought to be treated fairly.'

This was a commendable attitude, though George had little alternative but to adopt it. Even MacDonald acknowledged that, had the King cold-shouldered the first Labour government, it would have returned the treatment with interest. All the sovereign could do was to put on a show of even-handedness, while working behind the scenes to preserve the essentials of the status quo, or, as the Duke of Windsor later put it, to conduct his 'private war with the twentieth century'. Occasionally the King permitted himself to be provoked by Labour. He was furious, for example, when left-wing MPs derided the Duke of York's Australian tour as an expensive 'joy ride'. It was being made, they said, by 'mere figure-heads instead of the representatives of democratic Government', and they sneered at the 'sob stuff' about the Duchess's leaving behind her child, the future Queen Elizabeth II.

The King feared that the General Strike of 1926 'smacked of revolution' and wanted the government to proclaim martial law and arrest union leaders. But, conscious of the deep rift between the classes which the strike both reflected and exacerbated, he told his children 'to abstain from all public or private comment on the issues and to remain more or less out of sight until the trouble blew over'. Far from heeding this counsel, his eldest son travelled round London with 'friends in the Metropolitan Police'. He also lent his chauffeur to help distribute copies of Winston Churchill's inflammatory newspaper, the *British Gazette*, which was demanding the 'unconditional surrender' of the strikers. The King himself was more cautious. Indeed, true to his paternal appearance and to his paternalistic leanings, he at times urged a degree of moderation on the government. He commiserated with his poorest subjects, though he rejoiced at the eventual 'victory for law & order'.

After the strike, the King issued an appeal for national unity. He pleaded, as he had done so effectively to the Irish in 1921, that the bitterness should be forgotten. Instead, all 'able and well-disposed men should cooperate' to build the future. George's own contribution to this work was limited. He was inclined to refuse important public engagements when they clashed with his holidays at Sandringham. He would not pay state visits – 'Abroad is awful. I know. I have been.' He badgered his ministers about trivial breaches of decorum – MPs' deportment, the Lord Chancellor's hat. (F. E. Smith riposted rudely: 'I don't like the King's brown bowler, but I'm not always ringing up to say so.') When Gandhi came to confer over the fate of India the King almost refused to receive him. 'What! Have this rebel fakir in the Palace after he has been behind all these attacks on my loyal officers?' Finally the Mahatma was admitted, the King glaring indignantly at his bare knees and sending him off in due course with the injunction: 'Remember, Mr Gandhi, I won't have any attacks on my Empire.' Naturally, as both King and Emperor, George V wanted unity in his dominions and reconciliation among his subjects. But it had to be on his own – deeply conservative – terms.

This was particularly apparent when it came to the formation of the National Government in the summer of 1931. Faced by the 'run on the pound', Ramsay MacDonald was able to convince only a bare majority of the Labour cabinet to support the cuts in unemployment pay deemed necessary to restore financial confidence. His only course, if he wanted to preserve the unity of his party, was to resign. Certainly this was the course which his colleagues expected him to follow. But MacDonald allowed the King to persuade him instead to construct a coalition government to deal with the crisis. More of a romantic than a radical,

MacDonald was flattered by the royal importunities, and he did not consult his own rank and file. Thus he found himself presiding over a 'National Government' of Conservatives and Liberals, which was opposed by most Labour MPs. The autumn general election made his position even more anomalous. For although different elements of the National Government could only agree to disagree, all calling for a 'doctor's mandate' and each recommending different cures, they won a huge victory at the polls. Labour was reduced to a rump of 52 seats, while MacDonald, though still nominally prime minister, had to follow the lead of the 473 Conservatives behind him. The King pronounced the result of the general election 'marvellous'.

Labour bitterness at the electoral débâcle expressed itself in dark suspicions of conspiracy and betrayal, and many Socialists criticized the Crown for its part in creating the National Government. They claimed that a Patriot King had jockeyed them out of power by spurious appeals to the national interest. Harold Laski declared that the sovereign's proper role was 'that of dignified emollient rather than of an active umpire between conflicting interests'. According to Laski, George V had chosen MacDonald as George III had chosen Bute. The National Government was the product of a palace revolution. The King's intervention was an affront to British parliamentary democracy. However, Laski himself acknowledged that 'The metaphysics of limited monarchy do not easily lend themselves to critical discussion.' Constitutional judgements are, more than most, matters of predilection and prejudice. This is because the political functions of the modern monarch are shrouded in mystery and there is no written constitution from which logical inferences can be drawn. Still, although this was perhaps the most important intervention in his reign, it is fairly clear that, at the very least, the King did not sin against the canons of Bagehot. He merely advised and encouraged MacDonald, who responded with his humble duty.

Instead of complaining that the royal prerogative had been misused, Labour would have done better to recognize that it was fulfilling its invariable function. This was to resist change, or, better still perhaps, to ensure that the more things changed the more they remained the same. George had little scope for taking the initiative except at times of political crisis or stalemate. But when the opportunity arose he naturally acted in the spirit of Balfour's famous declaration that the Conservatives 'should still control, whether in power or whether in opposition, the destinies of this great Empire'. Sometimes those destinies were best served by a puppet-show of progress, when Conservatives were pulling the strings of Labour marionettes. From the King's point of view, the National Government, fronted by a congenial Socialist and dominated by staunch Tories, was admirably balanced.

George had little else to gratify him as the devil's decade advanced. He was distressed by the rise of fascism, thought Mussolini (who was using the Italian monarchy to dignify his dictatorship) a 'mad dog', loathed the violence of the Nazis. But he feared above all things another war and threatened to demonstrate for peace in Trafalgar Square, or even to abdicate, rather than countenance it. For much of the time the King's health was poor and, having few inner resources, he was bored and irascible. He cursed his servants. He called loudly to a lord in waiting who was ushering out Emir Amanullah of Afghanistan: 'Shut the door! I can smell that damned nigger from here!' He shouted at his family and expressed particular displeasure at the conduct and appearance of his eldest son. 'He has not a single friend who is a gentleman,' lamented the King. To the Prince he would vociferate: 'You dress like a cad. You act like a cad. You *are* a cad. Get out!' And to Baldwin the King prophesied with startling accuracy: 'After I am dead, the boy will ruin himself in twelve months.'

From inside the charmed circle not a whisper of discord reached the public. As the Duke of Windsor later recorded, 'The British Press still abstained from commenting on the private doings of the Royal Family.' Indeed, this reticence added to the King's fury when he read familiar accounts of his son's activities in vulgar American rags. In any case, the British people were increasingly in the thrall of a new medium, the wireless, a powerful organ of royalist propaganda. They responded eagerly to the 'aural pageants' broadcast by the BBC, whose director-general, Sir John Reith, quite deliberately set out 'to serve the House' of Windsor – his old age was embittered by the fact that he was left off the guest list for Buckingham Palace garden parties. What transfixed listeners most were the King's own Christmas broadcasts, none more successful than the first, in

1932, which was written by Kipling. The air waves proved to be the ideal means of humanizing the monarchy while actually enhancing its mystique. In fact, everything conspired to give the public the most favourable view of their King. What is more, after his death no retrospective lèse-majesté was permitted. George's official biographer, Harold Nicolson, was instructed to 'omit things and incidents which were discreditable to the royal family'. King George VI's private secretary told him: 'You will be writing on the subject of a myth and it will have to be mythological.' When Nicolson asked Sir Owen Morshead what he should do if he unearthed a major scandal he was told firmly: 'Your first duty will always be to the Monarchy.'

So both the Silver Jubilee of 1935 and the King's funeral the following year were splendid opportunities for a massive demonstration of loyalty to the Crown. Confident that the British ceremonies were more ancient and more dignified than the strident and sinister performances of the fascist dictators (though Mussolini did make various bogus attempts to resuscitate Roman rituals), the British rallied round their King. Only republicans like H. G. Wells disparaged the Jubilee display of uniforms, banners, bands and bunting. He was amazed that 'For millions these shows are naturally accepted as the realities.' But as the cheering and singing throng demonstrated, their feelings were real. George himself was modestly surprised and profoundly moved by their obvious enthusiasm. Certainly there was no disguising their grief at his death. A million mourners filed past the catafalque as he lay in state in Westminster Hall. Perhaps many shared the feeling of Duff Cooper who, when he heard the famous final bulletin – 'The King's life is drawing peacefully to its close' – concluded tearfully and 'without any logical justification, that we were passing another milestone on the road to disaster'. The growing Nazi menace made such apprehensions understandable. But there were other reasons for anxiety. As his father's cortège jolted through the streets of London the new King, Edward VIII, observed the jewelled Maltese cross from the crown on his father's coffin fall to the ground (to be retrieved by one of the bearers). He was not alone in wondering 'if it was a bad omen'. Probably the old King himself had been haunted by such fears. After all, as Harold Nicolson estimated, the quarter of a century in which he reigned witnessed the disappearance of five emperors, eight kings, and eighteen minor dynasties. Royal last words are more apocryphal than most and, though it is often stated that George V's were 'Bugger Bognor', he apparently did ask: 'How is the Empire?' Only cynics suggest that what he really said was: 'Who is the Umpire?'

Seven

Royal Quisling?

King George V forecast that his eldest son would ruin himself within twelve months. But at Edward's birth, in June 1894, an equally startling prophecy was made – by Keir Hardie. The Labour leader predicted in the House of Commons:

> From his childhood this boy will be surrounded by sycophants and flatterers by the score, and will be taught to believe himself as of a superior creation. A line will be drawn between him and the people he is to be called upon some day to reign over. In due course, following the precedent which has already been set, he will be sent on a tour round the world, and probably rumours of a morganatic alliance will follow [Loud cries of Oh! Oh! and Order] and at the end of it all . . . the country will be called upon to pay the bill.

Hardie was not just uncannily prescient about the future King's marital crisis, he correctly pointed to an essential element in his more fundamental 'identity crisis'. A modish phrase, yet in response to his father's exhortation, 'You must always remember your position and who you are,' Edward himself asked the question: 'Who exactly was I?' He was, of course, heir to the throne, and thus expected to be treated with respect bordering on reverence, exactly as Keir Hardie had suggested. On the other hand, King George had always insisted that he should not think himself different from, or better than, anyone else. Moreover the 'levelling process' of a naval apprenticeship at Osborne and Dartmouth, followed by a relatively normal Oxford career and 'the democracy of the battlefields', induced an 'unconscious rebellion' in Edward against his exalted position. As he wrote in his autobiography: 'The idea that my birth and title should somehow set me apart from or above other people struck me as wrong.' It certainly did some of the time. However, Edward's trouble was that, like other members of his family, Princess Margaret for example, he wanted to have his cake and eat it. He was eager to enjoy the intimacy fostered by equality and the idolatry due to royalty. He liked cocktails mixed with incense. When he entered the Junior Common Room at Magdalen College, Edward told the other undergraduates not to stand up as he wished to be treated without ceremony. On the next occasion, he berated them for their disrespect in remaining seated.

Doubtless Edward's partial revolt against the standards of his parents owed much to his loveless and unimaginative upbringing. One of his first nannies used to pinch him and twist his arm before taking him down from the nursery at tea-time. His parents were thus always presented with a squalling brat, and it was some time before they discovered the reason. George occasionally showed his offspring the cheery, chaffing side of his nature. But usually he was a domestic Captain Bligh, demanding faultless conduct and, when his orders were not instantly obeyed, issuing a peremptory summons to the Library (which housed his guns). As the Royal Librarian, Sir Owen Morshead, remarked, 'The House of Windsor, like ducks, produce bad parents – they trample on their young.' The King expected his children to act in accordance with the mottoes which adorned his walls – don't cry over spilt milk, a stitch in time saves nine. Oddly enough, crocheting, as taught by Queen Mary, was something which Edward and his brother George (known to the family as David and Bertie) did learn to like, and they continued the practice into adulthood. But this was about the limit of the culture they imbibed from their parents. King George rejoiced in his insularity and philistinism, deliberately mispronouncing French words on menus to indicate his contempt for that effeminate language. As for the French tutor, everyone thought it hilarious when he was persuaded to eat a new savoury, tadpoles on toast. And Queen Mary thoroughly approved when he burnt Balzac's 'indecent' novels. For the children music was a popular tune on the bagpipes, a folk-song on the piano, a jingoistic air played by a brass band, or everyone in the family standing stiffly to attention during 'God Save the King'. Art and literature were unknown quantities. Later Edward was fond of repeating the saddest cliché of the illiterate, that he learnt not from books but from life.

Sometimes life took on an alluring hue. Edward was taken to

see Queen Victoria, 'a divinity of whom even her own family stood in awe'. He was also much spoilt by his grandparents at Sandringham. There the governesses and tutors, who found Edward and George dispiritingly backward, were waved away and the children were given a rare taste of sybaritic splendour as only opulent Edwardians could produce it. In the big house, crammed with bibelots and overrun with dogs, they encountered 'the quintessence of all that was amusing and gay' and witnessed feasting of a sort which made Lucullus seem anorexic. Edward (or rather the ghost-writer of his autobiography) later described Christmas at Sandringham as 'Dickens in a Cartier setting'. But back at York Cottage strict discipline was reimposed. It was typified by the way in which, later on, King George greeted his third son, Henry, who arrived home after months abroad just as the family were sitting down to dinner: 'Late as usual, Harry.' In 1921, as Prince of Wales, Edward told a bereaved Lord Mountbatten: 'I envy you a father whom you could love. If my father had died, we should have felt nothing but relief.' When Queen Mary did eventually die, in 1953, her eldest son remarked: 'I somehow feel that the fluids in her veins must always have been as icy-cold as they now are in death.'

Handsome, engaging and relatively nimble-witted, Edward always outshone his brother George, who was reduced to a tongue-tied nervous wreck by his father's treatment. Edward could 'always manage' George, whom he would eventually dismiss as incurably dim. But as children they relied heavily on one another and their parting was a traumatic one. Aged twelve and a half, Edward was pitched from the segregated seclusion of York Cottage into the brutal mêlée of Osborne. There he survived homesickness, the bullying of his fellow naval cadets and the chivvying of his father when he did badly. This was often, though he was more successful than George, who was invariably at the bottom of his class. Even so, by the time Edward left Dartmouth, the navy, far from having taught him everything he needed to know (as his father expected), had scarcely equipped him to be much more than a proficient Sea Scout.

After Dartmouth, his grandfather's funeral, his admission to the Order of the Garter, his father's coronation and his own investiture as Prince of Wales, Edward served on a battleship for a short spell. Then it was decided that he should go up to Oxford.

While his parents attended the Delhi Durbar he 'swotted', which seemed mainly to involve his going to Sandringham and helping Queen Alexandra with endless jigsaw puzzles. The student Prince was hardly treated as an ordinary undergraduate, though he was not expected to endure the cloistered conditions which had been designed to keep his grandfather free of social contamination. Edward's room was freshly decorated and he was honoured with the first undergraduate bathroom in Magdalen. He also had a personal tutor, a valet and an equerry. Finally, the president of the college took a personal interest in him. This was Dr Herbert Warren, who was such a crashing snob that, when the future Emperor of Japan said that he was the son of God, he allegedly replied that many Magdalen men had distinguished relations. At Oxford Edward moved into a fast set, quickly learning to drink, gamble and carouse – though not learning much else. His relationship with his father did not improve, and he could have gained little inspiration from the King's parrot-like answers to his letters. Reporting on undergraduate behaviour at a Bullingdon Club dinner, Edward wrote: 'Most of them got rather, if not to say very, excited and I came back early [because, as he did not reveal, he was so inebriated that he could hardly stand up]. There was a good deal of champagne drunk and that accounted for it. It is interesting for me to see the various forms of amusement that undergraduates indulge in.' King George replied: 'I was amused by your description of your dinner at the Bullingdon Club, it appears that a good many of the young men drank more champagne than was good for them and became very noisy and excited, different people have different ways of enjoying themselves.'

While at Oxford, the Prince of Wales experienced the first stirrings of revolt against his father's authority. It must be said that Edward was scarcely the stuff of which revolutionaries were made, and that the causes of contention were not calculated to rock the state to its foundations. But in the royal scale of values his recalcitrance seemed grave enough. First, and most important, he began to resist the King's dictation in the matter of clothes. The Prince was even more obsessed than the King about this subject, later designing himself a special pair of safari shorts and writing a book about clothes. Unhappily, though, the royal tastes differed. The Prince made plain his dislike of the frock-coat. He wore his top hat at a rakish angle. Most momentous of all, he took to sporting turn-ups on his trousers. This provoked explosions of regal wrath and sarcastic questions about whether it was raining. Jeeves could not have been more deeply affronted by one of Bertie Wooster's sartorial aberrations. Almost as subversive were the Prince's views about the formal trappings and functions of royalty. After a banquet which he attended in honour of the King and Queen of Denmark, Edward wrote in his diary: 'What rot & a waste of time, money & energy all these State visits are!! This is my only remark on all this unreal show & ceremony!!' Edward increasingly came to prefer the more relaxed delights of the London season, when he could flirt, hunt, be a 'glorified clothes-peg' in his own fashion, and play Prince Charming to his heart's content.

He took less interest in those outside the pale of high society, evidently despising 'the dense crowd which was airing its patriotism in front of the Palace' and making a 'fearful shindy', on 3 August 1914 – the eve of Armageddon. The First World War increased Edward's revulsion with the artificiality of his public role. Having obtained a commission in the Grenadier Guards, he yearned to prove himself in combat. Occasionally he did manage to get up to the front line. He even came under fire and his chauffeur was killed by a shell. But for nearly all his term of service, to his real chagrin, he was kept safely away from the fighting. For the most part he did boring and unimportant staff work, complaining to Lord Stamfordham: 'I have no *real* job except that of being P. of Wales.' He was right. But that job gave him considerable scope for helping to secure the position of the monarchy in the troubled years after the war. As Edward told his father: 'This can only be done by keeping in the closest possible touch with the people & I can promise you . . . that I am & always shall make every effort to carry it out as I know how vitally it will influence the future of the Empire.'

For a time the Prince appeared to make an effort to live up to these professions. Aiming not only to bind the Empire more closely to the throne but also to drum up foreign trade, he engaged in an incessant round of tours, functions, visits and ceremonies. According to his own testimony, he shook so many hands that his right hand turned black and blue, planted enough trees to make a 'substantial forest', and laid enough foundation stones to build a 'sizable city'. In the course of several years he travelled all over the world, pursued by letters from King George, complaining, as often as not, about his clothes. In the New World he was a particular success. Edward recognized that people 'wanted, if not a vaudeville show, then a first-class carnival in which the Prince of Wales should play a gay, many-sided role'. In Canada he smiled what Chips Channon called his 'dentist's smile' and was mobbed by enthusiastic crowds – 'they just go mad & one is powerless!!' In the United States he was greeted with ticker-tape and welcomed as a 'Democratic Prince', a 'good sport' and a 'Prince with no pretence'. In Australia he was, he said, passed about as 'an Imperial souvenir' and 'a lucky talisman'. In India there was some attempt at a boycott but the government countered by inducements advertised in Urdu: 'Come and See the Prince and Have a Free Ride.' What with his prowess at sport and the splendid 'public spectacles to impress the native masses', the Prince proved almost as triumphant an ambassador in the subcontinent as elsewhere. He thought, understandably enough, that only a 'lunatic' would have suggested that 'the brightest jewel' in the imperial crown would be lost during his lifetime.

Like the Empire, the Prince presented a handsome façade to the world, but behind it the rot had set in with a vengeance. He grew increasingly impatient with his duties. He complained of having to deliver thousands of speeches and never being able to say what he thought. He never had a moment to himself and when he arranged a day's hunting Bonar Law was inconsiderate enough to die on him. He became more cavalier in selecting the functions which he would attend, refusing official business but finding the energy to go to flamboyant evening parties or to disturb fellow guests by playing his ukelele into the small hours. Often, as though to cock a snook at his father, he was late. Sometimes he failed to appear at all. When obliged to endure some particularly tedious occasion he might sulk like a graceless schoolboy. In India he found his life bounded by 'protocol so rigid that it astonished even me' and his irritation was frequently apparent. He scarcely bothered to hide the bored contempt he felt for the minor functionaries and their status-conscious wives whom he met at interminable, and apparently identical, functions. They were shocked by his attempt to break out of the prison house. And, indeed, his efforts to 'procure informal companionship' on his travels did lead to some lamentable breaches of decorum. The Japanese, for example, were willing to cater for his sexual needs but, as the British ambassador reported, 'with their usual excess of precaution they subjected every female thing that could come near him to medical examination. . . . There was nearly a terrible scandal because two missionary ladies who wished to present him with a Japanese Bible were hurried off by the police on the ground that they had not been inspected and disinfected.' In Africa a few years later, the Prince's habit of stopping his safari periodically while he had casual affairs with local ladies provoked the resignation of his assistant private secretary, Captain Alan Lascelles. And after 1924 King George, who took a quiet pride in never having set foot in the United States, virtually forbade Edward to go there because he was appalled by headlines like 'Prince Gets In With Milkman'.

By comparison the English press was so restrained that the *Spectator* seemed quite to be committing lèse-majesté with its suggestion in 1925 that the 'unduly restless' Prince 'exhausts himself in giving to amusements too many of the hours which might be spent on preparation for work'. However the *Spectator* did not blame his lapses on the Prince of Wales, who 'excels in courtesy and consideration', but on poor staff work. It thus revived the ancient excuse of kings who could do no wrong, namely, that their 'evil counsellors' were culpable. Moreover, the journal pontificated, harsher criticisms of Edward's conduct were doubtless 'traceable to non-British foreigners', a particularly sinister breed. Certainly, true Britons permitted no breath of scandal about the Prince's private life to get into the newspapers. His long infatuation with Mrs Freda Dudley Ward, which began in 1918, went unmentioned. The incidental philanderings were not noticed. There was scarcely a hint that the Prince spent his leisure hours leading the life of a Bright Young Thing, drinking cocktails with painted ladies, dancing to jazz in nightclubs, going off for louche weekends. Although the King privately inveighed against his son's mistresses, nicknaming them 'the lacemaker's daughter' or 'the South American whore', he was surprisingly permissive about the 'damn weekends'. He even gave Edward Fort Belvedere, a grace and favour residence near Windsor, for the purpose. But there were constant eruptions about other matters. The King disapproved of Edward's making jokes in his speeches, humiliated him in front of others about his attire, harassed him about his conduct abroad. The trouble was that everyone, including Queen Mary, was terrified of the King. When glared at by his father for being late for breakfast, Prince Henry, then aged nineteen, literally fainted. Edward could only rage and talk about renouncing the throne. To Mrs Dudley Ward he exclaimed:

> What does it take to be a good king? You must be a figurehead, a wooden man! Do nothing to upset the Prime Minister or the Court or the Archbishop of Canterbury! Show yourself to the people! Mind your manners! Go to Church! What modern man wants *that* sort of life?

Of course, the Prince did not want the responsibilities of that sort of life; but he did want the pleasures. He disliked being a performer in what he called 'the decorated circus'. He loathed being 'chained to the banquet table'. But he adored the perquisites of his position. Perpetually immature, he thrived on being spoilt and caressed in the gilded salons of the smart set. A plutocratic Prince in a democratic society, he enjoyed being able to pursue his fleeting hobbies, many of them energetic, some of them dangerous, all of them expensive – hunting, flying, golfing, gardening. He happily, and rightly, assumed that he would come first and get the best of everything and do what he pleased – he thought nothing of smuggling his dogs back into the country in defiance of the strict quarantine laws. Above all he revelled in the virtual *droit de seigneur* which he could exercise over women. Always easily led – he was supposed to 'reset his watch by every clock he passed' – Edward preferred his mistresses to dominate him. It was as if he yearned to alloy with tenderness the strict régime he had always known. Freda Dudley Ward, the only 'mother' he had ever had, according to Lord Mountbatten, said: 'I could have done *anything* with him! Love bewitched him. He made himself the slave of whomever he loved and became totally dependent on her. It was his nature; he was a masochist. He *liked* being humbled, degraded. He begged for it!'

So, in 1934, Edward became captivated by Wallis Warfield Simpson. She was a somewhat 'fast' and flirtatious American divorcée of such fascination that he brutally ostracized Mrs Dudley Ward and, forsaking all others, clove only to her. Mrs

Simpson, in turn, was excited as never before by the glittering new world into which he was the 'open sesame'. As she wrote, 'Trains were held; yachts materialized; the best suites in the finest hotels were flung open; aeroplanes stood waiting. What impressed me most of all was how all this would be brought to pass without apparent effort; the calm assumption that this was the natural order of things.' Edward later claimed that he was entranced with Wallis because she talked to him about his work. But it is clear that she actually provided him with an escape from it. She bubbled like champagne. A social animal with well-developed skills, she was vital, frivolous, amusing, superficial, attractive, modern. She was aptly described as 'a coquette . . . chic rather than feminine, half artifice, half steel'. For her the essence of sophistication was an exquisite cocktail party or a sumptuous dinner. She had an insatiable passion for antiques, bijouterie, ornaments, porcelain, objets d'art. Her first ambition was to storm Society, into which she now had such a gold-plated entrée. But very soon she began to feel her power. Edward abased himself before her. His letters were full of baby-talk as he apparently sought the maternal tenderness which had been denied him in his youth. To this infantile passion Mrs Simpson responded affectionately but firmly. She would forbid Edward to smoke or drink, order him to fetch things for her, even criticize his clothes. She also took to lording it over his servants; and his lifelong retainer, Finch, who resented her, was put out to grass. Perhaps prompted by the Prince, she was soon behaving like a future queen, presenting her cheek to be kissed, seeming to expect a curtsy. Edward became increasingly besotted and indiscreet. The King, who warned him that he could not go on leading a double life and would eventually be exposed, grew more and more perturbed. Perhaps worry hastened his death. Certainly once his father had died, Edward made a sudden and symbolic gesture. He immediately ordered that the 'bloody clocks' at Sandringham, which were always set half an hour ahead of Greenwich time in order to save daylight for shooting, should be put right. It was a flagrant slap in the face for tradition, the first of many.

The second was his appearance at a window in St James's Palace overlooking Friary Court, where he was being proclaimed King Edward VIII, a ceremony which the sovereign never attends. He was snapped by a newspaper photographer; in the background, but not identified when the picture was printed, could be seen the blurred outline of a woman. Those on the inside recognized Mrs Simpson, and recognized the extraordinary sway she exercised over the new King. As Edward's private secretary, Alec Hardinge, wrote: 'Before her the affairs of state sank into insignificance . . . every decision, big or small, was subordinated to her will.' Actually the King did take a serious interest in his official duties. In the words of his lawyer, Walter Monckton: 'He had a genuine desire to exercise the influence and prerogatives of kingship.' Indeed, fancying himself as 'Edward the Innovator', he wanted to extend them. But he had 'an equally strong desire to live as he pleased'. So Edward began by reading and initialling all the government papers he was sent. But soon his attention wandered, and he told Mrs Simpson that his red boxes were 'full of mostly bunk'. His lateness in returning them and a lack of initials betrayed his negligence. He was even more impatient with ceremonial. From the first he cut down his formal functions. He attended church infrequently. And he cast the first faint shadow over his lambent popularity when he was photographed looking bored and cross at a presentation. Once he climbed out of a window of Buckingham Palace in order to avoid seeing his private secretary, and sloped off to visit Mrs Simpson. The King's servants were outraged not only by his behaviour but by his mean-spirited dismissals and economies – their beer allowance was cut while he drank champagne. One footman at Fort Belvedere gave notice when he saw the King painting Mrs Simpson's toenails by the swimming pool.

Edward not only appeared in public with Wallis, though the English newspapers tactfully air-brushed her out of photographs, he even accompanied her to the legal chambers of Walter Monckton. This was an astonishing indiscretion in view of the fact that her second divorce, from Ernest Simpson, was already in train and the King might have been cited for collusion or adultery, or both. Even more reckless, however, was his Mediterranean cruise with Mrs Simpson and friends aboard the luxury yach *Nahlin* in the summer of 1936. Without consulting the government, he planned to start from Venice. However, he was with difficulty persuaded that such a move might imply that Mussolini's dictatorship had gained the royal seal of approval. Ungraciously the King agreed to embark from the Dalmatian coast, subjecting himself, he complained, 'to an indescribable night journey by train into Yugoslavia with a clanking and jolting such as I had never before experienced'.

The King was equally reluctant to oblige the Foreign Office when he visited Turkey. Indeed, he appalled the British ambassador in Istanbul by saying that he wished to see no one from the government and had only come to play golf. At last he was convinced that Anglo-Turkish relations would be irreparably damaged if he refused to meet Mustapha Kemal. That encounter proved surprisingly successful, perhaps because Mrs Simpson thought he was like 'fifty Hitlers'. What was disastrous about the supposedly incognito tour was the fact that at each Balkan port or bay where the *Nahlin* stopped, the King was photographed, in poses of almost exhibitionistic informality, with Mrs Simpson. Sometimes, a boyish figure with buttercup yellow hair, he was wearing nothing but gold ornaments and a pair of shorts. Once or twice he was caught in attitudes of dog-like devotion, his 'poached' Hanoverian eyes filled with sentiment, his entire mien alert for the sound of his mistress's voice. Nothing like the cruise of the *Nahlin* had been seen since the lewd Pergami took ship with Queen Caroline of Brunswick.

At this stage the British government was more preoccupied by suspicions about the nature of Mrs Simpson's hidden influence than it was about fears of a public scandal, for, again, the domestic press printed no compromising pictures. King Edward himself had never made any secret of his pro-German feelings. As Prince of Wales, in 1933, he had told Count Mensdorff: 'Of course it is the only thing to do, we will have to come to it, as we are in great danger from the Communists here, too.' 'Dictators [are] popular these days,' he had observed, 'we might want one in England before too long.' In June 1935 he had made a speech to the British Legion in which he advocated extending 'the hand of friendship' to Germany – and had been roundly rebuked by his father for expressing controversial views and for not getting government sanction. To his intimates Edward was much more outspoken, criticizing the Foreign Office's attitude to the Nazis and supporting a policy of appeasement more craven even than that espoused by ministers. Chips Channon speculated that the Prince's 'alleged Nazi leanings' were reinforced by Mrs Simpson. Nearly eighteen months later Channon elaborated: 'The King is insane about Wallis, insane. He, too, is going the dictator way, and is pro-German, against Russia and against too much slipshod democracy. I shouldn't be surprised if he aimed at making himself a mild dictator, a difficult task enough for an English King.' Difficult, indeed, but Baldwin's government was taking no chances. The content of Edward's red boxes was silently censored so that no royal indiscretions or initiatives could endanger the state. And for most of his reign the King himself was under surveillance by the security services. The American ambassador, Robert Bingham, told President Roosevelt that the King was not only surrounded by a 'pro-German cabal' but that 'many people here suspected that Mrs Simpson was actually in German pay'. However unlikely this was, there was no question about her pronounced Nazi sympathies.

Mildly antisemitic and inclined to worship strength, the King himself simply thought fascism was fashionable. Occasionally he mouthed dictatorial menaces: for example, when Duff Cooper mentioned the independence of the BBC, Edward replied: 'I'll change that. It will be the last thing I do before I go.' But he had no power to implement such threats. Still, Ribbentrop, the German ambassador – admittedly so stupid that even Goering called him 'Fathead' – did regard the King as a significant piece in the diplomatic game. Berlin was informed that Edward 'did not hold his father's view that the King must blindly accept the Cabinet's decisions. On the contrary, he felt it to be his duty to intervene if the Cabinet were to plan a policy which in his view was detrimental to British interests.' Edward actually did offer some slight opposition to Foreign Office policy, as when he refused Anthony Eden's request to meet the deposed Emperor of Ethiopia, Haile Selassie, on the grounds that it would be unpopular with the Italians. Furthermore, the King did constitute a grave nuisance to the government. In the autumn of 1936 Baldwin was so distracted by the Simpson divorce and the prospect of the King's marrying her that he begged Eden not 'to trouble me too much with foreign affairs just now'. When the abdication crisis did break, the country shared his preoccupation. As the writer H. N. Brailsford observed, 'While England chatters about a lady from Baltimore, Germany marches forward to the conquest of Spain.' Brailsford added that the King might have 'brought Fascism upon us in a peculiar English guise, with a Royal Führer'.

Others also thought it possible that Edward might exploit his immense popularity, like Bernard Shaw's King Magnus, and establish a royal dictatorship. Later the Duchess of Windsor would say that if only he had hired a first-class New York public relations man he might at least have ended up as prime minister. However the nearest he came to taking power was when he nobbled the British press. Probably because he got a kick out of fixing things for a king, perhaps because he wanted 'to bugger Baldwin', Lord Beaverbrook heeded the royal appeal. He persuaded his fellow newspaper proprietors virtually to ignore Mrs Simpson's divorce. Even the Communist *Daily Worker* complied with this 'gentleman's agreement', thus confirming Lenin's view that the English proletariat is incurably bourgeois. So, at the end of October, Mrs Simpson was given a decree nisi, the King's hand being plainly apparent in the favourable treatment which she received at Ipswich Crown Court. And there were no headlines in England like the famous American one, 'King's Moll Reno'd in Wolsey's Home Town'. References to the whole affair were cut out of American newspapers and magazines sold in England. But rumours abounded. They were fed by such notorious *faux pas* as the King's refusal, in September, to open some new buildings at an Aberdeen infirmary; instead he was seen greeting Mrs Simpson and other guests at Aberdeen station, prior to their visit to Balmoral. The Duchess of York, who with her husband had deputized for the King at the hospital, was particularly outraged. At Balmoral, apparently, she swept past Mrs Simpson, who was acting as hostess, announcing icily to the company at large: 'I came to dine with the King.'

During the autumn there was growing anxiety about where the King's relationship with Mrs Simpson would lead. Baldwin himself warned Edward that the respect which had grown up for the monarchy over the previous three generations stemmed from its integrity. That respect 'might not take so long, in face of the kind of criticisms to which it was being exposed', to disappear – 'and once lost I doubt if anything could restore it'. Others lamented that the honour, dignity and moral authority of the Crown had been 'cast into the dustbin'. Most English people in the know would have agreed with Harold Nicolson, who was indignant that 'that silly little man *en somme* should destroy a great monarchy by giggling into a flirtation with a third-rate

American'. But, of course, most English people were not in the know. When the King took part in his first state opening of parliament, on 3 November, he was almost overcome by the smell of mothballs from the peers' robes, but the public sniffed only the reassuring odour of tradition. When the King visited distressed areas in South Wales on 18–19 November, his celebrated declaration that 'something must be done' and his pledge that 'you may be sure that all I can do for you I will' seemed to be guarantees of continuing royal concern. However, by then he had privately expressed a firm intention to abdicate.

The matter had been virtually settled a few days before when the King's private secretary, warning that the press could not be kept quiet for much longer, had urged him to send Mrs Simpson abroad. The King, increasingly paranoid about an Establishment conspiracy against him, suspected that the issue was being brought to a head. He therefore told Baldwin that if the government opposed his marriage to Mrs Simpson, he would go. Edward was deaf to arguments that his personal inclinations should not take precedence over his royal responsibilities. To the appeals of his mother, who was appalled by the humiliation which his renunciation of the throne in such circumstances would bring to the family, he simply answered: 'All that matters is our happiness.' While the government was consulting the dominions to confirm its own view that Mrs Simpson was unacceptable even as the sovereign's morganatic wife, the press broke its silence. The avalanche was precipitated by an obscure bishop who, apparently referring to Edward's laxity as a churchgoer, commended the King to God's grace.

Edward was shocked by the publicity. But although the provincial papers and the quality London ones were hostile to him, he did have quite a lot of press support and he was treated with universal deference. Moreover, on 3 December most London newspapers, including *The Times*, forbore to mention Mrs Simpson by name. Nevertheless Edward was so accustomed to adulation that anything in the nature of objective appraisal smacked of the wildest iconoclasm. About the reports he later expostulated: 'Could this be the King or was I some common felon?' Edward was, as Chips Channon noted, always 'at his worst with Fleet Street – off-hand, angry and ungracious; he never treats them in the right way or realizes that his popularity largely depends on them'. Now, at any rate, he realized the press's capacity for destroying the image it had created. Unmanned by the experience, he sent Mrs Simpson to France and prepared to follow her with as little fuss and as much dignity as he could muster.

The abdication crisis was in every respect a nine-day wonder. Before the King left the country, on 11 December, a bizarre 'King's Party' had begun to coalesce. It was led by Winston Churchill, whose romantic attachment to the sovereign was tempered by the ambitious hope of somehow using the royal matter to lever Baldwin out of power. And it was supported by a motley crew of press barons, liberals, Catholics, communists and fascists. Crowds gathered shouting: 'God Save the King from Mr Baldwin!' However, the opposition, a solid phalanx of Tories, Socialists and Nonconformists, soon flexed its muscles and proved much stronger. Harold Nicolson found that most people were not angry with Mrs Simpson, 'but I do find a deep and enraged fury against the King himself. In eight months he has destroyed the great structure of popularity which he had raised.' Lord Salisbury spoke for the Establishment when he confessed that what shocked him was not that a man should want to marry his mistress or a woman with two husbands living, but that 'a man born to sublime responsibilities should be ready to jeopardize them, as it seems, to gratify a passion for a woman of any sort'.

The King was shaken by the animus against him. Churchill recorded that during one conversation Edward had two 'marked and prolonged "black-outs" in which he completely lost the thread of his conversation'. Churchill counselled delay and resistance. He whimsically advised the King to 'Retire to Windsor Castle! Summon the Beefeaters! Raise the drawbridge! Close the gates! And dare Baldwin to drag you out!' Not for nothing did Clementine Churchill call her husband the last believer in the divine right of kings. Edward did not share his faith or his fortitude. Behind the scenes he was negotiating the terms of his abdication with the government. It included a favourable financial settlement for himself: he got £60,000 from the Civil List, sold Sandringham and Balmoral to his brother George for a million pounds and took abroad very large sums of money from other sources. With such a nest-egg it was not surprising that, as Beaverbrook memorably informed Churchill, 'Our cock won't fight.'

There were also serious doubts about the capacity of Edward's successor. George's stammer was a severe handicap for one who would have to make so many public addresses. It was compounded by such patent slow-wittedness and lack of self-confidence that he seemed incapable of carrying out even the vestigial functions of limited monarchy. So, apparently, some official consideration was given to bypassing George and putting one of his younger brothers on the throne. Unfortunately, on closer examination, they seemed to be even less qualified than George. The Duke of Gloucester, known as 'Potty' to his friends, was a Hanoverian throwback. Stolid, wooden, given to liquor and tantrums, he was barely competent to be a professional soldier, let alone a king. When, during the war, an MP suggested that he should be made commander-in-chief of the army, the House of Commons just roared with laughter. The youngest brother, the Duke of Kent, was handsome and intelligent. But he had what was regarded at that time as an unfortunate penchant for black women and white men. He had also, in youth, been addicted to drugs and one of his paramours had almost driven him to suicide. It was therefore deemed better not to interfere with the hereditary principle. At least the new King was malleable and his wife was reliable. Indeed, there was every hope that the Queen, attractive, sensible, smiling, would keep her husband up to the mark. Though a commoner – née Elizabeth Bowes-Lyon – she seemed much more regal than he did. Once, when he pulled down the blinds of their railway saloon, she snapped them up again, saying: 'Bertie, you must wave.' A disappointed Chips Channon might grumble that the new King and Queen were 'the puppets of a palace clique' and 'too hemmed in by the territorial aristocracy'. Queen Mary had good reason to assert that 'The Yorks will do it very well.'

In the heat of the abdication crisis George evidently promised that, when his brother married, Wallis would receive the title of Royal Highness. However, to their perpetual chagrin – a chagrin worthy of Saint-Simon himself, the climax of whose life occurred in 1718 when Louis XIV's bastards were reduced from princely to ducal rank – the undertaking was broken. The Duke and Duchess of Windsor, as they became when her divorce decree was made absolute, also resembled the Bourbons in learning nothing and forgetting nothing. In fact, their exile, an empty quest for gracious living and elegant self-gratification, was made up of nothings. In England they became as nothing: there was not so much a revulsion against them as an act of national amnesia. After the first terrific shock waves had travelled round the world – H. L. Mencken said it was 'the greatest news story since the Resurrection' – not a wrack was left behind. Edward's celebrity vanished like that of a passé film star, while all attention was focused on the new leading players. To be sure, many people bitterly resented the real damage which the Windsors had done to the monarchy. The unctuous noises made by *The Times* and the Archbishop of Canterbury, about the betrayal of royal trust in the pursuit of 'alien' and 'exotic' pleasure, were widely echoed. A poll conducted at the time revealed that half the population wanted to do away with the monarchy altogether.

A Tory MP, Sir Arnold Wilson, said that in a free vote at least one hundred members of the Commons would have plumped for a republic. When the whips were out, however, Socialists joined Liberals and Conservatives in rallying round the throne. James Maxton moved that the abdication showed 'the danger to this country and to the British Commonwealth of Nations inherent in an hereditary monarchy, at a time when the peace and prosperity of the people require a more stable and dignified form of government of a republican kind, in close contact with, and more responsive to, the will of the mass of the people'. But his amendment to the Abdication Bill was defeated by 403 votes to 5. In the first issue of the left-wing journal *Tribune* Aneurin Bevan declared: 'The Labour Party has too much reverence.' Still, many of those who had fawned on King Edward now spurned the Duke of Windsor. Hector Bolitho's biography, which was being serialized during the abdication, performed an illuminating volte-face, from sycophancy to antipathy, in the middle. Even Churchill became disillusioned with the Windsors. He admitted to Baldwin that Mrs Simpson as Queen would have been 'an eventuality too horrible to contemplate', acknowledged to Beaverbrook that they had both been mistaken and disparaged the Windsors' 'court of dagoes on the Loire'.

Nursing their grievances, most of them imaginary, resenting their all too genuine boredom, the Windsors returned to the limelight when they visited Germany in 1937. The Duke gave the

Nazi salute, formed the opinion (which nothing ever changed) that Hitler was not 'such a bad chap', and belittled George VI to Goering. Whether the ex-King was a fool or a knave remains unclear. The British government's obsessive secrecy about captured German documents, and claims that Anthony Blunt owed his immunity from prosecution on charges of spying to the fact that he retrieved the Nazis' dossier on the Windsors after the war, suggest that the full story has yet to be told. However, in the light of the present evidence, Edward appears to have been neither a traitor nor a Nazi, simply an innocent abroad. Boyishly naïve, intellectually jejune, intensely egocentric, he unwittingly allowed himself to be used by Goebbels's propaganda machine. Had things turned out differently he could have been employed for more sinister ends. For after the outbreak of war in 1939 he made no attempt to hide the fact that he favoured a negotiated peace. Lacking any grasp of the principles involved, he forecast a 'disaster to the whole of civilization unless it ends soon'. The Führer had some reason to hope that he might make the Duke a Quisling King of England.

When France collapsed in June 1940, the Windsors fled to Spain, where they devoted most of their energies to securing the property they had left behind. The Duchess told her aunt that 'one's time is spent trying to communicate with France to make some arrangements for one's houses'. The Duke went so far as to ask the Germans, through a Spanish intermediary, for permission to bring his belongings out of France, thus shocking even Franco's brother: 'A Prince does not ask favours of his country's enemies.' The Duke's defeatist indiscretions were a serious embarrassment to the embattled Churchill. As one government memorandum put it, 'his inclinations are well known to be pro-Nazi and he may become a centre of intrigue'. While stoutly maintaining that the Duke's loyalties were 'unimpeachable', the prime minister nevertheless decided to pack him off to the Bahamas as governor. Reluctantly the Duke accepted what he called this 'futile appointment' to 'St Helena 1940!' He blamed his 'utterly stupid' brother, who was supported by the 'clever' Queen, for encouraging Churchill to use 'dictator methods' against him. And he badgered the British authorities about releasing two soldiers from combat duty to act as his servants – he eventually got one of them. Altogether the Duke behaved, as courtiers and ministers at home agreed, like 'a petulant baby'. Yet he was also an officer who knew, when reminded by Churchill, that he must obey orders. So he and his wife gritted their teeth and awaited their ship in a luxury seaside villa outside Lisbon, where one visitor, Sir David Eccles, described them as the 'arch-beachcombers of the world'.

Meanwhile a web of conspiracy was being woven round them, as Hitler decided that the former King was a political pawn worth capturing. Accordingly pressure was put on Spain, anxious to conciliate a Germany whose panzers were at the Pyrenees, to inveigle the Duke across the border where he would be kidnapped by Nazi commandos. Among the emissaries sent to persuade the Duke to leave Portugal was the playboy son of Spain's former dictator, Primo de Rivera, who apparently believed that if he succeeded he might be able to supplant Franco. German spies were dispatched to Lisbon to scare the Duke into cooperating – one scheme was to suggest that Churchill planned to have him assassinated. All these manoeuvres failed, though the Germans did achieve the signal triumph of abducting the Duchess's maid as she struggled through occupied France with trunks full of her employers' clothes. By 1 August the good ship *Excalibur* had gone with the Windsors. This did not stop all concerned from sending Ribbentrop highly imaginative reports, some of which have fuelled speculation concerning the Duke's loyalty, about how close they had come to success.

As governor of the Bahamas, the Duke himself helped to fuel speculation that he was pro-Nazi by openly advocating American isolationism. Churchill's patience was tested to the utmost by a series of such indiscretions, by demands from the Duke to take leave in America, by complaints that his residence was unsatisfactory, and so on. Though he could still be suave and debonair, the Duke palpably lacked judgement. He made no attempt to conceal his distaste for the majority 'coloured' population of the Bahamas, imposed rigid segregation and made blacks enter Government House by the back door. His preference for a white liaison officer over a black may even have precipitated a riot in which two people died and twenty-five were injured. He made a mess of a murder inquiry by inviting unqualified Miami policemen to investigate it. And he infuriated local opinion by censoring press criticism.

The Duke's blunders were compounded by the Duchess's tactlessness. She made little secret of her resentment at his being chained to a 'double-zero' job in 'this lousy hole'. 'I really do wish,' she said, 'we could move somewhere inhabited at least by our own class.' She also poisoned the Duke's mind still further about his own family, emphasizing that he was the victim of a 'Palace vendetta'. Alec Hardinge referred to her 'anti-British activities' and her 'efforts to avenge herself on this country'.

After the war the Windsors' feud with Buckingham Palace continued. They called Queen Elizabeth (George VI's wife) 'the Loch Ness Monster', 'that fat Scotch cook', or 'the dowdy Duchess'. The Windsors, of course, were anything but dowdy. They lived in sybaritic splendour surrounded by the gorgeous remnants of his royal heritage. True, theirs was merely a fashionable parody of court life. The Duke's realm had shrunk to domestic proportions while he found himself doing chores, like one of his liveried footmen, for an implacable favourite. His retinue was an unlovely mélange of playboys and toadies. The privileges which the Duke unblushingly claimed for himself were seldom granted. But, for reasons best known to itself, the government of the French republic allowed the ex-King tax-free status, despite his dealings in black-market currency. Even so, although the Windsors lavished luxury upon themselves, there was no regal largesse to spare. The Duke, who had once been prone to fits of generosity, was now pathologically mean. He sponged ruthlessly on rich and poor alike, explaining without embarrassment: 'The profession into which I was born has been losing ground for centuries. I have better cause than most to make provision for a rainy day.'

That day never came. The life of idleness palled. The petty jealousies and the drunken squabbles got worse. The Windsors found their pampered, shallow, banal existence barely supportable. A high point in the Duke's day might be watching the Duchess buying a hat, and sometimes she sent him to bed in tears. But, sustained by his grand passion, and with no other choice available, he put a brave face on it. And, strangely enough, the British public seemed to bear the Duke no malice, even to retain something of its old affection for him. He had shattered a dream. He had exposed the tawdriness behind the glamour of kingship. He had revealed the seamy side of royal family life. He had illustrated the hopelessness of a system of hereditary succession. Yet when he returned to England, he was often greeted with enthusiasm. Crowds would gather round his car shouting: 'Good old Ted! Good old Teddy! Glad to see you back!' Before his death in 1972 the Duke was cheered in London theatres and there was popular pressure for a rapprochement between the Duchess and the two Queen Elizabeths. When the Duchess died in 1986 there were curious manifestations of public grief, sternly discouraged by the Palace, which to the last had denied her the coveted title HRH, and gave her a very private funeral indeed. It was the culmination of fifty years' vindictiveness, something which the royal image-makers had difficulty in reconciling with the saccharine benevolence they attributed to the Queen Mother. But somehow they managed to incorporate the Duchess into the beatific myth. The nation liked the notion of royal happy families.

Eight

The Model of a Modern Monarch

King Edward VIII's abdication may have been quickly forgotten by a public preoccupied with such momentous crises as depression and war, but the royal family has been haunted by it ever since. King George VI's terrors were at first particularly acute. In October 1937, for example, the British ambassador to Washington recorded that 'The King does not yet feel safe in his throne, and up to a certain point he is like the medieval monarch who has a hated rival claimant living in exile.' In fact, the entire history of the British monarchy since 1936 may be seen as a protracted attempt to exorcize the ghost of the abdication and to ensure that nothing so potentially fatal ever overtakes the dynasty again. It is this trauma which accounts for the long ostracism of the Windsors, for the adamantine conservatism of the Palace, and for the sustained effort to ensure that the royal name is unblemished by any hint of impropriety. Apart from a few minor scandals this effort has been outstandingly successful. But one of its incidental results has been to make it even more difficult for any student of the subject to undertake an informed and objective analysis of the sovereign's role. For the lesson which the monarchy learnt from the abdication débâcle was that it should surround itself with more secrecy, not less. And the newspapers, having abdicated their own responsibilities, did not now see it as their duty to publish and be damned. Even the rare critical cartoon about the monarchy was censored, as David Low found to his cost. When newsreel cameras were allowed into Westminster Abbey for the first time, to record George VI's coronation in 1937, the professedly radical *Daily Mirror* wrote, apparently without irony, that the Archbishop of Canterbury, 'ever vigilant of public interest and good taste', would view the film and 'cut out anything which may be considered unsuitable for the public at large to see'.

Even Churchill acknowledged that the 'well-meant, but unwise stifling of the British press' caused sudden 'blasts of public opinion'. But he had no real conception of a truly independent 'fourth estate'. Like most members of the British ruling class, he thought it quite proper that Fleet Street should now try, in John Gunther's words, 'to "build up" the Duke of York' and 'bury Edward and his memory at once'. This campaign began immediately, as Chips Channon noted: 'The press is trying to work up popularity for the new régime and perhaps in time will succeed.' The new King, who was initially greeted with a marked lack of public enthusiasm, was hard to promote. It could have been said of him, as Harold Macmillan said of John Foster Dulles, that 'his speech was slow but it easily kept pace with his thought'. Plagued by his stammer, by a consciousness of his own inferiority and by nervous inhibitions of all sorts, George found it difficult to carry off his functions with dignity, let alone with panache. This was a major reason why Queen Elizabeth wanted the Windsors kept out of the way. As Walter Monckton recorded in his emollient fashion, 'She naturally thought that she must be on her guard because the Duke of Windsor, to whom the other brothers had always looked up, was an attractive, vital creature who might be a rallying point for any who might be critical of the new King, who was less superficially endowed with the arts and graces that please.'

Nevertheless, writers were soon discovering in George hidden depths and capacities which had somehow escaped the scrutiny of his tutors. They were abetted by readers eager to believe the best about their new sovereign. When the maverick Tom Driberg reported the coronation in the sceptical manner of a dramatic critic instead of the hushed tones of an acolyte (there was a characteristic hint of ribaldry in his description of the King's unbuttoning before being anointed with holy oil), he 'excited a storm of shocked rage among the middle-class readers of the *Daily Express*'. But even Driberg could not deny the fact that the King had one trump card – his Queen. Journalists played her for all they were worth. She was charming, poised and apparently, behind that radiant exterior, she possessed a steely will. So she was admirably equipped to take over the role of royal matriarch from the septuagenarian Queen Mary, who, to the amazement of her wig-maker, was now almost completely bald. Lord Tweedsmuir could perhaps have been pardoned for resorting to the kind of hyperbole which royalties always attract: he declared that Queen Elizabeth had 'a perfect genius for the right kind of publicity'.

Thus the modern British monarchy goes far to prove Shaw's point that kings are not born but made by universal hallucination. Certainly the trivial and sycophantic frothing of the press is matched by such a dearth of hard information about the sovereign that often historical judgements are not far removed from the realm of gossip and speculation. The novelist Penelope Mortimer was recently commissioned to produce a biography of the Queen Mother because she could write with 'imagination' – something she certainly managed to do. Edward VIII is the last British monarch about whom it is possible to pronounce with a fair degree of authority. There is only the sketchiest kind of documentation on King George's reign. Admittedly a long official biography does exist, written by Sir John Wheeler-Bennett in 1958. But it is not only profoundly boring – little more than a catalogue of public engagements – it is also blandly un-informative. If Wheeler-Bennett knew anything worth knowing about his subject he was clearly determined not to share that knowledge with his readers. His is a courtier's book, full of trumpery statements like this: 'The people of Scotland derived particular satisfaction from the fact that King George [V] con-ferred the Order of the Thistle upon his son on his wedding day.' Needless to say there is even less authentic information available about Queen Elizabeth II. Still, it is possible to give a tentative, interim account of the modern monarchy without resorting to the anodyne platitudes which the subject normally attracts.

Like his father, George VI had not been trained for kingship, and he had no thought of receiving what his mother called that 'intolerable honour'. George – 'Bertie' to the family – was brought up to be a naval officer and there was some question about whether he could qualify himself even for that profession. Demoralized by his father and eclipsed by his elder brother, he struggled hard to overcome his handicaps. Desperately shy and abnormally homesick at Dartmouth, he languished at the bottom of his class but was said never to shirk his duty. One of his tutors described him as 'quite unspoiled and a nice, honest, clean-minded and excellent-mannered boy'. At times, though, George became so frustrated by his failures that he gave way to fury – when playing badly at golf or tennis he would sometimes simply stalk off in a huff, abandoning the game and the other players. Like all his family, he was personally courageous and he saw active service during the First World War. Apparently he even enjoyed taking part in the battle of Jutland. But for much of the war he was incapacitated by a duodenal ulcer. This did not stop him from qualifying as a pilot in 1919, even though he was terrified of flying and his father (who never flew) had no faith in aeroplanes.

After the war George became 'the Industrial Prince'. His task was to secure the loyalty of the toiling masses, who were suspected of being dangerously disaffected in the aftermath of the Russian Revolution. He did so by touring many industrial areas and by organizing camps in which public schoolboys, whose wholesome social attitudes were presumed to be contagious, met working lads. According to Wheeler-Bennett, Prince George's success in holding these camps overcame objections that they were simply traps to catch young communists. Wandering around in football shorts immunizing proletarian youth against the bacillus of Bolshevism was enough of a strain, but George found his more formal functions almost unendurable. He nearly collapsed when taking his seat in the House of Lords in 1920, only to be steadied by Lord Birkenhead's curious whisper: 'Been playing any tennis lately, sir?' George quailed at the prospect of making public speeches, especially, as occurred at the opening of the British Empire Exhibition in 1925, in front of his father: 'I shall be very frightened as you have never heard me speak and the loudspeakers are apt to put one off as well. So I hope you will understand that I am bound to be more nervous than I usually am.'

Though George was almost a carbon copy of his father – their laboured handwriting was identical, they had the same taste in clothes, they were both typical Norfolk squires – the young Prince was made miserable by the King's constant criticism. But instead of rebelling, he was, in his older brother's opinion, 'agreeably weak'. Certainly he was unnaturally dutiful, as King George admitted in a rare and revealing tribute: 'You have always been so sensible and easy to work with and you have always been ready to listen to any advice and to agree with my opinions about people and things, that I feel that we have always got on very well together (very different to dear David).' Luckily George V thoroughly approved of his second son's marriage in 1923 to Lady Elizabeth Bowes-Lyon, daughter of the fourteenth Earl of Strathmore. The Duchess of York, as she became, was as attractive as she was patrician, and she had apparently agonized long and hard, during Bertie's gauche courtship, about whether to accept him. However, once her mind was made up, she brought him a degree of domestic happiness which he had never believed possible.

The Duchess captivated almost everybody, from George V downwards; to the amazement of his family the King even indulged her when she was late for meals. Queen Marie of Romania found her 'one of the dearest, sweetest, most gentle . . . and most agreeable women I have ever met'. Chips Channon, despite his homosexuality, was half in love with her – she was 'always charming, always gay, pleasant and smiling . . . mildly flirtatious in a very proper romantic old-fashioned Valentine sort of way'. Kenneth Clark, later Keeper of the King's Pictures, also experienced romantic feelings for her, though his first impression was that 'she was not much better than the kind of person one met at a country house'. Duff Cooper, though conscious that there was 'a leaven of snobbery, or I should prefer to call it loyalty, which magnifies the emotion' he felt towards royalty, said that she was 'sweet' and 'affects no shadow of airs and graces'. Virginia Woolf considered the Duchess 'delightful, incredibly gay and simple. It was a tragedy that she should be royal. She was clever. She talked to Harold [Nicolson] perceptively about *Some People*, whereas the Duke had only read the Arketall story and got it wrong.' Sir Ronald Lindsay agreed about her attractiveness but not her cleverness: she was 'not a great intellect but had any amount of "intelligence du coeur"'. So transcendent was the Duchess's charm that she was credited with working miracles. Wheeler-Bennett cites the conversion of an (unnamed) 'Communist agitator' in Australia. When the Duchess waved and smiled – 'right into my face' – as he stood in the crowd, he vowed never to say another word against royalty. A few sceptics felt that the Duchess was too miraculous to be true, and there were dark tales about her ruthlessness and insincerity. She was said to be a 'tartar' at home and there is no doubt that her views were extremely right-wing. According to the American diplomat William Bullitt, 'her sister-in-law, the Princess Royal, goes around England talking about "her cheap public smile"'.

There was something well-nigh miraculous about the Yorks' eldest child, too. Princess Elizabeth was born in 1926 and within a couple of years Churchill discovered in her 'an air of authority and reflectiveness astonishing in an infant'. Certainly she attracted extraordinary devotion. The Duchess of York wrote to Queen Mary: 'It almost frightens me that people should love her so much. I suppose it is a good thing, and I hope that she will be worthy of it, poor darling.' Princess Margaret Rose, who was born in 1930, was her father's favourite. She was warmer and more demonstrative than her elder sister, though less conscientious and less neurotically tidy. But if both girls were brought up to expect unusual adulation, they did not anticipate the prominence which was to be their lot after 1936. Until then the Yorks lived an unsophisticated, countrified sort of existence. The girls were educated in an old-fashioned way, as seemed appropriate to their station. The Duchess set little store by academic excellence. But she did think it important for her daughters to 'spend as long as possible in the open air, to enjoy to the full the pleasures of the country, to be able to dance and draw and appreciate music, to acquire good manners and perfect deportment, and to cultivate all the distinctively feminine graces'. The parents seldom dined out, preferring to play racing demon or rummy with their children at home. They were not even smart enough to receive invitations from the leading hostesses of the day, Lady Cunard and Lady Colefax. The Duke's preoccupations were well illustrated by the letter he wrote to the master of fox hounds at the Pytchley Hunt in the middle of the Depression: 'It has come as a great shock to me that with the economy cuts I have had to make my hunting should have been one of the things I must do without. And I must sell my horses too. This is the worst part of it all.'

Needless to say, the abdication crisis came as a much greater shock to George. Edward treated him with characteristic lack of consideration, singularly failing to take his brother into his confidence in a matter which would revolutionize George's future. But by 25 November 1936 the Duke of York feared the worst. Assuming that he would become King, he wrote: 'I will do my best to clear up the inevitable mess, if the whole fabric does not crumble under the shock and strain of it all.' When, on 9 December, it became clear that his regal fate was sealed, George went to see his mother at Marlborough House where (in Walter Monckton's presence) he 'broke down & sobbed like a child'. Queen Mary wrote: 'It is a terrible blow to us all & particularly to poor Bertie.' Two days later George became the third monarch to reign in 1936. In a state of intense distress he told 'Dickie' Mountbatten how hopelessly unqualified he felt for the role, only to be informed that his father, George V, had said the very same thing to *his* father, Prince Louis Mountbatten. The handover occurred with due ceremony. George recorded: 'When D[avid] and I said goodbye we kissed, parted as freemasons & he bowed to me as his King.'

The rumours about the new King's poor health and lack of ability continued to circulate. Some people claimed that he would never be crowned, others that even if he endured the arduous ceremony, he would be a recluse and a 'rubber stamp'. In order to counter this gossip there was a concerted effort to make the coronation a spectacular affirmation of loyalty to the Crown. The newspapers did their best to associate George VI with George V: 'We have not known him long, but long enough to discover in him some of the steady, sterling stuff that made his father the most beloved Englishman of his generation.' Such was the persuasive power of the press that wags professed to see on the new King's chin the first sproutings of a nautical beard. The great London stores competed with one another to produce the most gorgeous decorations, doubtless encouraged by trade journals exhorting them to 'Cash in on the coronation. Give your shop a patriotic effect.' The West End was festooned with red, white and blue bunting, filled with massive portraits and plaster casts of the royal couple, not to mention gigantic tableaux of Empire. The display at Selfridge's was so picturesque that it was afterwards bought by an Indian prince, who used it to embellish his palace.

The authorities, keen to gauge the public response to the royal procession, installed a measuring apparatus at Whitehall: it recorded eighty-five decibels of cheering for Queen Mary and eighty-three for the King and Queen. In the Abbey, Channon noted, even the few Socialists were impressed by 'the grandeur of the feudal capitalistic show', though they complained of having to sit behind 'these Peer Johnnies'. Channon retorted: 'It's their show, after all. You are lucky to be here at all.' The coronation celebrations were larger, though less spontaneous, than those of the Silver Jubilee, and they seemed to have the desired effect. Unquestionably the disenchantment caused by the abdication lingered on. An anonymous 'American Resident', in a pamphlet optimistically entitled *The Twilight of the British Monarchy* (1937), claimed that the coronation was 'a sort of whistling in the dark'. At the abdication people had glimpsed the emptiness of the pageantry and the artificiality of the royalty worship. The spirit of republicanism was 'probably stronger than it had been since the days of Joseph Chamberlain'. According to the 'American Resident', the 'taboo is off', the 'sickening cant about royalty has already been appreciably reduced, the Hallelujahs have been soft-pedalled'. The press itself warned against deifying the monarchy and acknowledged the present disillusionment which, as one newspaper said, even 'the luscious Coronation propaganda cannot dissipate'.

In all likelihood the 'American Resident' was guilty of wishful thinking. At the coronation the rain did not dampen the carnival spirit. The bus strike failed to dispel the patriotic euphoria. The anthropologist Malinowski reckoned that the coronation 'generated an increased feeling of security, of stability, and the permanence of the British Empire'. This was doubtless very comforting at the time. Whether it was desirable for the British people to dwell in such a cloud-cuckoo-land while real perils loomed ever larger on the global scene, is another matter.

According to that magisterially discreet but eminently well-informed royalist, Dermot Morrah, after the abdication Queen Elizabeth 'insisted that the unbending must be left to her, and that the crowned and anointed King must not be too ready to step down from his pedestal'. This suited George very well, though it also reinforced the antiquated social exclusiveness of the monarchy. Of course, it was in any case virtually impossible to bridge the great gulf fixed between royal personages and ordinary mortals. Queen Mary always referred to royalties as 'dear so-and-so' and to commoners, however rich, as 'poor so-and-so'.

As one British grandee put it: 'The important thing to remember is that in the eyes of the royal family we're all glorified footmen and ladies' maids.' The 'American Resident' wrote: 'In no other western country in Europe is royalty less democratic, so widely separated from the people, so aloof, so profoundly snobbish socially as in this politically most democratic of countries.' So, partly as a matter of policy and partly through his own incapacity, George ensured that the monarchy would remain remote from the people. As Harold Laski wrote in 1938, the King had no real contact with the working class and it would have caused astonishment if he had stayed with a trade unionist rather than a peer. George talked vaguely of somehow managing to retain 'the common touch'. But, in his own modest way, he continued the war which his father had waged against the twentieth century.

The extent to which George allowed himself to be made the prisoner of a Palace clique is unclear. He certainly employed the dourly Establishment-minded Alec Hardinge as his private secretary. Between them, Hardinge and the Queen probably insisted that the Duke of Windsor's importunate telephone calls from exile, which reduced the King to inarticulate fury, should cease. Chips Channon, who wrote with some animus but rightly prided himself on being intimately acquainted with the doings of high society, maintained that a clique was also responsible for purging Edward's supporters from the new royal retinue. However, whether 'court minions' or the King himself bore the responsibility, there is no doubt that during the late 1930s the Palace did, in Channon's words, 'intrigue' and 'dabble in politics'. This intervention was of doubtful constitutional propriety. It was also sadly misguided. For, having 'boundless confidence in Mr Chamberlain' and being on 'very cordial terms' with Lord Halifax, the King did all he could to strengthen the policy of appeasement. He even proposed a number of more or less fatuous personal initiatives. George wanted to send an appeal to Hitler for peace as 'one ex-serviceman to another'. He was anxious to dispatch 'a friendly message direct to the Emperor of Japan'. To his disappointment, the Foreign Office turned down such suggestions.

More successful were the official engagements that the King and Queen undertook. Admittedly, their programme was not too strenuous. Staying at Windsor, Kenneth Clark was 'shocked' by how little the King and Queen 'did with their day; she never rose before 11'. Still, they did the usual royal chores, touring factories, inspecting troops, visiting exhibitions, opening hospitals, laying cornerstones, unveiling monuments, launching ships and the like. Of course, there was always an air of artificiality and stiffness about such occasions, not to mention a taste of slumming. But the British people actually liked being patronized by royalty. The 'American Resident' went so far as to claim that although the democratic British were shocked by the 'slavish adulation' which Germans and Russians gave to their dictators, it was surpassed by their own 'sheepish adoration of the King and Queen'. Ironically enough, though, their visit to the United States in 1939 seemed to prove Lord Stamfordham's old dictum that 'Americans are the greatest worshippers of Royalty'.

As always, the preparations were made with meticulous care. Roosevelt was amused by royal requests that eiderdowns and hot water bottles should be provided in Washington in June, though his wife was somewhat less happy about implementing the protocol – the White House servants had to be taught to serve the Queen exactly thirty seconds after they had served the King. The President was interested by William Bullitt's confidential report on the couple: 'She resembles so much the female caddies who used to carry my clubs at Pitlochry in Scotland many years ago that I find her pleasant. . . . The little king is beginning to feel his oats, but still remains a rather frightened boy.' Bullitt advised the President not to mention the Windsors because the Duke had recently written to Queen Mary severing relations with Bertie on the grounds that he had behaved towards him in such an ungentlemanly way – thanks to 'the influence of that common little woman', the Queen.

Roosevelt duly charmed the royal pair, and they in turn did their best to charm him. Citizens of the republic greeted the first English King ever to set foot on their soil with delirious enthusiasm. Half a million people packed Pennsylvania Avenue and the newspaper headlines blared (what else?): 'The British Re-take Washington.' Queen Elizabeth stole the show, anticipating Princess Diana by almost half a century, though she did so by being gracious and regal from more of a distance. When a journalist suggested to the British ambassador that she might 'do something human while she is here, like going shopping', he was frostily informed that if any purchases became necessary Her Majesty would send her maid. The Queen later said: 'That tour made us! I mean it made us, the King and I. It came just at the right time, particularly for us.' From the public relations angle, this was undoubtedly true. Unfortunately it was less satisfactory from the diplomatic point of view. The King returned home with the soothing but misleading impression, which Roosevelt had conveyed to him and which he presumably conveyed to the government, that 'If London was bombed [the] U.S.A. would come in.' George was even indiscreet enough to communicate his misplaced confidence to a journalist: 'It's in the bag.'

The King had congratulated Chamberlain after Munich. When the war made manifest the bankruptcy of the prime minister's foreign policy, George's admiration for him by no means faltered. Although suffering from bouts of mild defeatism, he supported the government vigorously, issuing no stern warnings about its inept handling of the 'phoney war'. Indeed, when Socialist criticisms grew too loud, he called in Clement Attlee and rebuked him – the Labour leader was said to have left the Palace in 'a chastened mood'. More sinister, when the Jewish war minister, Leslie Hore-Belisha, attempted to make the army more democratic and complained that British defences on France's frontier with Belgium were inadequate, the King 'insisted' (according to Chips Channon) on his resignation. George was furious with the Tory rebels who caused Chamberlain's own resignation in May 1940. Left to himself, he would have chosen as Chamberlain's successor the congenial Lord Halifax, a mediocrity who at the prospect of the premiership got a 'bad stomach ache', rather than the genius with fire in his belly whose finest hour it was. Winston Churchill, not King George VI, emerged as Britain's inspiration during the Second World War.

Staunch royalist that he was, Churchill lauded the achievement of the King and Queen: 'The war has drawn the Throne and the people more closely together than was ever before recorded and Your Majesties are more beloved by all classes and conditions than any of the princes of the past.' This was certainly the received wisdom. Books invariably cite the Queen's bold refusal to send her children to Canada as many hundreds of affluent parents (including the Mountbattens) did: 'The Princesses cannot go without me; I cannot go without the King; the King will never go.' They quote her brave remark after part of Buckingham Palace was damaged in a raid: 'I'm so glad we've been bombed. It makes me feel I can look the East End in the face.' They describe arduous royal tours of the blitzed areas, and the pathetic shows of loyalty. They affirm that because of 'King George VI's high visibility to his subjects during [the war], the House of Windsor became even more popular and secure'.

The reality was somewhat different. Although the royal family appear to have spent some nights at Windsor Castle,* driving up to London in the morning, the King, who had seen the bombs falling, was badly shaken by the raid on Buckingham Palace. He recorded: 'It was a ghastly experience & I don't want it to be repeated.' A week later he was still suffering from shock. According to the press and the BBC, the British people were not only shocked but outraged by this attack. However, as Philip Ziegler demonstrates in his book *Crown and People* (1978), the mass media issued mendacious propaganda about the enthusiasm which the royal family generated during the war. Drawing on the records of Mass Observation, an early (and not entirely reliable) form of opinion poll, he was able to show that the King and Queen were regarded as unprecedentedly irrelevant at a time when the nation confronted perhaps the greatest crisis in its history. A typical opinion was that people 'don't dislike them or anything – they just don't think about them'. Another common view was: 'I think it's all a bit silly – kings and queens in wartime.' Nor were Londoners unduly sympathetic about the assault on Buckingham Palace. One housewife said: 'It's all very well for them, traipsing around saying how their hearts bleed for us and they share our sufferings, and then going home to a roaring fire in one of their six houses.' This disrespectful attitude was expressed to the sovereign himself. When he told one victim of

---

* Queen Mary, accompanied by a staff of sixty-three and mountains of baggage, spent the war at Badminton in Gloucestershire, where she reduced the Duke and Duchess of Beaufort to the status of guests in their own home. She kept four suitcases packed, one full of jewellery and tiaras, in case of invasion. Her main objection to Hitler, it seems, was that he spoke such abominable German.

the blitz that 'My house was bombed too', the disconcerting response was: 'Which one?'

The fact was that the royal couple were out of their element, exiles from the realm of happy fantasy which they normally inhabited. Instead of being Ruritanian figures waving benignly from a golden coach during some more or less factitious occasion of national rejoicing, the King and Queen were associated with a reign of terror and tribulation. Furthermore, in the crucible of conflict the traditional social distinctions and conventions tended to dissolve. Inherited privilege of any sort seemed particularly indefensible. In this people's war there was a marked growth of egalitarian feeling, an acute consciousness that sacrifices ought to be fairly shared at the moment and properly rewarded afterwards. Hence the remarkable public response to the Duke of Kent's death in an aeroplane accident in 1942, reflected in this comment on his widow's plight: 'She won't have to work to keep those children. *We* will.' Hence the tremendous enthusiasm for the Beveridge Report (1942), which advocated full social security. Hence the radical mood which resulted in the Labour landslide in 1945. Hence the feeling that illusions, however grand, were a distraction when the state was in danger. Even a robust Tory like Oliver Stanley could wax sour about royalty in his wartime diary: 'The King is fundamentally a weak character and certainly a rather stupid one. The Queen is a strong one out of a rather reactionary stable.'

The Queen's intervention was frequently evident. In 1943, for example, she played an important part, according to Stanley, in causing the resignation of Sir Alec Hardinge as the King's private secretary and his replacement by his assistant, Sir Alan Lascelles, who was less overbearing though hardly less reactionary – he resigned from the Reform Club when it voted to admit women. However, this change did not mean that the personal influence of the Crown increased during the war, far from it. Churchill treated the monarch with elaborate courtesy, though he incensed George by being late for his regular weekly audiences. But the prime minister made it clear who was boss. He insisted that his disreputable ally Brendan Bracken be made a Privy Councillor despite royal objections. He also vetoed as inopportune the King's proposal to go to India – 'A visit from me would buck them up' – in 1944.

In any case George was preoccupied with the minor matters which invariably obsess royalty. He was determined, for example, that 'all questions relating to uniforms must come before me before any alterations to it are discussed, let alone settled'. His functions were largely ceremonial. He inspected troops abroad as well as at home – in North Africa and later Italy, where he made an excellent impression. It is true that he could be temperamental and obstructive, that he tired easily and that his health was fragile. He was also apt to fuss about slight inconveniences, such as the 'defective and erratic' plumbing in his villa at Algiers. But he was able to relax more easily with military men than with civilians. His ministers found him 'stiff and speechless', incapable of grasping complex arguments and so shy that he had great difficulty in terminating meetings. With senior officers, though, he revealed his retentive memory for detail, he joked and chaffed, and he even talked a little wildly when he got excited. General Eisenhower was amused when the King said he was delighted to discover that General Montgomery was not after *his* job. The royal comments on military strategy were less happy. In October 1943, for instance, just when it was becoming plain that the Italian campaign had bogged down and that all possible Allied efforts should be devoted to making a success of the Normandy invasion, the King encouraged Churchill to persist in his ambition to slit open Europe's 'soft underbelly'.

Luckily this advice was not heeded. Where the King did score, though, was in helping to frustrate Churchill's rash scheme to sail with the D-Day armada – George threatened to come too. By this time he was devoted to his volatile prime minister. He supported him in his attempt to maintain the coalition government until Japan was defeated, even though the country had not had a general election for ten years. When Labour refused to agree and then won so crushingly at the polls, the King was surprised and shaken. Indeed, like Queen Victoria, he seemed to question whether the popular vote reflected the popular will. He wrote to General Smuts: 'It was a great shock to me to have to lose Churchill as my chief adviser, and I am sure the people did not want to lose him as their leader, after all the years of stupendous work he did on their behalf in the war.' George found relations with his new premier, the laconic Attlee, awkward and said that all his Labour ministers were 'rather difficult to talk to'.

According to Wheeler-Bennett, the King was 'not pro-Conservative or anti-Socialist'. He simply feared the prospect of an untried Labour government and was 'distrustful of undue haste'. This is scarcely a correct summary of George's views, even on the meagre evidence which Wheeler-Bennett himself provides. Like Edward VII after the Liberal landslide of 1906, King George did his best to delay and to thwart the radical new measures which his government proposed. He 'told Attlee that he must give the people here some confidence that the Government was not going to stifle all private enterprise'. He urged him to take a strong line against industrial stoppages: 'the liberty of the subject was at stake if a strike interfered with home life'. He told Herbert Morrison that 'he was going too fast in the new nationalizing legislation'. He tried to foist his kingly fads on the Labour administration: 'I said we must all have new clothes & my family are now down to the lowest ebb.' He even succeeded in having the Order of the Garter de-politicized and placed in the personal gift of the sovereign. According to Wheeler-Bennett, he hoped that this would add to the '*mystique* of monarchy, of which the Fount of Honour was so vital an attribute'. All told, it is clear that the King was about as much of a dyed-in-the-wool Tory as his father had been, though he was less confident about expressing his views. Chips Channon was categorical: 'I do not think he concealed very skilfully his dislike of the Socialists for all the ones who had been in waiting are vitriolic about him.'

Many members of the Labour government were indeed privately prepared to disparage all aspects of the monarchy. Sir Stafford Cripps dismissed royal pageantry as 'all bunk and bunting'. Hugh Dalton wrote that King George was 'as nearly inanimate as an animate monarch can be'. But Attlee himself was an unrepentant royalist. He did, to be sure, complain of the 'vulgar snobbery' with which the sovereign was surrounded and he accused the press of 'enveloping the Royal Family with a continual round of obsequiousness'. But he seems to have been willing, in 1945, to defer to George's strongly expressed advice that Bevin would make a better foreign secretary than Dalton. (Here the King may well have been right, though his hostility to Dalton – the one Labour minister, he told Gaitskell, 'I cannot abide' – probably stemmed from the fact that Dalton was the son of George V's tutor and had 'let down the side' by joining the Socialists.) Attlee was a staunch foe of republicanism, describing it as the creed not of Socialists but of 'bourgeois radicals'. He always resorted to the standard Labour argument that his party 'would not raise a finger to turn a capitalist monarchy into a capitalist Republic'. He was particularly concerned that, if India were allowed to stay in the Commonwealth as a republic after independence was granted in 1947, it 'would lead to the spread of Republicanism'.

Needless to say, the King had always insisted that 'we must not lose India'. But when it became clear that there was no hope of retaining the jewel in the imperial crown and, indeed, that the tide of Empire was ebbing inexorably, the monarchy adapted itself to the new circumstances of Commonwealth with protean swiftness. Since Queen Victoria's time the British sovereign had been the incarnation of Empire. The monarch, his status enhanced by elaborate ceremonial and his name invoked to justify every imperialist action, seemed to invest British dominion with his own quasi-divinity, to endow it with ultimate legitimacy. Now, all of a sudden, the King ceased to be an Emperor, signing himself after 1947 simply 'George R[ex]' instead of 'George R[ex et] I[mperator]'. Of course, the British are adept at discovering contemporary justifications for obsolete institutions. So occurred an astonishing metamorphosis. In 1949 the King, having lost an Empire, found a role. He became Head of the British Commonwealth, which today consists of forty-nine countries, twenty-six of which are republics.

The Commonwealth is the ghost of Empire. It was conjured up to mask the fact that the great days of British pre-eminence were gone. The royal 'magic' (as Churchill called it) invested this chimerical organization with some substance. But, as the historian Nicholas Mansergh suggested, the Commonwealth resembled the Trinity in testing the faith of its devotees to the utmost – it involved 'a new Athanasianism of many crowns in one monarchy'. Some could not believe. In 1948, for example, Eire left the Commonwealth and broke its connection with the Crown. The new Taoiseach, John Costello, declared: 'Friendship with Britain did not depend on archaic forms, but on principles of association unrelated to outworn formulae.' The Commonwealth's dignified disguise could not conceal the fact that it was a mass of anomalies. Its existence comported uneasily with the 'special relationship' between Britain and the United States, not to mention Britain's growing involvement with Europe. The economic relationship between Britain and Commonwealth states brought fewer benefits than problems. Britain was often embarrassed by the exigencies of the novel partnership with lesser breeds over whom she had formerly held sway. The Crown could be put in an impossible position if it received conflicting advice from different Commonwealth countries. In fact, the Commonwealth survived by sentiment not sense.

It was the kind of sentiment in which General Smuts wallowed when the royal family visited South Africa in 1947 – a tour, incidentally, disapproved of by almost a third of the British people, who regarded it as an expensive holiday in the sun at a time when conditions at home were particularly fraught. Smuts thought that the King and Queen would have the 'blessed and fruitful function' of healing the racial rifts in South Africa. As Smuts's biographer observed, 'It was a wistful dream.' So, in essence, was the Commonwealth, a dream of past glories given an air of plausibility by the Crown. The association was, and remains, about as incoherent as King George's verdict – a mixture of Commonwealth loyalty and connoisseurial candour – on South African brandy: 'It is, of course, m-magnificent, except that it is not very nice.'

Lady Diana Cooper observed that George VI transformed the 'operetta' monarchy which he inherited from his brother into an 'institution'. In fact, all he did was to adhere slavishly to what Penelope Mortimer called his father's 'high standards of mediocrity'. It is true that he permitted some modernization to take place. Since Edward VIII's time the Beefeaters had been allowed to shave off their beards. Buckingham Palace now had electricity. Its enormous staff was better treated. Servants no longer lived in 'beetle-ridden basements', largely because they had, to George's shock and anger, organized a trade union and demanded improved pay and conditions. However, they were still expected to accommodate their personal lives to their employers' needs. Queen Elizabeth was quite firm that her daughters' gushing governess, Marion Crawford, should postpone her wedding because 'it would not be at all convenient'.

Royal convenience also impinged on the life of the Crown's political servants – the timing of the 1951 general election was partly determined by Attlee's wish to fit in with the King's programme.

Still, even during the war, when the royal family apparently ate rationed food off gold plates (though it seems doubtful whether they had ever seen a coupon and it is surely inconceivable that their diet was not supplemented from their country estates), nothing fundamental was allowed to change. The butter pats were monogrammed with the royal coat of arms. The countless clocks were kept ticking away punctually. A man was employed full-time to keep down the vermin. The gilt chairs, untouched since Queen Victoria's day, were liable to disintegrate when anyone sat on them. According to Miss Crawford, living in Buckingham Palace was like 'camping in a museum'. Its vast rooms, decorated in pink and gold, and bursting with priceless heirlooms, 'resembled the setting of a luxurious pantomime'. When in festive mood, during private dances, the King would sometimes even lead the 'Conga' through the halls and corridors of the Palace. However, like his forebears, George took no interest in higher culture. Lord Crawford's protest about his 'boycott of science and art' made no impression on him, or on his elder daughter – token visits to the opera scarcely conceal the modern British monarchy's arrant philistinism.

In the main, then, George was a royal retrogressionist. He had his family's customary obsession with clothes. During the war he designed a new livery for his pages and footmen. He had an eagle eye for sartorial impropriety and roundly ticked off people, including royal personages, for being 'damned sloppy'. He went so far as to visit Anthony Quayle's dressing room at Stratford, where he was playing Henry VIII, and show him how the Garter should be worn. In his latter years, with Labour in power, George was oppressed by the change of standards and the decay of values which he had been brought up to regard as sacrosanct. When the writer Vita Sackville-West told him that her family mansion, Knole, had been given to the National Trust, he responded despairingly: 'Everything is going nowadays. Before long I shall also have to go.' To the end he remained a simple country squire, devoted to his family, patriarchal towards his estate workers (he put pressure on senior ones to attend church at Sandringham), and preoccupied with shooting. Even when stricken with cancer, the King would not be deprived of his sport and he spent the last day of his life happily killing hares. Shortly after the King's death Chips Channon sketched the character of this shy, dull, well-intentioned man:

> He had no wit, no learning, no humour, except of a rather schoolboy brand. He was nervous, ill at ease, though slightly better after some champagne. He had no vices and few interests other than shooting. He had few friends and was almost entirely dependent on the Queen whom he worshipped: she was his will-power, his all. He was an affectionate father and a loyal friend to the very few people he liked . . . no one hated him – he was too neutral; hence he was a successful and even popular sovereign.

It was a fair epitaph, or, at least in the present state of know-ledge about the King, it seems a plausible one. There is no doubt that the nation felt a sense of loss. The crowds at George's funeral, an elaborate ceremony modelled on his father's, were vis-ibly subdued and some people wept openly. Richard Dimbleby's florid broadcast about the royal lying-in-state apparently summed up the general feeling: 'Never safer, better guarded, lay a sleep-ing King than this, with a golden candle-light to warm his resting place, and the muffled footsteps of his devoted subjects to keep him company.' The fact was that by doing his duty with stolid unimaginativeness the King had rescued the institution which he embodied from the parlous state in which his brother had left it. By the simple expedient of adhering rigorously to the standards of a bygone age, George VI had restored, and to some extent made, the modern monarchy. Never has such an un-inspiring figure been such an inspiration.

Nine

Our Own Dear Queen

Since 1952 Queen Elizabeth II has presided with all, and some-times more than all, her father's dignity, his devotion to duty and his instinctive reliance on fossilized tradition, over the remorseless decline of Britain. Unlike George VI, Elizabeth knew that she was destined for the throne from quite an early age. She was brought up to regard the prospect with the high seriousness of a zealot. Unfortunately, the only authentic glimpses of the young Princess are provided by the maudlin memoir of her former governess, Marion Crawford. (For all 'Crawfie's' adulation of her charges, she was never pardoned for breaking the menial's code of secrecy – the royal family thought she must have taken leave of her senses, which did not stop them from evicting the hapless governess from her grace and favour cottage.) Anyway, through the goo of Miss Crawford's prose it emerges that 'Lilibet' was a preternaturally solemn little girl. In this, she afforded a striking contrast to her sister Margaret, who was frivolous and flirtatious even as a child, and in some ways resembled her uncle Edward. Their father was intensely posses-sive about his daughters, but whereas Margaret was spoilt – she was his 'plaything' – Elizabeth was trained to have an elevated, almost Victorian, view of her role. Even King George V was impressed by her grave demeanour. 'Grandpapa England', as she was said to call him, hoped that Edward would not marry and have children and that nothing would come between Elizabeth and the throne. Another member of the family expressed the same feeling in a different way: 'God's tooth, what a narrow squeak Margaret wasn't the eldest daughter.' With Elizabeth as queen, Britain might not enjoy a new Elizabethan age, but at least the nation's decadence would proceed with decorum.

The romance of royalty is so pervasive that even the most level-headed witnesses are liable to have their judgement warped by it. But observers as different as the Countess of Airlie and James Lees-Milne, Marion Crawford and Queen Mary, said that Princess Elizabeth reminded them of Queen Victoria. Attending the Princess's confirmation in 1942, Lady Airlie observed her 'grave little face under a small white net veil' and opined: 'The carriage of her head was unequalled and there was about her that indescribable something which Queen Victoria had.' Lady Airlie concluded that the indescribable something was an 'air of Majesty'. Lees-Milne implied that it was imperiousness. He recorded that, shy though she was, the Princess made no bones about telling a vicar that she had disliked part of his sermon. And she went so far as to twit her own mother for being a commoner. Miss Crawford recorded that after an inspection of the Grenadier Guards in her new role as Colonel, Elizabeth gave vent to some ringing criticisms. An officer had to explain, via Crawfie, that this was not quite appropriate. In due course, incidentally, half the guardsmen opted out of a levy imposed on them to buy Elizabeth a wedding present, saying that the royal family never did anything for anyone. Queen Mary, too, noted the resemblance between her grand-daughter and her grand-mother-in-law. From her youth up, apparently, Elizabeth adopted the regal habit of staring hard at a person who said anything she disapproved of, and ignoring the remark completely. It was her way of saying: 'We are not amused' . . . or, rather: 'One is not amused.'

There was little enough to amuse the royal children during the war years, though they scarcely suffered like their contemporaries, despite the cosy implication of Elizabeth's famous BBC Children's Hour Broadcast. Being incarcerated in Windsor Castle, where they were protected with as much care as the Crown Jewels stuffed into hatboxes in the cellars, only added to their social segregation. Occasionally, during the Christmas pantomimes they organized, the Princesses met ordinary people, but they played supporting cast to the royal stars. For the most part Elizabeth and Margaret were confined to their own tight family circle, diluted only by the company of courtiers and servants. The last, of course, were scarcely intimate companions. Indeed, the relationship was typified by Elizabeth's eating her lunch on one side of a large boulder while the ghillie with whom she was out deer-stalking ate his on the other. The Princesses' education seemed to fit them better to enjoy the company of animals, dead or alive, than that of human beings. Elizabeth grew up fully equipped to make a good squire's wife. There is an air of poignancy in her oft-quoted remark that, had she not been Queen, she would have liked to be 'a lady living in the country with lots of horses and dogs'. During Elizabeth's youth the only remotely normal experience she had was joining the Auxiliary Territorial Service at the age of eighteen. As she said years later, 'one had no idea how one compared with other people'. But even in the ATS she was carefully sheltered. It was hardly surprising that she fell for the first suitable man who presented himself.

This was, of course, Prince Philip of Greece, at that time a serving officer in the Royal Navy and known, when he took British citizenship to assuage the xenophobia which his suit provoked, as Lieutenant Mountbatten, his mother's maiden name. Philip was of Danish and German descent, junior member of a royal house which the Greek people treated as a political shuttlecock, regularly knocking it on and off the throne. Attractive, arrogant and ambitious, he was perhaps seeking a permanent billet. At any rate he unmistakably set his cap at the young Princess. Unfortunately he proved as unpopular with George VI as he was alluring to his daughter. The King did not want his family broken up and he thought Elizabeth too young and in-experienced to wed. So every sort of obstacle was placed in the way of their marriage. The details are unknown. But it seems that in spite of the paternal discouragement the couple got engaged in the autumn of 1946. This was kept secret, however, and the Palace issued a statement denying newspaper rumours about the match.

Evidently the King found good reasons of state to support his personal preferences. For when the royal family toured South Africa in 1947 Philip did not accompany them. And Elizabeth, in the celebrated broadcast made to mark her coming of age, dedicated her life to her people, which she would scarcely have done without prompting from her father. It was an awkwardly juvenile performance, one which she evidently regretted later. For she subsequently explained that it had occurred when she was 'green', during her 'salad days', though she would not retract a word of it. Anyway, across the aether, in her fluting Pont Street voice (whose cut-glass vowels are now out of fashion even among royalty), she said:

> I declare before you all that my whole life, whether it be long or short, shall be devoted to your service and to the service of our great Imperial Commonwealth to which we all belong. But I shall not have strength to carry out this resolution unless you join in it with me, as I now invite you to do; I know that your support will be unfailingly given. God bless all of you who are willing to share it.

It was, to quote Philip Howard's attractive simile, 'like Peter Pan appealing to the audience to shout that they believe in fairies in order to save the life of Tinkerbell'.

However naïve these sentiments sound today, they have surely remained, for forty years, Elizabeth's watchword. While she is alive the spirit of service will not die, though that spirit, as royally interpreted, evidently implies servility on the part of the masses. For Elizabeth to serve her subjects they must also serve her – royalty in the castle, commonalty at the gate. Still, even if it is a somewhat patronizing, *de haut en bas* ideal, it does at least acknowledge that feudal privilege implies feudal duty. The young Princess Elizabeth returned home. In 1947 she married, amid the usual ballyhoo – the wedding provided a splash of colour in a drab era and it was described by one newspaper as 'England's answer to *Oklahoma*'. Then she started a family and settled down to perform her functions as heir to the throne.

Her sister Margaret, meanwhile, was learning that it was possible to enjoy the perquisites of her position without meeting the responsibilities. After her sister's wedding, Margaret's life became a long round of entertainment. Of course, the King and Queen had always indulged and seldom disciplined her, and after the war they wanted her to enjoy life. So, as Miss Crawford sadly observed, they failed to impose any 'definite work' or any 'definite routine'. At home a bored Margaret 'mooned about her room getting more and more depressed'. But increasingly she went out . . . and stayed out. Every night of the week her dumpy figure, dressed to the nines, could be seen cavorting in some fashionable haunt. The late hours made her crosser and ruder and more inconsiderate than ever. There was drinking and later, to the horror of polite society, smoking in public, assisted by an ornate cigarette holder. There were hints of early indiscretions. Chips Channon detected 'a Marie Antoinette aroma' about Margaret. Pretty, surprisingly intelligent, possessing a lively sense of fun, artistic interests and a talent for mimicry to match the Prince Regent's, Margaret was flattered by her set into believing that she was a paragon of talent and charm. Unfortunately, like some royal Judy Garland, she also cultivated a temperament. She insisted on being the centre of attention and threw scenes if for some reason she failed to attract the limelight. She wanted to enjoy both the deference prescribed by etiquette and the familiarity afforded by bohemianism. She wished to revel in the delights of chic rebellion – 'Disobedience is my joy,' she told Jean Cocteau – and to benefit from the advantages of polite convention. Socially, like so many royalties, the Princess invited intimacy and then pulled rank. When someone incautiously referred to 'your father' she retorted witheringly: 'You mean, His Majesty the King.' Margaret liked servility but she would not give service. In 1984 the Queen Mother, who is as old as the century, undertook more public engagements than she did.

By the end of George VI's reign, what perturbed the family most was the fact that his younger daughter had become enamoured of his favourite equerry, Group Captain Peter Townsend. Unfortunately Townsend was married, though in 1951 he separated from his wife and in 1952 he obtained a decree nisi on the grounds of her adultery. The spectre of the abdication crisis once more stalked the corridors of Buckingham Palace. Elizabeth had publicly declared in 1949 that divorce 'caused some of the darkest evils in our society'. Yet she was devoted to her sister and is said to give way to emotion only over Margaret. After their father's death the new Queen was faced with the problem of how to respond to Margaret's wish to marry Townsend. It was a problem compounded by the fact that in the annexe of Westminster Abbey, after the coronation service, Margaret was observed proprietorially brushing a speck of dust or a bit of fluff from Townsend's uniform and looking adoringly into his eyes. This gave the foreign press a peg on which to hang the rumours of their attachment which it had been sedulously purveying. The British press, to paraphrase Lord Northcliffe, stuck to its traditional opinion that royal news, like good wine, improves by keeping. But, after a decent interval of silence, British newspapers did publish the story, while simultaneously declaring that such a match was unthinkable – a sure sign that it was under active consideration.

Margaret's *faux pas* was about the only thing to mar Queen Elizabeth's coronation. This glittering spectacle, with its attractive and youthful principal, seemed to banish the cares of the pinched postwar world and to usher in an exciting new era of hope and prosperity. At the same time it was an earnest that Britain was still Great, that the ancient splendours of the realm had by no means vanished. Enormous care was taken to foster this impression. The military parade, the imperial fanfare and the religious symbolism were played up by a press which had never been more deferential to the monarchy. As Harold Laski wrote, 'Eulogy of its habits has reached a level of intensity more comparable with the religious ecstasy of the seventeenth century, when men could still believe in the divine right of kings, than of the scientific temper of the twentieth.' The electronic media of communication were, if possible, even more ingratiating. Doubtless advised by Lascelles, who thought that even the Christmas wireless broadcast impaired the mystique of monarchy, the Queen seems initially to have opposed televising the ceremony, though opinions differ on this score. However, it did emerge that public opinion would not tolerate the TV cameras' exclusion and the propaganda value of including a mass audience became manifest. So although no close-up shots were permitted of the most solemn parts of the service, the populace was involved in this aristocratic affair.

There had been some popular hostility towards the coronation before it was held, and complaints were heard about the huge cost. Some Labour politicians felt alienated from the proceedings: Barbara Castle described it all as a 'neurotic outburst' and John Freeman saw it as wasteful ballyhoo and 'the glorification of every kind of anti-socialist belief'. But a combination of media coverage, love of processions, holiday junketings, rampant commercialism, as well as the sacred character of the ceremony itself, generated an immense enthusiasm. It did not seem absurd for sociologists to talk of a 'national communion service', or for the Archbishop of Canterbury to pontificate that on the great day the country and the Commonwealth had not been 'far from the Kingdom of Heaven'. Low's *Guardian* cartoon 'the morning after', featuring a blimp-like figure with a paper crown awry on his head, the remains of tinsel littering the room, a television set in the corner and a reminder of the £100 million bill, provoked a storm of denunciation. It was spitting in church. Low had sneered at 'a unique and inspiring experience'.

Paradoxically, though, as the festivities receded the hangover got worse. Thoughtful citizens could not but consider that the coronation, with its archaic formalities and its patrician congregation, with its coaches, postilions, robes, tiaras and coronets, was a distinctly feudal occasion, a sort of medieval pantomime. It hardly symbolized the life of a modern, unified, democratic nation. Rather it emphasized the privilege of the 'Abbey Happy' few who were invited to attend, and the great gulf which divided them from the populace at large. As the euphoria wore off, the coronation seemed to have been the pageant of the Establishment. It survived in the memory as a romantic holiday from mundane preoccupations, a theatrical extravaganza profoundly irrelevant to the real world. Lord Altrincham, a loyal monarchist, concluded that it had been 'an interlude of solemn pretence, an orgy of make-believe, in which the mass media were in league with the most blindly conservative forces in our society'.

Altrincham's view was reinforced by Queen Elizabeth's tenacious adherence to royal practice and protocol which seemed increasingly outmoded. There were the state banquets, where footmen wore gold-braided scarlet liveries, knee-breeches and pink stockings, the guests processed from the music room to the ballroom, and the Lord Chamberlain and the Lord Steward entered backwards in front of the monarch. There were the court presentations of debutantes, the Crown setting its seal of approval on a grotesque rigmarole of snobbery. There was Royal Ascot, where admission to the Royal Enclosure was restricted to those who could obtain the very expensive tickets issued by the Lord Chamberlain. There was the socially exclusive and rigidly hierarchical court, full of wealthy Old Etonians and propertied ex-Guards officers. There was the press secretary, Sir Richard Colville, who treated journalists like tradesmen and declared: 'My job is for the most part to keep stories about the Queen out of the press.' Experienced reporters learnt to believe nothing about royalty until it was officially denied by 'a Buckingham Palace spokesman'.

Nothing seemed to convict Queen Elizabeth's court of bland dissimulation and po-faced stuffiness more than its attitude to the Margaret/Townsend affair. When, shortly after the coronation, in June 1953, newspapers began to ventilate the rumours, the private secretary and the press secretary combined to avert a scandal. Lascelles, who had so disapproved of Edward VIII's louche behaviour, was horrified by the prospect of a repeat performance, even on a minor scale, of the abdication crisis. When Townsend admitted his passion for Margaret, Lascelles replied: 'You must be either mad or bad.' Now he and Colville advised the Queen that Margaret and Townsend should be separated. Lascelles got Churchill's support and, with a great show of official innocence, Townsend was packed off to Brussels as British air attaché. Margaret herself was sent on a tour of southern Africa, where her sullen looks afforded a striking contrast to her mother's beaming smiles. The 'royal romance', as the papers called it, hung fire for two years, though the couple continued to meet surreptitiously.

When it became clear that, aged twenty-five, Margaret still wished to marry Townsend, the Establishment once again closed ranks. Sir Anthony Eden, who had succeeded Churchill earlier in 1955, advised against the marriage, advice buttressed by a threat of resignation from the High Anglican reactionary Lord Salisbury, who was Secretary of State for Commonwealth Affairs and Lord President of the Council. The Church and *The Times* (to say nothing of the *Church Times*) combined as they had done in 1936. The Queen Mother, who wept in front of her household at the prospect of such a mésalliance, insisted that George VI would never have sanctioned it. Margaret was faced by the stark choice: reject Townsend or lose caste. If the Princess did marry him she must cease to be a Princess. This meant giving up her Civil List income, waiving her rights to the succession, and ceasing, as a private person, to enjoy the delicious perquisites of royalty. Such a course was inconceivable for one who had declared: 'I cannot imagine anything more wonderful than being who I am.' Rather than renounce royalty, Margaret issued a statement renouncing Townsend. It was a somewhat brazen exercise in Palace humbug. For Margaret, after having been obviously involved with a married man, now announced that she was 'mindful of the Church's teaching that Christian marriage is indissoluble'.

In Fleet Street editors chewed over the affair and dog ate dog. The *Daily Mirror*, which had given its adulation of the monarchy a democratic veneer by inviting its readers to vote on whether the Princess should be allowed to marry Townsend (nearly 97 per cent said yes), lambasted *The Times*. It had spoken for 'a dusty world and a forgotten age' and the *Mirror* wondered whether it would prefer Margaret to marry 'one of the witless wonders with whom she had been hobnobbing these past years'. But *The Times* had no doubt that it thundered for the nation when it praised the Princess for sacrificing personal happiness on the altar of public duty, unlike her uncle, and for 'taking the selfless royal way'.

There could have been few better illustrations of the great social divide in Britain than this episode. It was a case of gentlemen versus players, of the old, hidebound, traditionalist Establishment versus the masses, of the secular and sacred guardians of propriety versus the rest. In so far as people thought about it at all, most of them had no objections to a minor royalty marrying a divorced person. As for the traditional teachings of the Church on the subject of holy matrimony, few in an increasingly irreligious society paid them a moment's heed. Even among those top people who took *The Times*, the antique standards which Princess Margaret was now supposed to embody were more professed than practised. Eden himself was a divorcé. In short, the furore caused by Margaret's thwarted nuptials was largely a matter of hypocrisy. The affair treated the world to the ridiculous spectacle of a section of the British public in one of its periodical fits of morality. Queen Elizabeth may well have been personally tolerant, anxious even to secure her sister's happiness. But no one at court could remain unaffected by the paranoia caused by Edward VIII's abdication. Royal personages therefore had to abide by the outward forms of respectability, be those forms never so outmoded. It was not for nothing that in 1957 Lord Altrincham launched his famous attack on the social exclusiveness of the monarchy. Queen Elizabeth thought he must be mad.

Actually Altrincham's criticisms did the monarchy a signal service, just as he intended. For they led to reforms in an institution which is so resistant to change that it is always in danger of lagging fatally behind the temper of the age. His thesis was that republics were now the rule and monarchies the exception. 'When someone now asserts his belief that the British Monarchy will endure he is not asserting a proposition which is self-evident and unassailable; he is almost saying *Credo quià impossibile* [I believe because it is impossible].' In order to survive, Altrincham argued, the monarchy should transcend class as well as race. At the moment the royal entourage was dominated by a 'single social type' and the court was a 'tight little enclave of British "ladies and gentlemen"'. The royal sisters themselves bore the 'debutante stamp', particularly the elder, with her stilted and artificial style of speaking. '"Crawfie", Sir Henry Marten [of Eton, who taught Princess Elizabeth constitutional history], the London season, the race-course, the grouse-moor, canasta, and the occasional Royal Tour – all this would not have been good enough for Queen Elizabeth I.' He concluded that by having a classless and Commonwealth court the monarchy could accommodate itself to the modern age without losing its romantic appeal or its numinous power.

Altrincham's article, printed in *The National and English Review* (which he owned and edited), was couched in respectful though direct terms. But such were the mealy-mouthed conventions of the day that he was accused of having perpetrated the grossest lèse-majesté. Royalists were particularly indignant that he had criticized a person who could not answer back. This was absurd, as Altrincham later pointed out. Obviously the 'Palace spokesman' is as talkative as his royal ventriloquist wants him to be; the Crown has countless self-appointed defenders to reply on its behalf; and the right to ignore criticism is a privilege not a penalty. Ironically, though, when the rumpus had abated, a *Daily Mail* poll revealed that a majority of its young readers agreed with Lord Altrincham and that a majority of all its readers thought that the court's social circle should not be so narrow. It was a point reinforced in Malcolm Muggeridge's rather more wide-ranging polemic about the 'royal soap opera', which he described as an 'ersatz religion', a couple of years later. Referring to the ineffably snobbish Colville, Muggeridge remarked that even the Queen's 'press-relations officer must be out of the top drawer – a fact which makes them quite exceptionally incompetent'.

Far from being deaf to criticism, as their studied silence in the face of it suggests, the modern British monarchy has been acutely sensitive – and responsive – to it. Indeed, this is one of the secrets of the institution's survival. Princes cannot afford to be weather-cocks, blown about by every gust of fashion. Rather they must be barometers, slowly reflecting the climate of opinion. Being the nominal leader of her people, the Queen has to follow them – but at a distance. So, almost imperceptibly, the court has been modified to fit in with the democratic spirit of the age. Luncheon parties were begun at which the Queen could meet a slightly more varied class of person. In 1957 Prince Charles was sent to school – admittedly to an exclusive fee-paying school, but at least he would not be educationally segregated in quite the way his predecessors had been. In the same year it was announced that the presentation of debutantes would be abolished and that life peerages would be created. The last was an assault on the hereditary system which might be thought to have cut at the root of the monarchy. But the general feeling was that it would help to revitalize an upper house which seemed increasingly archaic and yet was undoubtedly a vital buttress to the throne. It was noticeable that when the Queen gave her first television Christmas broadcast, in 1957, even her voice and delivery had improved. Other changes followed. Buckingham Palace chapel was rebuilt as an art gallery and the public was permitted to view a selection of the royal treasures. In 1960 an Australian, William Heseltine (subsequently knighted), was appointed as Colville's assistant. In due course Heseltine succeeded him, and in 1986 he became the Queen's private secretary, an office which has traditionally been occupied by old-style members of the Palace mandarinate. Nowadays the Queen actually indicates that she is human not only by 'going walkabout' but by making the occasional coy little joke in her speeches – something of which her Grandpapa England would never have approved.

To a great extent these reforms are cosmetic. Nothing can alter or conceal the fact that the Queen has the conventional prejudices and predilections of her caste. With her passion for horses and dogs, for parlour games and jigsaw puzzles, for long walks in sensible shoes and Scottish picnics on blasted heaths, she is the very model of an Edwardian country lady. Having such a vested interest in the status quo, the Queen is bound to resist any fundamental change, such as the abolition of the House of Lords. There was much talk about the democratization of royalty in 1960 when Princess Margaret married a commoner, a diminutive photographer called Anthony Armstrong-Jones. But the prospect that their children might be born without a handle to their name prompted his ennoblement, as Lord Snowdon – thus making, said the wits, a mountain out of a molehill. The Queen's personal influence, based not only on incomparable experience at the centre of affairs but on patronage which, though vestigial, counts for so much in status-conscious Britain, is inevitably directed towards conservatism, if not Conservatism.

Such is the monumental discretion of prime ministers that very little is known about the way in which the Queen has carried out her political functions. It seems that she and Churchill established a doting relationship, similar to that between Lord Melbourne and Queen Victoria. Churchill, whose romantic passion for royalty was clearly roused to a new pitch by the pretty young monarch, would doubtless have harked back still further – to his great ancestor the Duke of Marlborough and Queen Anne, whom he had once described, with characteristic hyperbole, as 'a great Queen championed by a great Constable'. Queen Elizabeth indulged Churchill, allowing his audiences to last much longer than their scheduled time, apparently so that they could discuss racing – her genealogical expertise extends to horses. The Queen also indulged Eden. If ever there was a time when the royal prerogative of warning should have been employed it was before the invasion of Suez in 1956. According to Eden, however, the Queen did not disapprove of this operation, even though she was *au fait* with the collusion which occurred between Britain, France and Israel.

The Queen later told Alastair Hetherington that the Palace was riven by squabbles over Suez. Official secrecy being what it is in the United Kingdom, the full truth about this episode will not be known for many years, if at all. But evidently the monarch, like *The Times*, was privy to, and failed to protest about, what can only be described as Britain's Watergate – a sordid conspiracy of the rulers to deceive the ruled. Not long afterwards the Queen bestowed the Order of the Garter, which is in her own gift, on Eden.

There is also a marked dearth of information about the way in which the Queen employed her most important remaining prerogative when, in 1957 and 1963, she had to select Tory prime ministers. Eden's resignation after the Suez débâcle left two main contestants for the premiership. They were Harold Macmillan, a hawk against Egypt, and the more moderate R. A. Butler, who was firm favourite. The Queen took advice from two Tory elder statesmen. Winston Churchill preferred Macmillan. He was older than Butler, had married a duke's daughter, had resisted appeasement during the 1930s and was less imbued with the kind of liberalism which had made his rival happy to be a reforming education minister in wartime, something incomprehensible to Churchill. Salisbury, also a hawk over Suez, took soundings among senior Tories and was delighted to find that Macmillan was the more popular. Butler was regarded as being half-apologetic about Suez and too clever by half. So the Queen appointed Macmillan. Having held such limited consultations with such elevated personages, she laid herself open to the charge of being part of an 'Establishment ramp'.

The charge was repeated more vehemently in 1963 when Macmillan resigned, due to ill health, in the wake of the Profumo scandal. On this occasion Butler was again the favourite, though he was closely pressed by Iain Macleod and Reginald Maudling. Now that members of the upper house could renounce their peerages, two other candidates entered the field, Lord Hailsham and, a rank outsider, the fourteenth Earl of Home (pronounced Hume). Last and least, he was foreign secretary, appointed, to everyone's astonishment, simply as Macmillan's protégé. An amiable sprig of the nobility – 'Home sweet Home', Churchill called him – he seemed more suited to shooting grouse than to entering the hurly-burly of the House of Commons. Moreover, his political record was better forgotten – he had been Neville Chamberlain's parliamentary private secretary and was still desperately searching for a compromise peace after Hitler had invaded Poland. Nevertheless, from his hospital bed Macmillan pushed for his preferment. He made out a (very shaky) case for Home and advised the Queen to send for him. This she was apparently pleased to do. It was, in the *Mirror*'s argot, the most remarkable appointment since Caligula made his horse a consul. Thanks largely to the magnanimity, or to the feebleness, of Butler, Home was able to take up the reins of government. But many Tories were perturbed and Enoch Powell and Iain Macleod refused to serve under someone who seemed better qualified to be a member of the Drones Club than a modern prime minister. With his plus-fours and his plummy drawl, Home looked and sounded like an anachronism. His wife had to remind him where he was when he was about to make a speech. He hardly added to his political stature by admitting that he tried to solve the nation's economic problems with the aid of matchsticks. And in 1964 he led the Tories to defeat in the general election.

The Queen did not emerge well from either of these episodes, simply because she was seen to leave the realm of romance and enter the domain of politics. There is little doubt that she behaved with constitutional propriety for, as Richard Crossman later noted, the Queen is almost neurotically sensitive to the charge that she takes sides politically. But she did not remain above suspicion. For she failed to consult widely enough and, no more able to escape the natural bias of royalty than her forebears, she seemed to favour the more reactionary elements in the Tory Party. Certainly she enhanced its unfortunate grouse-moor image. Home was a frequent guest at royal shooting parties and he manifestly belonged to what a disillusioned Iain Macleod called the 'magic circle'. During the 1960s old inhibitions were breaking down and there was an increasing tendency to cavil about what was everywhere known as 'the Establishment'. This was defined by its supporters as an 'incorporate thinking organism ... dedicated to the survival of England through any and every crisis of history and arrogating to itself, as some outsiders have thought, an influence capable of transcending the executive power'. Its critics simply regarded the Establishment as (in Richard Rovere's phrase) 'the legitimate Mafia'. In England it possessed no godfather (not even the Archbishop of Canterbury or the editor of *The Times*) but its fairy godmother was surely none other than the Queen. Kingsley Martin, editor of the *New Statesman*, devoted an entire book to showing that the Crown was head of the Establishment rather than of the nation. Nothing had changed, he argued, since Gladstone told Queen Victoria that 'the powerful circles in which Your Majesty has active or personal intercourse contain hardly any persons who understand the point of view of the majority of the electorate'. It was still true, as the 'American Resident' had observed in the 1930s, that the monarchy was the 'secret well from which the flourishing institution of British snobbery has been drawing its nourishment'.

Usually the monarch was shielded from such strictures, avoiding controversy by the simple expedient of remaining politically invisible. The orb and sceptre are symbols bereft of real meaning. The speech from the throne is an acknowledged charade. The sovereign belongs, in Bagehot's terminology, to the dignified rather than to the efficient part of the constitution. She is a ceremonial presence only, a gloved hand in a gold coach, an animated icon. The best way to preserve her in that venerated role and, incidentally, the best way for the Tory Party to become master of its own destiny, was for Conservative MPs to elect their own leader. So, in 1965, that change was made. The royal mystagoguery was removed from what is, after all, the most fundamental and elementary process of democracy – counting votes. The Crown's prerogative of choosing a prime minister is not quite defunct. It could still operate in the case of a hung parliament, something which, with the advent of the Liberal–SDP Alliance, seems to be a growing possibility. But modern monarchs know that safety lies in exerting influence from behind the scenes rather than wielding power at the centre of the stage. The less power the Queen has, in fact, the stronger she becomes.

Nothing better illustrates this than the increased security of the Crown's position after 1964. According to Anthony Sampson, the Queen was nervous about the arrival in office of people she saw as revolutionary Socialists. She must have been all the more delighted to find the institution of which she is the avatar so lovingly protected by those ardent royalists Harold Wilson and James Callaghan. As that flail of the monarchy, the MP Willie Hamilton, observed, Labour became 'an alternative Establishment'. His view is that the 'political parties are in a conspiracy' to keep the institution of monarchy out of party politics and out of public scrutiny. There is a lot of evidence for this view. In opposition Harold Wilson was apt to indulge in radical rhetoric, asserting, for example, that the 'Tories can afford reverence and idolatry. A reforming party cannot.' But in power Wilson worshipped at the royal shrine with as much devotion as the most ardent Conservative. Subsequently, on all possible occasions, he waxes lyrical about his cosy relationship with the Queen, about the happy days at Balmoral, and about the astounding fact that the sovereign is capable, on occasions, of washing the dishes. Even Barbara Castle, loud in her left-wing protestations, was easily seduced by the charm of royal occasions. After a Buckingham Palace garden party, where she and her husband had enjoyed their privileged status, she wrote in her diary: 'I am glad to say that Ted and I share all the interests of normal people. No intellectual snobbery about *us*. Ted in particular adores ceremonial and will never willingly turn down a festivity.'

Mrs Castle was probably here thinking of the animadversions on 'the mumbo-jumbo of royalty' so often voiced by her donnish Wykehamist fellow-minister, Richard Crossman. He was appalled by the royal hoops through which hard-working ministers, self-proclaimed Socialists, happily jumped in order to fulfil the requirements of feudal protocol. In October 1964, for example, Crossman recorded a 'fantastic episode' in which new Privy Councillors had to attend a rehearsal for the formal kissing of hands:

> I don't suppose anything more dull, pretentious, or plain silly has ever been invented. There we were, sixteen grown men. For over an hour we were taught how to stand up, how to kneel on one knee on a cushion, how to raise the right hand with the Bible in it, how to move back ten paces without falling over stools – which had been carefully arranged so you did fall over them. Oh dear!

After the ceremony proper, the Queen remarked: 'You all moved backwards very nicely.' Crossman was not mollified. He continued to protest about having to dance attendance on royalty as a Privy Councillor. It was, he said, 'the most idiotic flummery and I must admit that I feel morally superior to my colleagues for despising it'.

Crossman did his best to avoid meeting his obligations. But the Queen 'strongly objected' to his absence from Privy Council meetings. He himself strongly objected to the fact that four busy men had to take a day and a night to go up to Balmoral in order to stand in front of the Queen for two and half minutes while a list of titles was read out. He was also indignant when a previously arranged meeting was put off because she had a 'private engagement'. However, even Crossman mellowed towards the monarch in time. At first he found the Queen a bore, shy, tongue-tied, only capable of talking about corgis. Crossman apparently achieved a reform whereby she could get to know her Privy

Councillors better, and later she became more relaxed and less inclined to stand on her dignity. Crossman recorded that the Queen was sometimes 'in tremendous form', able to describe quite vividly and amusingly, for example, the performances of all-in wrestlers which she had seen on television.

Whatever their private feelings about the monarchy, though, few politicians were willing to risk public hostility or electoral disaster by openly criticizing the institution. Willie Hamilton, the right-wing Labour MP for East Fife, was, needless to say, an honourable exception. He reckoned his own party guilty of 'cowardice' on the subject, and many of them refused to speak to him after his sharp comments on the 'royal pay claim' during the parliamentary select committee inquiry into the Civil List in 1971. Yet, oddly enough, almost everyone in the Labour Party resented the manner in which Prince Philip first raised the financial issue. The Prince has always been something of a bugbear to Labour. A bluff, opinionated sailor, he is inclined to give vent not just to clichés but to Tory clichés – without apparently seeing the force of the obvious ripostes. Thus he urges British businessmen to pull their fingers out, while Buckingham Palace continues to be run on medieval principles. He recommends emigration for the unemployed, though not if they are royal. He advocates taxation for large families, his own, of course, excluded. He favours the conservation of wild life, in such time as he can spare from blood sports. Indeed, he claims that shooting conserves the birds, an argument that he would scarcely care to extend to royalty. Philip consequently infuriated government ministers and supporters in 1969 when he said on American television, NBC's *Meet the Press*, that the monarchy would shortly be going 'into the red'. He himself would probably have to give up playing polo and his family might have to 'move into smaller premises'. Since he liked to refer to Buckingham Palace as 'our tied cottage' this would mean moving to a very humble abode indeed.

The royal family's financial crisis must therefore have been acute, at least by its own far from modest standards, and soon the papers were full of it. Probably Philip's remarks had not been part of a carefully laid plot to embarrass the government into coming up with more cash. As Richard Crossman surmised, he was more likely to have been led into indiscretion, as he so often was into rudeness, by a natural tendency towards exhibitionism. It seems, in fact, that Philip himself initially regarded it as a gaffe because there were futile endeavours to have the NBC tape cut. But it was obvious that too many journalists had heard what he said. It was equally obvious that he would be accused (not for the first time) of unconstitutional interference in politics. For once the Labour cabinet was almost unanimous. Even the sebaceous Harold Wilson was moved to indignation: 'Most rich men feel that part of the job of a rich man is spending a good part of his wealth for charitable and public purposes. It takes royalty to assume that all their private income is to be kept to themselves and accumulated and that they are not obliged to spend any of it on seeing themselves through their public life.' Others went further. Crossman suggested referring the royal pay claim to the Prices and Incomes Board, but this was laughed out of court. Barbara Castle thought Philip's behaviour 'absolutely outrageous'. 'Why, after all, should the Civil List be increased to enable Philip to play polo, when his wife was one of the richest women in the world, and who enjoyed tax concessions that other people were denied?' At least there ought to be a Select Committee to 'look into the private fortune of the Queen'. Only Jim Callaghan demurred: 'I am a loyalist. I wouldn't want to see the royal family hurt and I think Philip is a very fine fellow.' Still, the case for having a Select Committee was overwhelming. Wilson skilfully outmanoeuvred the Tories in the House of Commons by arguing that it was in the Queen's own interest. There should be some proper assessment of royal financial needs so that the monarchy would not be exposed to controversy and criticism.

The Select Committee was set up and duly reported at the end of 1971. Its recommendation that the Civil List should be raised from £475,000 to £980,000 was implemented by Edward Heath's government the following year – within a decade it had risen to £4.2 million. This was a significant victory for the royal family, as the whole business of submitting their finances to the scrutiny of MPs had proved traumatic. Previously all had been shrouded in mystery. Even someone as well informed as Kingsley Martin could presume that the Queen's investments were 'taxed like other people's'. Whether by accident or design, the Palace had fostered a number of illusions. Perhaps this was just due to the obsessive secrecy which pervades the British Establishment – for years no one would reveal how many people there were in the royal household. Probably there was also some deliberate obfuscation. Until 1967 the Palace underestimated the revenue from the Duchy of Cornwall and claimed that it was subject to tax. In Andrew Duncan's trenchant words, the cost of the monarchy 'provides a classic example of how an old-fashioned court can entwine itself in excruciating double-think, side-track legitimate enquiry, and become involved in complicated arrangements that in any other sphere would charitably be called hanky-panky'. The Select Committee did at least tweak back the royal curtain, though its members were, for the most part, too submissive to demand a full and proper accounting. As the *Financial Times* said, the committee 'has not made any serious attempt to find out all the relevant facts about Her Majesty's private income'.

There was the rub. It was clear from the figures that the Civil List, which had not been raised since 1952 and covered the Crown's expenses as head of state, was now inadequate to maintain her in the standard to which she had become accustomed. In other words, she was faced with the prospect of having to economize on servants, by far the greatest expense. However, the Select Committee did not discover how much money the Queen was receiving in the way of hidden subsidy through not paying income tax, surtax, capital gains tax or capital transfer tax on her vast private fortune. Speculation about the size of the fortune grew so extravagant that the Lord Chamberlain, Lord Cobbold, was authorized to tell the committee:

> Her Majesty has been much concerned by the astronomical figures which have been bandied about in some quarters suggesting that the value of these funds may now run into fifty to a hundred million pounds or more. She feels that these ideas can only arise from confusion about the status of the Royal Collections, which are in no sense at her private disposal. She wishes me to assure the Committee that these suggestions are wildly exaggerated.

So the Crown Jewels, pictures, palaces, even George V's prized stamp collection, belonged to the nation.

Still, this left a treasure trove of huge but unspecified proportions in royal hands. It was known to include the private estates of Sandringham and Balmoral as well as the Duchy of Lancaster, which consisted of over 52,000 acres and yielded an income of some quarter of a million pounds. In addition there were enormous amounts of jewellery, antiques, furniture, shares and cash, all deemed private though acquired by virtue of the monarch's public position. And this is not to mention the Prince of Wales's untaxed income of about £100,000 from the Duchy of Cornwall, which owns large tracts of Kennington (including the Oval) as well as thousands of acres in the west country. Incidentally, these two duchies, Lancaster and Cornwall, have only a tenuous claim to be considered private, based on a curious judgement by the government's law officers in 1913 which suggested that the less said about 'these awkward and delicate matters' the better. The trouble was that there was no clear distinction between the monarch's public and private income or expenditure. Thus some public funds were spent on the 'upkeep and improvement' of the Queen's private estates at Sandringham and Balmoral. Similarly, she had been topping up the Civil List from her own resources. By failing to sort all this out, and by allowing itself to remain in blissful ignorance of the totality of royal finances, the Select Committee, and parliament after it, perpetuated and endorsed a muddle.

Nevertheless there was much self-congratulation about the British genius for pragmatism, for illogical compromises which mysteriously worked. Many thought it was anyway lèse-majesté to inquire too closely into the Crown's portfolio, be it never so large. Royal riches were fine, provided they were not flaunted. If the sovereign were taxed she might come to resemble the undignified 'bicycling' monarchs of Scandinavia, or the Dutch royal family (actually immensely opulent), which in 1972 relinquished many of its financial privileges. However, a surprisingly large number of people reckoned that the Queen should live a more ordinary life. A *Daily Mirror* poll revealed that eight readers opposed the royal 'pay rise' for every one who supported it. A typical statement ran: 'If we cannot afford free milk for our kiddies, we can't afford any increase for a very wealthy family.' Several other journals considered that it was quite wrong to give lavish public subventions to royalty without a full disclosure of their private assets – a means test. The *Guardian* argued that 'A constitutional monarchy needs to be democratic in form as well as in good intent.' The *Observer* supported Douglas Houghton's proposal to turn 'the working aspects of the monarchy into a public department open to continuous parliamentary scrutiny'. Richard Crossman caused offence by writing an article in the *New Statesman* entitled 'Royal Tax Avoiders'. Willie Hamilton provoked outrage by describing Princess Margaret as 'this expensive kept woman'.

The deferential majority on the Select Committee reckoned to avoid such a furore in future by establishing a system of automatic increases which could be paid without any embarrassing parliamentary discussion. However, they did not anticipate an inflation rate which robbed the pound of forty-five per cent of its value in the three years after 1972. Thus in 1975 Harold Wilson was once again faced by the prospect of having to increase the royal allowance. It was an awkward task, because he was simultaneously appealing to everyone else for voluntary wage restraint at a time when standards of living seemed about to decline. The Labour prime minister appeared to be propounding one law for the rich and another for the poor. He thus provoked a further 'national debating orgy', as the *Guardian* called it:

> between the monarchists, the not-so-monarchists, and the republicans: all the loyal retainers – the gold sticks, the comptrollers, the constables, the ushers, even the bargemaster, the swan upper, and others medieval in style, if not in job description – are trundled across the stage for the derision of the toiling masses. This frequent performance has become a symbolic re-enactment of the French Revolution, with Mr Hamilton as chief tricoteur.

Parliament, supposedly the forum of free speech, did its best to stifle Willie Hamilton; many of his questions, which have to be submitted to the Table Office, were judged to be not 'in order' because they involved royalty in politics. But in 1975 disquiet about the Civil List claim was so general that the government could not avoid a short debate. In it Michael Stewart declared that the 'example of a Head of State who is immune from that part of the law that requires us to pay tax is unfortunate'. It would be less 'slovenly and undignified', and would save the Crown from much criticism, if a proper distinction were made between the Queen's public and private resources, and full information be provided about both. She should then be granted an adequate Civil List to cover official costs and she should pay tax on her private income like anyone else. After all, the sovereign's personal fortune, as the *Guardian* said, 'had been acquired only in the process of governing' and had been augmented because, by virtue of his office, the sovereign could hand it on free of estate duty. Despite these arguments the Civil List was substantially increased, doubtless assisted by what Barbara Castle called 'a bit of royal softening up' of Labour politicians among the flesh-pots of Buckingham Palace. Even so, ninety MPs voted against it.

More than any other royal issue, the financial one continues to rankle in the public mind. There was much indignation in 1976 when the Companies Act was amended to exempt the royal family from the clause requiring owners of over five per cent of the stock of public companies to disclose their holdings. A growing body of royalist, as well as a hard core of republican, opinion regards the royal exemption from tax as an indefensible anomaly, if not a public scandal. For it means that the monarchy is unaccountable in more senses than one. Its total cost today is in the region of £25 million per annum. This includes everything from the royal yacht *Britannia* to the upkeep of palaces like Holyrood House, in which the Queen spends an average of ten days a year. But this figure does not mean much, partly because it is impossible to disentangle the monarchy's private from its public finances and partly because it does not include the loss to the Treasury of the taxes which should, in reason and justice, be levied on the Queen. The points made by G. O. Trevelyan in relation to Queen Victoria remain strikingly apposite. The present Queen apparently likes to joke – apprehensively or complacently? – that when the republican tocsin sounds, 'We'll go quietly.' No doubt they will – like the Shah of Persia, or President Marcos, or 'Baby Doc' Duvalier, who cried all the way to their numbered Swiss bank accounts. Meanwhile it is difficult to see how a monarch whose throne rests on an ever-growing pile of private wealth can identify with her lowly subjects, let alone be regarded as a symbol of national unity.

Perhaps sensing that she was in danger of becoming too remote from the masses, perhaps responding to the more relaxed mood of the 1960s, Queen Elizabeth and her advisers made continuing endeavours to bridge the gap between Crown and people. Their best-known effort was the television film *Royal Family* (1966). Irreverently nicknamed 'Corgi and Beth', it cleverly revealed the fact that the Queen was a creature of flesh and blood – so much so that some wondered whether too much light had been let in on her magic. In 1970 the Queen began to go on 'walkabouts', meeting just folks instead of the usual dignitaries. Here, certainly, was a sign of the 'democratic monarchy' which Queen Victoria had said that she never would tolerate. But other attempts to popularize and modernize the monarchy were less fruitful. Indeed, the whole conception of modernizing the monarchy is something of a contradiction in terms, for it is the embodiment of tradition, however spurious. As Philip Howard points out, the Queen's Awards to Industry, which were instituted in 1966, scarcely ring with the language of the white-hot technological revolution:

> Greeting! We being cognizant of the industrial efficiency of the said body as manifested in the furtherance and increase of Export Trade and being desirous of showing Our Royal Favour do hereby confer upon it the Queen's Award to Industry.

A notable attempt to streamline an anachronism occurred in 1969 when the Prince of Wales's Investiture took place at Caernarvon Castle. The pageantry was as spurious as it had been when Lloyd George first conceived of the project – in some ways more so, for Lord Snowdon concocted a green uniform for himself which reminded some people of Buttons and others of Robin Hood. The Poet Laureate thought the Investiture 'idiotic' but duly versified for his supper. Even Prince Philip expressed doubts about the extent to which 'this sort of virtually medieval revival was relevant'. But the canopy over the Prince's dais was made transparent so that the entire ceremony could be a television spectacular. Even so, almost half the population of Wales (who have recognized royal propaganda for what it is since the first English prince was foisted on them) thought the Investiture a waste of public money. Feeling perennially neglected by Westminster, they reckoned it might have been better spent on improving their lot.

Yet, paradoxically, attempts to bring the monarchy up to date tend to undermine its appeal. In some respects the institution, increasingly isolated in the world, increasingly lonely on its social and financial pinnacle at home, has a better chance of survival as a fairy-tale entity. From their own point of view royalists would be wise to harp less on the Queen's incomparable political experience, for her activities at the centre of affairs are unaccountable and thus bound to be suspect. She exercises power, or at any rate influence, without responsibility. The royal family would be better advised to endure the charges that they are old-fashioned and irrelevant, and carry on performing with gracious condescension the gorgeous ceremonial which the British have learnt to mount with such rare attention to detail. As the heroine of a saga set in Never-Never Land, the Queen is infinitely glamorous. Even critics of the monarchy can only make mild mock of pageantry. Richard Crossman, for example, condemned the State Opening of Parliament in 1967 for not being splendid *enough*. It was 'like *The Prisoner of Zenda* but not nearly as smart or well done as it would be at Hollywood. It's more what a real Ruritania would look like – far more comic, more untidy, more homely, less grand.' Barbara Castle found state banquets 'pure Ruritania' too, but all the same she was impressed: 'gold plate, knee-breeched gentlemen advancing in an organized phalanx to serve the courses, roses everywhere, minstrels in the gallery, and the dining-room dominated by a huge canopied throne'. For its own sake, as Bagehot intimated, royalty cannot bear too much reality.

The trouble is that reality will keep breaking in. Hedged about more securely by protocol than the Sleeping Beauty by thorns, the Queen is largely immune. But members of her family and 'royal hangers-on' are less well protected. Prince Philip, for example, has frequent painful encounters with life outside the idyll. He is notorious for outbursts of rudeness, attacks on the press, dogmatic pronouncements and philistine attitudes (he once referred to a Henry Moore sculpture as 'a monkey's gallstone'). And this is to say nothing of his distressing absences from home, which have fed rumours about what Andrew Duncan delicately calls 'the women who play doormat to his vanity'. For all his hail-fellow-well-met heartiness, Prince Philip manages to be particularly offensive to members of the Commonwealth. In Canada he crossly declared: 'We don't come here for our health. We can think of better ways of enjoying ourselves.' In New Zealand *Truth* dubbed him the 'Prince of Arrogance'. An Australian journalist was moved to describe him as a 'fatuous ninny' with 'the brains of a polo pony'.

Actually, in some ways Philip is rather well-meaning. In his patronizing way he manifestly does care about youth, conservation and technology. Of course, he is forthright to the point of tactlessness, but probably this is just because he is frustrated by the fact that he has no real job to do. Similarly, he asserts himself because he feels unmanned by having to play second fiddle to a woman. Still, the fact that Philip is condemned (without hope of a reprieve) to be a kind of royal Denis Thatcher may explain, but it cannot excuse, his hectoring behaviour. When Dr Allende attended a state banquet in Chile wearing a lounge suit, Philip seemed to take it as a personal affront. 'Why are you dressed like that?' 'Because my party is poor and they advised me not to hire evening dress.' 'If they had told you to wear a bathing costume, I suppose you'd come dressed in one?' 'Oh, no, sir,' replied Allende. 'Our party is a serious one.' Allende later demonstrated its seriousness at the sacrifice of his own life. The British Labour Party was less serious: Jim Callaghan had little difficulty in persuading Anthony Crosland, who was initially reluctant to wear formal dress, that in the royal presence it was more important to be chic than radical. Some trade unionists were less amenable. When Philip announced that he was 'sick and tired of making excuses for Britain' abroad, Clive Jenkins said that the Prince was the best argument for republicanism since George III.

By the same token, Princess Margaret is its best argument since Queen Caroline of Brunswick. The rumours of drunken squabbles and compulsive infidelities might have been ignored. But the squalid post-marital escapades, notably her liaison with an aspirant pop singer and well-born gardener called Roddy Llewellyn, caused an open scandal. What with her 'alcoholic hepatitis' and her 'nervous breakdown', her extravagant indiscretions and her unedifying associates, the Princess must have caused her sister the most acute embarrassment. (She must also have caused the *Observer* an occasional twinge – in a marvellously oleaginous profile it once praised the Princess for 'fastidiousness in the choice of her friends'.) In fact, Margaret did for royalty what John McEnroe did for tennis. She might have brought her caste into less disrepute had she abandoned it and retired into private life. But the glamour, the adulation, and the sinecure, were clearly still too much for her to sacrifice. Consequently she gave critics a big stick with which to beat the monarchy. There could have been few who did not agree with the Scottish MP Dennis Canavan, when he denounced her jaunt to Mustique in 1978: 'Here she is, going away with her boyfriend to a paradise island while we are being asked to tighten our belts. The princess should be paying her own way in life – the taxpayer shouldn't be subsidizing her luxury trips abroad.' But in 1979 her Civil List allowance was raised to £82,000. She commented gratefully: 'The increase doesn't pay for the stamps.'

Princess Margaret is not the only controversial divorcée in the royal family. The attractive Princess Michael of Kent has an unenviable reputation, not least for disingenuousness about her origins. Her recent professions of ignorance about her father's career as an officer in Hitler's SS caused some surprise. Nor have the Kents' commercial ventures won them universal acclaim. Princess Michael, for example, reputedly earns £25,000 a year as 'non-executive director' of a commercial art gallery, and she was obliged to admit that the talk about her having a degree in the history of art from the University of Vienna was untrue. Others close to the Queen have introduced similar elements of actuality into dreamland. In 1976 Princess Alexandra's husband Angus Ogilvie was criticized by a Department of Trade report for his conduct as a director of Lonrho, itself branded by Edward Heath as 'the unpleasant and unacceptable face of capitalism'. Ogilvie was described as a weak man who, partly because of his financial relationship with Lonrho's chief executive 'Tiny' Rowland, had been negligent in his duties. In 1982 Prince Andrew, known in his premarital persona as 'Randy Andy' or 'One-Night-Standrew', was discovered going on holiday to the West Indies with an actress – named, improbably but suggestively, Koo Stark – who had appeared in 'soft' pornographic films. This adventure was scarcely the sex crime of the century (though it does seem a little incongruous to have its protagonist prating, as he recently did, about the 'moral pollution' afflicting Britain). But the popular press naturally made a meal out of it and the Queen undoubtedly felt that the royal image was further tarnished. Few of her relations seemed to fit in with Rebecca West's account of the royal family – 'a presentation of ourselves behaving well'.

Nevertheless, the royal future is bright. The abdication could do little to shake the fundamental loyalty which the British feel for their monarchy, and nothing since has made much impression on it. Indeed, royalism is akin to religious faith. It relies on the evidence of things not seen. People willingly suspend disbelief in the presence of their idol – not for nothing does the Queen say: 'I have to be seen to be believed.' The monarchy, in popular estimation, is a kind of self-fulfilling prophecy. Whatever is about it, is right.

Thus, for example, in a poll conducted by BBC *Breakfast Television* 79 per cent of those questioned thought that Miss Sarah Ferguson was the right woman to wed Prince Andrew (now disentangled from Miss Stark). They took this view despite the fact that his fiancée had an embarrassing Argentinian stepfather and a number of previous amours to her credit. All of a sudden, the case that royal brides should be pure as the driven snow, which was so pruriently canvassed *vis-à-vis* Diana Spencer, is turned on its head. In Prince Charles's case the traditional double standard operated with full force. His juvenile sexual adventures were indulged as 'sowing wild oats' or 'playing the field'. But no such latitude could be granted to his future wife – hence, apparently, the rejection of some earlier girlfriends and the virtual cradle-snatching of Diana Spencer. Perhaps there is less flexibility where the Crown itself is concerned. In matters like male primogeniture and the rule that younger sons come before their elder sisters in the line of succession, the monarchy flouts current ideas of sexual equality. But, possibly because no suitable virgin could be found for Prince Andrew, arguments are found to accommodate him. Now, according to the *Observer*, 'The idea that a royal bride must be a virgin and Caesar's wife rolled into one comes from earlier centuries.' It is good for a royal 'playboy' like Andrew to marry 'a woman of experience'.

No such logic-chopping is needed to justify the Queen, or indeed her two oldest children. Prince Charles is over his awkwardly protracted youth, with its fits of goonishness and its displays of naïveté (at one time he appeared to think that all children had nannies). Princess Anne now seems to share his good intentions. Having overcome much of the sulky selfishness which marred her early years (in 1970 a Washington paper suggested that she be limited to 'opening rhododendron shows in Kent' if she could not contain her irritation with the press and her boredom with foreigners), Anne is now making her way back into public esteem through her excellent work with the Save the Children Fund. Recent polls reflect the royalist enthusiasm generated by the Queen's sixtieth birthday celebrations. True, they indicate that a third of the population believes the royal family to be out of touch with modern-day Britain and that over half want its younger members to do proper jobs. But a staggering 89 per cent think that the monarchy should continue and only 7 per cent think it should be abolished. This compares with a figure of 16.4 per cent which supported a republic in 1977. During the earlier 1970s, when the royal finances were causing such a fuss, some polls showed that up to 53 per cent of the population favoured dispensing with the monarchy. Thus today, when the decline of Britain has never been more palpable, the cult of monarchy has never been stronger. The voice of reason may be powerless against the faith of multitudes. But now is certainly the time to strike a blow against the tyranny of conventional opinion.

Ten

Chinless Wonderland

'Is there any man now alive who would kiss the hem of that trumpery?' asked Thackeray, referring to King George IV's coronation robes, which were on display at Madame Tussaud's. Were the novelist to rise from the dead, well over a century after writing these words, he would be surprised to see that modern visitors, approaching the tableau of royal waxworks at Madame Tussaud's, lower their voices and adopt a respectful demeanour. Paying obeisance to stuffed dummies is evidently a conditioned national response. When the regal waxworks live and breathe, as primped and coiffed in the flesh as they are as models, public worship becomes an ecstasy – people thrust out their hands like lepers hoping for Christ's benison. Certainly Britain has the unenviable reputation of being the most socially deferential and differentiated of all the industrial democracies. Whatever Tennyson might say, the British seem to value kind hearts less than coronets, simple faith less than Norman blood. Observing the phenomenon, an American journalist exclaimed: 'In the age of the hydrogen bomb, the ghost of William the Conqueror strides the land.'

Of course, the roots of social deference go very deep, right back to the 'feudal subordination' of which Dr Johnson was such a doughty champion. By the nineteenth century snobbery and class division seemed to be engrained in the national character. Richard Cobden wrote: 'The insatiable love of caste that in England, as in Hindustan, devours all hearts, is confined to no walks of society, but pervades every degree from the highest to the lowest.' At the top of the scale it was a matter of loving lords. Harry Wilkins, a Merton don, was typical in aspiring to be a nobleman's chaplain as the next best thing to being a nobleman

himself: 'My dear fellow, think what it would be to be a Marquis
– a *Marquis*! my dear fellow.' But, as Bulwer Lytton indicated,
there was a degree of social mobility, a chance of removing in-
equalities, which exacerbated social snobbery at the bottom end
of the scale:

> With us the fusion of all classes, each with the other, is so general,
> that the aristocratic contagion extends from the highest towards
> the verge of the lowest. The tradesmen in every country town have
> a fashion of their own, and the wife of a mercer will stigmatize the
> lady of a grocer as 'ungenteel'. When Mr Cobbett, so felicitous in
> nicknames and so liberal in opinions, wished to assail Mr Sadler, he
> found no epithet so suitable as the disdainful appellation of '*linen-
> draper*'!

Plus ça change. The public-school satirists of *Private Eye* thought
it the acme of humour to nickname Edward Heath 'the Grocer'.

During the Victorian age it was perhaps reasonable to regard
deference as a useful social cement. Respect for rank was natural
and almost universal. Snobbery was a breakwater against revolution. With their wealth, land and education, their distin-
guishing clothes and physique (due to better diet), noblemen
really did seem to belong to a higher order of beings, ordained to
rule. They had that numinous quality known as breeding. Taine
quoted a self-confessed 'man of the middle class' in the 1860s to
the effect that aristocrats' 'titles and pedigrees give them a quality
of dash and style, and troops will more readily follow officers
who have that'. So would the electorate. Bagehot explained:

> England is the type of deferential countries, in which the numerous
> unwise part wishes to be ruled by the less numerous wiser part.
> The numerical majority . . . is ready, is eager to delegate its power
> of choosing its ruler to a certain select minority. It abdicates in
> favour of its *élite*, and consents to obey whoever that élite may
> confide in.

Well might Thackeray complain, in his *Book of Snobs*: 'What
peerage worship there is all through this free country.' Well
might Henry James declare, as he did in 1878: 'The essentially
hierarchical plan of English society is the great and ever-present
fact to the mind of a stranger; there is hardly a detail of life that
does not in some degree betray it.' But there were sound reasons

to defer to paternalists in what was still in many respects a patriarchal society.

After the 1860s, though, there was a steady erosion of aristocratic power and pelf. The franchise was extended. Land (less profitable at the end of the golden age of English agriculture) was more comprehensively taxed. New wealth challenged patrician predominance. Egalitarians undermined the traditional notion that aristocrats were a class of gentlemanly leaders, devoted to public service, living a wholesome life close to the land, embodying culture and honour. They presented them instead as a privileged vested interest. There were, indeed, counter-attacks, one of the more curious being A. M. Ludovici's *Defence of Aristocracy* (1915), which advocated patrician rule because the poor were so ugly. Still, the Parliament Act of 1911, which curtailed the powers of the House of Lords, symbolized the decline of the old order. Even more significant were the huge sales of land, mainly to tenant farmers, which occurred after the First World War, largely as a result of taxation. Perhaps as much as a quarter of Britain changed hands in two or three years. As the historian F. M. L. Thompson wrote: 'A transfer on this scale in such a short space of time had probably not been equalled since the Norman Conquest.' Writing in 1930, Winston Churchill, himself the scion of a ducal house, said that the passing of the territorial aristocracy which had occurred during his lifetime amounted to a silent revolution.

Yet the revolution was never completed. The aristocracy was constantly reinvigorated by transfusions of new blood and, more important, new money. Between 1916 and 1945, 280 new peers were created, many of them politicians, usually from wealthy, upper-class, public-school-going backgrounds, but some 66 of them successful businessmen. Today some three-quarters of the millionaires who die each year are noble by birth. Of course, there are market gardener, dentist and policeman peers, but the landed magnates still own a third of Britain. Only a bold man would now say, as Chips Channon did as late as 1939: 'It is the aristocracy which still runs this country although nobody seems to realize it.' However, the House of Lords does still trundle on and its ancient, somnolent members are now actually to be heard hoping that the televising of their proceedings might give them a new lease of life. It is not impossible, *pace* Bagehot: 'A severe though not unfriendly critic of our institutions said that "The *cure* for admiring the House of Lords was to go and look at it."' Nor does Labour seem unduly exercised by the ten-to-one Conservative majority in the Lords – much of it made up of backwoodsmen like the late Lord Mansfield, who wanted to bring back the stocks, the pillory and the treadmill, or Lord Radnor, who refuses to open his castle to the public on the grounds that 'you can even smell the people who come round'. Everyone agrees that heredity is an unsound basis on which to qualify for a seat in parliament, that a rational democracy demands the replacement of a disguised oligarchy by a representative legislature, and that a flagrant defiance of meritocratic principles at the centre of affairs is damaging to the state. But there seems to be a strange reluctance to reform the House of Lords.

Indeed, the British seem positively to enjoy the anachronism, just as they revel in the prominent social role played by the aristocracy. They have adopted *en masse* what Mark Pattison called 'the flunkey's estimate' – they measure worth by social status. Ramsay MacDonald was not the last politician to fawn over duchesses. The *Tatler*, that almanac of name-dropping and fop-fetishism, flourishes. Nancy Mitford's language game was all the rage with those who had pretensions to speaking in a U, as opposed to a non-U, fashion. There is a whole field of punditry devoted to the shape of peers' coronets, the marks of degree on their robes, the ceremonial gyrations they perform. Forests are laid low so that articles and books can appear explaining the finer points of etiquette – a life peer's son precedes a baronet's lady, an English duke takes precedence over the Aga Khan, even though he is a direct descendant of God. The late Sir Ian Moncreiffe of that Ilk ('a quaint name we have used since the Middle Ages because it gives other people such fun') found a ready audience for his preposterous opinions. (He, like Lord Mountbatten, was obsessed by genealogy – the snob's astrology.) The well-known story of the policeman who refused to rescue Bertrand Russell from a fracas when told that he was a famous philosopher but leapt into action on learning that he was the son of a peer, graphically illustrates the prestige which continues to be attached in Britain to blue blood. Snobbery is *par excellence* the British disease.

That the hereditary peerage has survived, despite all the odds, and still exerts an influence in the country out of all proportion to its numbers, is due in no small part to the monarchy. Traditionally lords, even more than bishops, were lions under the throne. They deferred to the monarchy so that their inferiors would defer to them. Sometimes, indeed, they grovelled, as Bagehot's famous description of Lord Chatham recalls: 'the most dictatorial and imperious English statesman' bowed so low before George III that you could see the tip of his hooked nose between his legs. Edmund Burke said of Chatham that the 'least peep into the king's closet intoxicates him and will to the end of his life'. Royalty and aristocracy lived in fruitful symbiosis. Although Queen Victoria liked to inveigh against the luxury and self-indulgence of the higher classes, she was quite clear that aristocrats were to be preferred and promoted above abler but humbler persons. Her descendants echoed her view, George V, for example, disparaging Asquith for not being quite a gentleman. Gentlemanliness was the most important criterion by which to judge suitable cases for advancement, for only thus could the social fabric be preserved. After all, princes as well as peers owed their position to heredity.

So when the aristocracy caught a cold the monarchy began to sneeze. It was not, of course, that the Crown, immune from personal taxation, was suffering from the financial ills which were afflicting so many peers. It was simply that as the magnates began to draw in their horns, as the great country houses were shut, or let, or sold, or vested in the National Trust, as the city palaces were knocked down to make way for blocks of flats, or transformed into museums or whatever, the lonely eminence of the sovereign became more exposed. The social hierarchy of which the monarch is the apex and the cornerstone was being undermined, and the throne was thus notably less well buttressed.

Naturally the royal family has done its best to preserve that hierarchy. It encourages members of the aristocracy to perpetuate the old ways. King George V delayed the shutting of Elveden, the stately home of the second Earl of Iveagh, by proposing himself for periodic visits. Despite the deep conservatism with which the present Queen has been infected by her mother, she welcomed the introduction of life peerages in 1958 because they would broaden the base of the upper house and help to justify its existence. Royalty fosters aristocracy most effectively by investing it with some of its own magic. The Queen and her family surround themselves with lords and ladies on official occasions, and associate with them almost exclusively in private. Best of all, royalties condescend to marry into families whose pedigrees are sufficiently distinguished. A list of young ladies thought suitable to consort with Prince Charles (who, admittedly, did some sexual slumming as well, and whose mother dearly wanted him to marry into the blood royal) reads like an extract from Burke's *Peerage*. It includes the daughters of the Dukes of Westminster, Northumberland, Grafton, Rutland, Wellington, the Marquis of Lothian, the Earls of Westmorland and Spencer (she carried off the prize), Lord Rupert Nevill, Lord Astor, Lord Balniel . . . and so on. After Prince Andrew announced his engagement to Miss Sarah Ferguson *The Times* was gratified to discover that her birth and upbringing placed her 'well within those charmed concentric circles which surround the royal family and which smell of saddle soap and old money'.

When, under the auspices of her royal lover, Mrs Simpson stormed the topmost pinnacles of Society, she described herself delightedly as 'Wallis in Wonderland'. It was a chinless wonderland. There intellectual endeavour was measured by jigsaw puzzles completed and lucky females grew 'wild with exaltation' because they had 'danced with the man who's danced with the girl who's danced with the Prince of Wales'. That wonderland survives, its glamour hardly faded, its attitudes only a little more defensive, its addiction to 'fun' unchanged. Monty Python's 'Upper-Class Twits of the Year' are barely distinguishable from members of P. G. Wodehouse's Drones Club (though the latter are much more amusing and endearing). Not for nothing did the Australian Richard Neville, when he came to England, feel 'transported back in time to a wonderland of wigs and starched collars, of liveried courtiers and secret passage-ways . . . deposited amidst an eternal, antique stage play'.

But is not all this carping just social sour grapes? Is it not an incautious flouting of Lady Bracknell's maxim never to criticize Society because only people who cannot get into it do that? What is wrong with the traditional respect for royalty and rank? Does it not actually augment the public stock of harmless pleasure? Are not critics of the present order, indeed, open to the charge that, like all puritans, they really object to social pleasures not social pains, that they protest not about the harm which the royal-aristocratic nexus allegedly does but about the evident enjoyment its members get and give? In any case, is it not futile to talk about abolishing class distinctions? Are they not endemic in all societies? Do not the sea-green incorruptibles who try to turn egalitarian principles into practice merely replace one set of distinctions with another, ending up like the pigs in *Animal Farm*? How do republicans answer these fundamental questions?

What must surely be apparent at once is that the whole royal racket and the system of social snobbery which it sustains are deeply corrupting both to those inside and to those outside the pale of Society. Nothing is more striking in the history of the monarchy than the flattery accorded to kings and queens by their attendant lords and ladies, who are themselves given their measure of obsequiousness by beings further removed from the hallowed purlieus of the court. 'He who meanly admires mean things is a Snob,' wrote Thackeray. And what is meaner than to invest the dazzling gewgaws of royalty and the frippery trinkets of aristocracy with a moral worth which they cannot bear? Sycophancy debases both the giver and the receiver. Moreover it is both contagious and vicarious: the associates of kings bask in their reflected glory. Witness the ingratiating letters which so many in prominent social and political positions sent to Wallis Simpson during 1936 – after the abdication most of them pretended scarcely to have known her. Lady Colefax's adulation was typical. She told the King's inamorata that she 'had grown every month more full of delighted admiration for not only your immense wisdom & lovely common (so miscalled!) sense, but also for your unfailing touch of being exactly right in all judgements & in all kinds of moments in life at every angle'. Evidently woman, as much as man, is a toad-eating animal. Yet, as Hazlitt argued with such devastating cogency, the worship of royalty is based on a transparent fiction. Unlike the ancients, the moderns

> do not think kings gods, but they make believe that they do so, to degrade their fellows to the rank of brutes. . . . This mock-doctrine, this little Hunchback, which our resurrection-men, the Humane Society of Divine Right, have foisted on the altar of Liberty, is not only a phantom of the imagination, but a contradiction in terms; it

is a prejudice, but an exploded prejudice; it is an imposture, that imposes on nobody; it is powerful only in impotence, safe in absurdity, courted from fear and hatred, a dead prejudice linked to the living mind; the sink of honour, the grave of liberty, a palsy in the heart of the nation.

In short, royalty is the opium of the people. It is a spurious religion designed to keep the masses happily singing hosannas to an apparition of majesty which insults their lowly lot.

That royalty today reduces those that come into its orbit to a state of humiliating subjection is attested to by none other than that *arbiter elegantiarum* among journalists, Peregrine Worsthorne. He recalls a visit which Queen Elizabeth paid to the offices of the *Daily Telegraph* and the joyous relief among the staff after everything had passed off smoothly. 'Absurd as it may seem, one was reminded of those stories of how officers and men in the First World War were brought into communion for the first time by the ordeal of battle.' Her Majesty had lowered everyone, from editor to office-boy, 'to the same condition of awed servility'. Because of its capacity to humble the proud and to cut the mightiest down to size, Worsthorne then asserts, the monarchy is an egalitarian institution. Such an audacious paradox fatally discredits itself, providing as it does clear evidence that the reactionary cupboard is bare of more plausible arguments. If the Queen enjoys such a *de haut en bas* relationship with her subjects, she cannot, by definition, be considered egalitarian. She may, indeed, regard everyone without royal blood as being beyond the pale, but she would scarcely surround herself with a phalanx of titled folk if she did not think such distinctions mattered. Egalitarianism as defined by Worsthorne – the reduction of everyone to 'the same condition of awed servility' – hardly comports with the human dignity normally associated with the concept. No doubt it is salutary, as Worsthorne further argues, for government ministers to be prevented from becoming too puffed up by their own importance. But an infallible mechanism for deflating them already exists – the ballot box. For them to be humbled by an insolent display of regal hauteur is a slur on democracy.

The cringing British reverence for royalty and rank is a symptom and, to some extent, a cause of a deeper malaise than mere social snobbery. For the past hundred years – a period roughly coterminous with the existence of the ornamental modern monarchy – Britain has been, relative to its economic competitors, in decline. In 1900 Britain dominated international trade, exporting one third of the world's manufactured goods. During the lifetime of the Queen Mother the figure has fallen to below eight per cent and Britain now imports more manufactured goods than she exports. Britain was once the first industrial nation; now she is the nineteenth.

Trying to explain what has caused Britain's economic stagnation is one of the few thriving industries the country has left. Amid the welter of fact and argument, academics engaged in this study have found it difficult to distinguish cause from effect. They have become embroiled in ideological debate about how far trade union power, or 'stop-go' policies, or nationalization, or monetarism, are responsible for the British sickness. They have failed to pinpoint any one of the multitudinous factors as being fundamental. However, what does emerge from their debate with striking clarity is that Britain's problems are so complex and deep-seated that they are not susceptible merely to economic explanations. Social, cultural and psychological factors are, as Arthur Koestler said, 'at the root of the economic evils'. This was certainly the conclusion of the authoritative Hudson Institute Report on Britain (1974) which declared that in the final analysis the country's declining fortunes were the result of 'aspects of British culture and an inheritance of particular British historical experience'. More specifically, as William Pfaff of the Hudson Institute declared, 'What's wrong in Britain is more what's wrong at the top than what's wrong at the bottom. They haven't been served very well by their élite.'

The *clou* of that élite is, of course, the monarchy. Far from being a unifying symbol as is so often claimed, it emphasizes the divisions which disfigure the social topography of Britain. The royal family is the embodiment of class privilege. It wallows in unearned income. It looks and speaks like the Hooray Henrys with whom it associates. It fosters and embodies the 'Them and Us' mentality which makes British enterprises so much less competitive than those of, say, Japan (where managers and workers wear the same overalls and eat at the same tables). Wherever the Queen goes, enormous expense and effort are devoted to mark her elevated status, to lay down red carpets, to redecorate her accommodation, to construct special lavatories for her personal use – so much so that she can have no conception, except through the medium of television, of what her subjects' lives are like. Thus royalty confirms and validates the social rifts which run through even relatively new industries in Britain. Paul Murphy, the supervisor of an aircraft factory, records:

> The tradition in the industry is of separate canteens, even separate toilets. It still exists today where on the toilet door you can see 'Ladies' and 'Gentlemen' on the staff side, and 'Male' and 'Female' on the shopfloor. There are four canteens still today at British Aerospace, Manchester. There's a special mess for the directors, there's a mess for middle management. Below them there's another mess for supervision, and ultimately the larger canteen on the shopfloor. And yet when things go wrong the directors tell us we're all working for the same company. I can't square that circle.

The gulf fixed between white collar and blue collar is further deepened by differences in pension rights, holiday provision, the way people are paid and so on. What is more, the stratifications are echoed throughout industry. One of Britain's dwindling number of shipbuilding workers likened the hierarchy in the yards to 'the Indian caste system'.

For all Prince Philip's homilies to industry and Prince Charles's efforts to drum up trade, the royal family typifies the cult of amateurism which helps to debilitate the British economy. This is partly because it is evident that royalty lacks a productive role. For the last hundred years or so the Crown has appeared to be purely decorative. 'The royal family works very hard,' so the cliché runs. Even if this is conceded – and when, say, Princess Margaret's exiguous 'public engagements' are set against her ample income the cliché looks distinctly threadbare – the sort of work which they are seen to do is supremely irrelevant. It is all inspection, never construction. It involves taking a patronizing interest instead of making a serious contribution, flaunting wealth instead of generating income. It is, inevitably, ceremonial rather than executive. Royal exhortations to British industry urging the introduction of up-to-date methods ring particularly hollow. Earnest and well-meaning they may be; but they are about as convincing as a pep talk from Ethelred the Unready.

Buckingham Palace, with its wasteful and archaic internal organization, with its footmen matched into pairs by size and dressed on ceremonial occasions in scarlet coats with gold trimming, red velvet breeches and black leather pumps, is scarcely a model of business efficiency. Nor does royalty set a Stakhanovite example on the domestic front. According to Stephen Barry, 'the Royals do absolutely nothing for themselves. Everyone who works in the Palace has a function and the end result is cosseting the Royals. . . . We used to say that the first thing that Nanny teaches a Royal is how to ring for service.' Surrounded by the flummery of the ages, the monarchy tends to validate old-fashioned practices. Teaching by example, it helps to foster the insouciant amateurism of management and the atavistic traditionalism of workers, which have made so much British enterprise fit only for display in a museum of industrial archaeology.

Part of the trouble, at least as far as Philip and Charles are concerned, was their education. Father and son were both sent to Kurt Hahn's more brutal and philistine version of the English public school, Gordonstoun. At such academies English boys, the sons of wealthy parents, were traditionally taught to be the leaders of the future. By means of competitive games, muscular Christianity, classical studies, sexual segregation, strict discipline, elaborate ritual and physical hardship, they learnt to become the governors or defenders of the British Empire. Alternatively they equipped themselves to live a life of decorous idleness, modelled on that of the Victorian royal family. Idleness conferred gentility: as Josephine Butler's aunt wrote in 1853, 'A lady to be such, must be a mere lady, and nothing else.' Ladies and gentlemen could be active, of course, busily engaged in what Winston Churchill once called the 'frivolous and expensive pursuits of the silly world of fashion', or living a 'natural' existence on the land, hunting, shooting and fishing. But they lost caste if they worked, particularly if they went into business. Box-wallahs were the lowest form of European life in India and at home commerce was a dirty word. In any case, lacking a scientific and technical education, public schoolboys were scarcely qualified to become captains of industry.

But has not all that changed today? Fee-paying schools have to give value for money, say their current defenders, and they now concentrate on training and motivating the élite who will restore the fortunes of Great Britain Ltd. To some extent this is true, though there are few signs of an economic revival and public schools are notoriously conservative institutions. In such backwaters change occurs slowly. In British society as a whole past patterns of deference determine present attitudes. Ideas outlive reality. What will never change, unless the public schools are taxed out of existence (while a decent level of investment simultaneously makes the state system more attractive), is the social cachet they confer. This, indeed, is their *raison d'être*. When public school headmasters pontificate about character building what they mean is the fostering of élite attitudes based on class advantage. When they talk about freedom of choice they mean the freedom to purchase social privilege (a corollary of the freedom of those without shoes to go barefoot). As R. H. Tawney said, 'The hereditary curse upon English education is its organization upon lines of social class.'

The public schools project their antiquated standards into the world of work. Boys emerge from them believing that the professions make more respectable careers than trade or industry, that gentlemen are preferable to players, that the old boy network will perpetuate the inequality of opportunity which they have hitherto enjoyed, that the old school tie will serve them as it always served Captain Grimes – as a lifeline out of the soup – and that the talented amateur is superior to the trained professional. (Sometimes, of course, he is, which may explain why the British are such good inventors and such bad entrepreneurs.) At their worst, too, public schools discourage notions about the dignity of labour and idealize the feudal style of life which stands in the way of economic advancement. Adam Smith – and before him, Defoe – noted that 'merchants are commonly ambitious of becoming country gentlemen'. The further away from working for their money they got, the higher they rose in the social scale. Their modern prototype is Lord Leverhulme, three generations removed from the grocery business and the soap factory, who became one of four stewards at Royal Ascot, where it was his duty to welcome the Queen as she progressed through the bobbing ranks of her top-hatted subjects into the Royal Enclosure. Here, incidentally, better than almost anywhere else, is to be seen in operation what one social critic has called the 'informal apartheid based on social rank rather than race' which pervades British life like a bad dream.

Perhaps apartheid is too strong a term. Certainly, defenders of the present social order would argue that, far from segregating its citizens, the honours system binds them together in a common loyalty to the throne. Moreover blue blood is not like white skin: anyone (anyone with white skin) can acquire it, or something which in a generation or two is indistinguishable from it. And just as the nuances of snobbery are the stuff of many novels, so the process of climbing the social ladder gives point and pleasure to many lives. To quote an extreme instance: Karen Blixen, the author of *Out of Africa*, thought it well worth catching syphilis from her husband to become a Baroness. Similarly the distribution of honours is not a mode of discrimination so much as a social cement. All societies recognize and reward outstanding merit in some way, and if the Crown were not the fount of honour some other source would have to be invented. The fact that the Queen herself annually decorates two thousand or so of her subjects informs the whole system with glamour and quasi-mystical significance. There is some truth in all this. As even Willie Hamilton acknowledges, being presented with the most meretricious of baubles can mark the peak of a humble life's ambition.

This is a sad state of affairs, for it suggests that honour is a social quality which is conferred rather than a moral one which is intrinsic. That is, of course, a fruitful confusion from the Crown's point of view because it implies that the Queen bestows honour in the ethical sense instead of just dishing out trinkets to those named in the Birthday Honours List. (As P. N. Furbank points out in his brilliant book *Unholy Pleasure: The Idea of Social Class* [1985], a similarly fruitful confusion occurs between 'nobility', meaning virtue, and 'nobility', meaning aristocracy.) The point is that the honours system may reward accomplishment (especially in certain rather narrow spheres, such as the civil service) but its more important purpose is to reinforce the social hierarchy of which the Crown is head. Hence the ceremonial kow-towing at Buckingham Palace. Hence, too, the debris of archaic distinctions, Imperial Service Orders to Commonwealth functionaries, knighthoods to people who have never ridden a horse let alone donned a suit of shining armour, Baths and Garters to backwoodsmen who barely know the meaning of the word chivalry. Probably such glittering prizes are all the more welcome for being so *recherché*. But they scarcely seem an appropriate way of acknowledging success in a modern industrialized democracy. It is like trying to promote Britain's reputation as a centre of advanced technology by advertising the tournament at Ashby de la Zouche.

The honours system as it now exists depreciates contemporary achievement at the expense of obsolete adornment – to say nothing of the opportunities it gives for political patronage and corruption. Those who have done the state some service are doubtless entitled to their laurel crowns. Churchill liked to say that medals were 'the poor man's escutcheon' – though, while the poor man might be gratified to receive a bit of tin and ribbon, together with a limp royal handshake and a few words of commendation in (what Patrick White called) the Queen's 'high-pitched, cold china voice', he might also wonder whether his heroism was cheaply purchased. Bob Geldof, too, might reflect that it was much cheaper for the Thatcher government, which earned his criticism for dragging its feet at the United Nations over famine relief, to award him an honorary knighthood than to improve its deplorable record on aid to the Third World. The present point is, though, that the rewards of virtue ought not to be such as will exacerbate social divisions. Royal participation in the system makes this inevitable, ensuring as it does that honour is translated from moral into social terms. It has always been so, as Mrs Simpson artlessly revealed when she complained to the Duke of Windsor at the end of 1936 that the new King and Queen would not 'give us the extra chic of creating me HRH'. Those magic initials were simply the last word in snobbery.

Yet snobbery of one kind or another is part of the human condition, say advocates of the old order. People will always want to demonstrate their superiority over one another and they will always find some means of doing so. Egalitarianism is a mirage. The attempt to reach it engenders new forms of dictatorship and a new kind of standardized citizen. Perhaps. But the fear of producing a worse social order ought neither to stifle criticism of the existing one nor to paralyse efforts to improve it. What is so pernicious about the monarchy is that it legitimizes artificial excellences, based on birth and breeding, as opposed to real ones, based on worth and achievement. It makes affluent parasitism respectable, thus undermining not only what remains of the Victorian work ethic but the principle of rewarding real merit or endeavour. It enjoys a hereditary monopoly of the headship of state, which suggests what the royal family think about careers being open to talent and equality of opportunity. Above all, it sustains an obsolete social hierarchy which at best perpetuates the 'two nations' division observed by Disraeli and at worst helps to stultify the open and efficient running of the country. Royalty is the germ of the British disease.

Even if all this were so, its defenders may say, there can be no question but that royalty gives pleasure to millions and that, surely, is what its puritanical detractors cannot stand. It is true that many people, like H. G. Wells's mother, live surrogate existences through the royal family. Sleeping and waking, or in that trance-like state induced by the cathode-ray tube, the British are fixated on monarchy like a junkie on a drug – as Brian Masters has shown, for many it is what dreams are made on. The satisfactions of royal fantasy are obviously intense, though whether more so than those promoted by addictive television serials like *Dallas*, or *Eastenders*, or *Coronation Street*, is not clear. The advantage of the fictional Never-Never Land, of course, is that viewers willingly suspend disbelief during the programmes but generally switch on to reality once they switch off their sets. However, royalty is a true-life romance and it is correspondingly more hallucinogenic.

What Muggeridge called the royal soap opera fosters weird and dangerous ideas about the monarch's position and powers. A survey carried out in 1964, for example, revealed that thirty per cent of the population believed that the Queen was specially chosen by God. For years successive governments were able to avoid improving the lethally unhygienic condition of kitchens in National Health Service hospitals because they could conjure with 'Crown immunity' from prosecution. And although, at the time of writing, legislation is going through parliament to end this disgraceful state of affairs, 'Crown immunity' will remain in operation in other spheres of the NHS. For example, hospitals which breach the health and safety regulations in other ways may not be prosecuted. Similarly, when magistrates assert that they are appointed by the Crown, or policemen claim to be acting

in the Queen's name, they are investing themselves with a mysterious accretion of authority for which there is no real warrant. It
is all part of a psychological nannying process which the
monarchy encourages. The masses must be treated like children
and taught to respect their elders and betters. Everything must
be left to the Crown's agents because they know best. Citizens
must be subjects.

Like a long-running advertisement, royalty has immense
power to promote retrogressive social values. It glamorizes
unearned privilege, sustains an archaic and unfair social order,
instils deference, saps innovative thought, fosters conservatism
and encourages superstition. Ultimately, of course, royalty gives
the public a wholly misleading impression of Britain's place in
the world. The gorgeous display of pomp and circumstance
which always surrounds the monarch induces a feeling of euphoria. It massages the national self-esteem and masks Britain's
steep decline in power and wealth. Escapist fantasies are one
thing – and perhaps because it is so mindless *Dallas* seems to fill
the bill quite satisfactorily. Delusions of grandeur are something
else altogether. The delusions inspired by royalty, however much
pleasure they may give, can seriously damage the nation's
health.

On the contrary, royalists aver, the monarchy is actually of
enormous benefit to the country both at home and abroad. It
acts as a magnet to foreign tourists, who flock to Britain in search
of living history. And members of the royal family, unsullied by
politics, are uniquely popular and effective as Britain's ambas-
sadors overseas. There is probably something in this argument,
though nothing can be proved either way. It is impossible to
calculate how many tourists would come to a republican Britain,
though they might be attracted by the prospect of being shown
round the royal palaces by their quondam occupants, now ex-
propriated and superannuated. It is also impossible to say
whether such good will as Britain enjoys in the world would
diminish without royal visits abroad. Similarly, the heavy cost of
the monarchy cannot be weighed against the income it generates,
for there is no way of computing it. There is evidence that trade
does not follow the royal standard. Indeed, British exports to the
countries concerned have a nasty habit of dropping after royal
visits. But, of course, they might have dropped anyway and they

might be in an even more parlous condition without the efforts of the sales representatives from Buckingham Palace.

What can be said, though, is that the monarchy does not project a progressive image of Britain. This may well account for much of the institution's popularity with foreigners, who are fascinated to encounter breathing anachronisms and to find that the past is, indeed, another country. They may also be gratified to see the past and discover that it barely works. With its Byzantine etiquette and its Jabberwock formulae, its fairy-tale coaches and its Ruritanian pageantry, Queen Elizabeth's world has less in common with a contemporary developed country than with Camelot. Yet while the monarchy keeps its hold on the public imagination, it will be difficult to rid Britain of the feudal attitudes and social divisions which degrade her character and impede her forward march. Only by dissolving nostalgic fantasies and applying their minds to the development of realistic policies can the British people hope to equip themselves to compete successfully in the global market-place. Only by cutting the royal umbilical cord which binds the nation to the past can Britain begin to convince its customers abroad that it is fit to face the future. Needless to say, a republic, while fostering economic advance and democratic ideals, would preserve what true patriots love about their country, its culture, its traditions of freedom, tolerance and justice, its loathing of political violence, its sense of humour and of what George Orwell called 'decency', its physical beauty. But until the republic comes Britain is surely doomed to remain an offshore island of dreams and decadence, a *tableau vivant* crowded with picturesque figures dressed in quaint, old-fashioned garments, the Madame Tussaud's of the world.

Eleven

Treason of the Clerks

In June 1982 Ronald Reagan became the first American President ever to stay overnight at Windsor Castle and journalists from both sides of the Atlantic arrived in force to cover the momentous event. Needless to say, there was little to report apart from a more or less vacuous exchange of civilities. But what did emerge, and it came as a revelation both to British and American newspapermen, was the startling difference of approach which the two heads of state adopted towards their respective press corps. It was dramatized when the Queen and the President went out after breakfast for a much-heralded horseback ride in Windsor Park. Mr Reagan obviously regarded the expedition as something of a publicity stunt. He posed for pictures and fielded a few of the questions which the hundred or so waiting reporters lobbed at him. But an expression compounded of rigidity and anxiety came over Queen Elizabeth's features and she pulled away from the press, Reagan dutifully following. According to the *Daily Mail*, 'The Queen couldn't believe people shouting questions at the President. She looked furious enough to call out the Guards.' American journalists, accustomed to being given every facility, were just about as angry and incredulous at the various niggling restrictions which Buckingham Palace successfully imposed on them during the visit. A White House aide commented feelingly: 'In the United States, the press plays a much stronger role in political life than it does in Britain, where there is a much more controlled environment. Over here it's like a bureaucrat's *dream*.'

This is not to suggest that the press has everything its own way in the United States. The President does all he can to manipulate the media. He employs a public relations staff of between 150 and 500 people (depending on how their jobs are defined) whose purpose is to 'stage' (his spokesman Larry Speakes uses the word without embarrassment) the presidential news. All Reagan's engagements on his visit to Britain, for example, were carefully calculated for the effect they would have at home, particularly on the viewers of prime-time television news broadcasts. Furthermore the relationship between the press and the presidency has invariably been one of antagonism. John F. Kennedy told his special counsel, Ted Sorensen: 'Always remember that their interests and ours ultimately conflict.' However, the American tradition is that the people have the right to know what their elected leaders are doing in their name, and freedom of the press is enshrined in the constitution. Despite recognizing the permanent conflict of interest, Kennedy, more than many chief executives, understood the nature and appreciated the necessity of the First Amendment. He noted that although totalitarian governments had the freedom to move in secret, they suffered by not exposing their activities to a constant, abrasive, independent scrutiny. So, 'Even though we wish they didn't write it, and even though we disapprove, there isn't any doubt that we could not do the job at all in a free society without a very, very active press.'

Like other presidents, Kennedy did not live up to these fine sentiments. His visceral attitude was typified in a scribbled note asking whether there was 'a plan to brief and brainwash key press' immediately after the Bay of Pigs invasion. Nevertheless, the United States does more than pay lip-service to freedom of information and Americans have no truck with the argument that newspapers must somehow be controlled for their own or for the public's good. They recognize that prior restraint in almost any form, whatever the motive for imposing it, is fatal. As Thomas Jefferson said, there is no remedy for the evil of bad newspapers, for 'Our liberty depends on the freedom of the press, and that cannot be limited without being lost.'

The British have espoused an entirely contrary tradition. Stephen Leacock was not far wrong in claiming that the difference between American and British newspapers was that when the former got the news they shouted it from the housetops, whereas the latter tried to break it to their readers as gently as possible. The British tradition is typified by an Official Secrets

Act which literally makes it a criminal offence to reveal how many cups of tea civil servants drink each day. After the failure to convict Clive Ponting for disclosing information to a Member of Parliament, something the jury obviously considered to be in the public interest, it seems clear that the Act is a dead letter. But, passed in thirty minutes, it has been on the statute book for nearly eighty years and the Conservative administration, like successive Labour administrations, appears to be in no hurry to reform it. Other measures, such as draconian libel laws and the Contempt of Court Act (1981), not to mention the D notice system, whereby newspapers agree not to publish anything officially deemed to be prejudicial to the national interest, further restrict the freedom of the press in Britain. And the government habitually keeps 'sensitive' information to itself. The British convention is that public information is the private property of the government and that what interests the public is not in the public interest. Trappist monks are freer with their asides than official spokesmen and, as even *The Times* acknowledges, confidentiality 'is a physiological disorder which afflicts ministers and civil servants' throughout the country. Instances are legion, from the covert way in which the decision was taken to build the Concorde to the refusal of government ministers to answer MPs' questions about white fish. The most notorious example concerns Attlee's authorization of the development of Britain's atomic bomb without the knowledge of most of his own cabinet. More recently there is the sorry tale of how the British nuclear industry has been bedevilled by official secrecy, not to say official lies – in 1984 the Friends of the Earth had to obtain a report on the dangers of nuclear reactors, written by the United Kingdom Atomic Energy Authority, from the United States under the Freedom of Information Act.

For every step which the British authorities take towards open government, an ideal for which they profess inordinate respect, they seem to take two steps back. For example, parliamentary select committees were established not only to keep a check on the executive but to expose matters which had hitherto been kept under wraps. Yet recently a select committee voted to ban a *Times* journalist from the precincts of parliament for reporting some perfectly innocuous information about its proceedings – a vote so absurd that the House of Commons itself would not endorse it. The Thatcher government's attitude towards secrecy involves it in Orwellian convolutions. In 1984, appropriately enough, *The Times* reported that the Cabinet Office had refused to release a study on its policy towards open government, on the grounds that it 'obviously would not lend itself to publication'. *The Times*'s headline read: 'Progress towards open government to be kept a secret.'

But surely the monarchy cannot be blamed for all this? Not directly, of course. However, as appeared again and again from the historical survey, royalty has always resisted the pretensions of the press to be the fourth estate of the realm. Its fundamental attitude was well summed up by King Charles II's press licenser, Sir Roger L'Estrange:

> Supposing the press in order, the people in their right wits, and news or no news to be the question, a public *Mercury* should never have my vote, because I think it makes the multitude too familiar with the actions and counsels of their superiors, too pragmatical and censorious, and gives them not only an itch, but a kind of colourable right and license to the meddling with the government.

From George III, who opposed the reporting of parliamentary debates, via Queen Victoria, who wanted journalists excluded from polite society, to Queen Elizabeth II, who never gives interviews and whose present press secretary, Michael Shea, thinks that no personal news about royalty is good news, the monarchy has hated, feared and despised the press. As Anthony Sampson says in his authoritative *Anatomy of Britain*, after the making of the television film *Royal Family*, the Queen and Prince Philip returned to their 'habitual aloofness and dislike of the media'. Whereas Scandinavian and Dutch royalty 'cultivated a commonsensical and accessible image, the courtiers at Buckingham Palace were acutely conscious of the magical element, enhanced by the British cult of secrecy'. The monarchy also enhances the cult.

The best recent example of its doing so was its extraordinary behaviour after the intrusion of Michael Fagan into the Queen's bedroom early one morning in July 1982. Fagan may have been deranged, but he had no difficulty in proving that the security system at Buckingham Palace was defective. Apparently he sat on the Queen's bed and although she twice rang for help none

204 Our Own Dear Queen

204 *Our Own Dear Queen*

was forthcoming for about twelve minutes. Yet Fagan was not the first intruder to be discovered within the Palace walls. At least one previous break-in had been hushed up, so it was clear that the policy of trying to put matters right in private did not work. Nevertheless, after the Fagan episode the sovereign and her advisers behaved like some curious cross between an ostrich and a Pavlovian dog. Their conditioned response was to keep mum once again, to forget about the incident as quickly as possible and to instruct the Palace press office to deny all knowledge of it. The story might not have been reported at all if a journalist on the *Daily Express* had not had a Deep Throat at court who believed that royal security would never be tightened up without proper scrutiny. And proper scrutiny required publicity, even a public scandal. *The Times* agreed. Only a 'sense of national outrage' would ensure that adequate security measures were devised and implemented. 'It is bad enough that the episode occurred at all. But it is even more disturbing that all the signs suggest that, but for the happy chance of a press disclosure, there would have been an official conspiracy of silence.'

Needless to say, the Queen and her family do not want complete silence to reign, otherwise there might be no cheers for royalty. They want it both ways; they want the publicity due to their public office and the privacy which a private person might expect. Of course, this is rather a tall order, for, as Americans recognize, the private lives of prominent figures, who largely owe their celebrity to the publicity which they otherwise encourage, are inextricably mixed up with their public lives. Everything about them therefore becomes a legitimate subject for the attention of the media. The royal family naturally do not accept this argument, and its members constantly complain about the intrusiveness of the press. Their strictures certainly give the lie to the cliché that the monarchy cannot answer back. Indeed, the press often publishes royal attacks on itself.

Prince Philip has likened journalists to 'mosquitoes', described them as 'bloody vultures' and turned a hose on them. Prince Charles, too, has taken the opportunity to douse them. But, recognizing that reporters have a job to do, he is generally more tolerant towards what he sometimes calls 'the bloody press'. Princess Anne's assaults on the 'pests' of the press were notorious, though recently she has undergone a mysterious transformation. As Auberon Waugh says, in his inimitable way, 'Either Princess Anne has been deceiving us all these years when she appeared as a demented llama whose poisonous spittle could blind a press photographer at 100 yards, or she's deceiving us now that she appears as a mixture of Brooke Shields, Dr Johnson and the Virgin Mary.' No doubt her metamorphosis is due to the need which she felt to get a better press, for in her early years even the staunchest Beefeater papers could hardly help reporting her combination of sulks, *hauteur* and ill temper. She seemed to think that she could behave like Queen Anne. Confronted by a group of protesters against blood sports when she was about to go hunting, she demanded angrily: 'Who's paying you to do this?' The riposte was obvious: 'Well *we're* paying *you* to do that!' Having been even less popular than her aunt Margaret, the Princess has climbed back into public esteem by dint of the good works so sedulously puffed by the media. She shows no disposition to complain about this sort of coverage.

Indeed, the press's function, from the viewpoint of Buckingham Palace, is to conduct an extended public relations campaign for royalty. The role is vital, for the Queen and her family believe, doubtless correctly, that invisibility fosters unpopularity. Thus when, as has happened, photographers protest against royal rudeness by ostentatiously downing cameras and refusing to take pictures, they receive instant cooperation. Similarly, according to Douglas Keay, who has written a book about the relations between the press and the Palace, the leader of an African state who proposed to ban overseas journalists during a royal tour was told that it would not proceed without them. Prince Charles is realistic about the matter: 'It's when nobody wants to write about you or take a photograph of you that you ought to worry in my sort of job. Then there'd be no great point in being around.'

There is little chance of this happening. So besotted is the public with royalty that all its activities, however trivial, are recorded *ad nauseam*. A minor journalistic industry is devoted to inventing stories about the royal family. On a slightly less fictional level, whole pages are given over to such portentous issues as whether Charles is going bald. A picture of the Princess of Wales on the cover of a journal is practically guaranteed to raise its circulation by 10 to 15 per cent.* Drivel about the royal corgis sells newspapers. Fleet Street therefore has the most enticing of all incentives for its royal drum-beating – lucre. In general newspapers act quite willingly as vehicles for royal propaganda. There is, in fact, no need for the legal and bureaucratic apparatus of restraint available to the Palace. Compulsion in this sphere, as in others, cannot achieve what sycophancy does. As Humbert Wolfe memorably concluded:

> You cannot hope to bribe or twist,
> Thank God! the British journalist.
> But, seeing what the man will do
> Unbribed, there's no occasion to.

It is true that (to paraphrase Ruskin) amid the so many square leagues of dirtily printed gossip and adulation there are occasional items that embarrass and even outrage the monarchy. Hence the royal abuse. Hence, too, the few occasions when the Palace protests or intervenes. Its continuing sensitivity about the Windsors, for example, was illustrated by an ill-judged complaint about Trog's cartoon in the *Observer* featuring the Duchess remarking that Queen Elizabeth did not seem to realize that it was to her (the Duchess) that she owed her throne. Royalty tends to ignore most of the spurious stories printed about it – these are virtually presented as fiction anyway – but it is extremely thin-skinned about material which is for one reason or another more plausible, even when it is also relatively trivial and innocuous. Thus in 1983 the Palace resorted to law to suppress the *Sun*'s mildly sleazy revelations about life behind its walls, written by a former employee, Kiernan Kenny.

Mistrusting the press, the monarchy prefers television, which seems to be staffed by the most blatant kind of journalistic flunkeys. Sir Alastair Burnet continues the tradition of Richard Dimbleby, Audrey Williamson and, still more, of Godfrey Talbot, whose awed tones filled the air-waves for so long. Significantly enough, one of the BBC's court correspondents,

---

* However, pictures of Princess Anne and Princess Margaret have been known to *reduce* sales abroad, according to the German magazine group which publishes *Bunte*. In Australia *Women's Weekly* used to find that pictures of Queen Elizabeth encouraged people to buy, but more recently her selling power has been overtaken by that of babies and kittens. It took Princess Diana to restore the royal appeal.

Ronald Allison, was later appointed to be the Queen's press secretary. It is easy enough for poachers to turn into gamekeepers if
they have had intimate relations with the gamekeepers all along.
The television court correspondents behave like public relations
officers for royalty. They adopt an ingratiating simper in
presumed collusion with their unseen audience and, after royal
items, their simper is invariably echoed by the news-readers.
They are also regularly granted privileges which print journalists
are denied. As the *Guardian* columnist Alan Rusbridger reported
during the Australian tour made by the Prince and Princess of
Wales in 1985, television

> is what the whole show is geared to, HRHs must perform for the
> bank of mirror-lenses that are lined up and cordoned off at a suitable
> distance. . . . The Palace, one assumes, is doing its sincere best to
> safeguard the mystique of royalty. The energies of the press man-
> agers are thus devoted to devising picture ideas – at which they are
> very good – while seeking to ensure that [the] fewest possible words
> will accompany those pictures.

If there is anything significant to report, the Palace calls the
BBC or ITN, not Fleet Street. Michael Shea and his assistants
can more easily focus the cyclopean gaze of television on what
they want seen than pull the wool over the Argus-eyes of the
print press corps – who are in general kept at a safe distance.

The irony is, though, that about 99 per cent of the items which
newspapers publish about royalty are favourable. Apart from
anything else, the system favours journalistic poodles. Just as the
parliamentary lobby correspondents are in bed with Mrs
Thatcher (or Bernard Ingham) so the court correspondents are
in bed with the Queen (or Michael Shea). They are carefully
scrutinized, as befits anyone who is to become an honorary
member of the Establishment, and picked for their discretion.
This is likely to be measured in terms of their social background.
Grumbles were heard at the Palace about the appointment of the
first woman court correspondent, Grania Forbes, but she proved
acceptable after it was discovered that her grandfather had served
as a colonel in the Coldstream Guards and her father had been
to school at Eton. In a curious way, too, even the journalistic
paparazzi, those trench-coated, binoculared news-hounds, are
sucked into the system. As their reports all too clearly indicate,

they fondly imagine that they enjoy the esteem, even the friendship and the confidence, of royalty. Beneath their brash posturings, they seem somehow to visualize themselves as the gentlemen-in-waiting of the press. Thus republicanism is to all intents and purposes taboo in Fleet Street, though sometimes a paper like the *Sun* might presume to suggest that the sovereign should (as well as visiting ducal houses) 'drop in for tea at a council house in Wigan'. It might also dare to assert that the '21st century may well demand that the Queen be truly a monarch of all the people'. But there are virtually no fundamental criticisms and no hard-hitting investigations of the strange feudal anachronism at the heart of Britain's supposed democracy. Fleet Street places its devotion to the Crown, as a sovereign circulation-builder, above its duty as the fourth estate.

Ultimately the British class sytem is responsible for the deference of the press. Until quite recently Grub Street hacks were reckoned by genteel people to possess not only the proclivities of poachers but the morals of actors. Certainly they were 'in trade'. Often, therefore, they lacked the prestige, or were simply too respectful, to challenge their social superiors, especially when those social superiors happened to be royal. Hazlitt denounced the sycophantic hireling of the press with his usual pungency:

> He measures the greatness of others by his own meanness; their lofty pretensions indemnify him for his servility; he magnifies the sacredness of their persons to cover the laxity of his own principles. He offers up his own humanity, and that of all men, at the shrine of royalty. He sneaks to court; and the bland accents of power close his ears to the voice of freedom ever after; its velvet touch makes his heart marble to a people's sufferings. He is the intellectual pimp of power.

Today, of course, he is more the intellectual pimp of pomp. Since the monarchy has become politically ornamental, the radical voices decrying it have grown fewer and fainter. Paradoxically, as the press has become more independent of the political parties over the last century or so, it has become more slavish towards the monarchy.

Actually, this has been less the fault of the journalists themselves than of the proprietors. Independent though they were in other spheres, they grovelled to royalty. Northcliffe's offer to print and omit what suited Edward VII has already been mentioned, and throughout his career the Napoleon of Fleet Street kow-towed to the Crown. Having climbed the social ladder, he and other press barons did not want to beat the system but to join it. Lord Kemsley, for example, owner of the *Sunday Times*, thought that there was something vulgar, if not downright improper, in the disclosure of the secrets of top people, and if they were royal such revelations were obviously out of the question. After its conversion to Toryism, the *Daily Telegraph* became, as one of its nineteenth-century rivals said, full of 'senile adulation for the powers that be'. It has remained so ever since. Between the wars its proprietor, Lord Burnham, apparently saw nothing odd about printing items like this: 'I was greatly struck by the deferential attitude of the man who was washing the face of Queen Victoria on the Temple Bar Monument.'

Even the mischievous Lord Beaverbrook, though he prosecuted a long vendetta against Lord Mountbatten, proved exceptionally accommodating where the monarchy was concerned. He was quite happy to help orchestrate the conspiracy of silence about Mrs Simpson and even to risk his credit by attempting to form a King's Party. In fact, Beaverbrook was as responsible as any of his fellow press barons for what the distinguished historian of the press, Stephen Koss, called its 'moral paralysis' during the 1930s. Those who controlled it, associating themselves with the upper class, refused to publish unpleasant facts largely because they believed that to do so would have a deleterious effect on circulation. As Beaverbrook said, 'A paper can't afford to prophesy disaster, can it?' Suppressing information not only about the state of the monarchy but about the imminence of war, British newspapers failed in their primary duty as the fourth estate. They behaved as organs of propaganda – in the national interest, naturally – instead of disseminators of news. They treated their readers as children who could not be trusted with reality but had to be told fairy-tales. The *Spectator* was typical in beginning the year 1936 with fatuous eulogies to Edward VIII – 'If there were no monarchy, he would be uncrowned King of England', wrote Philip Guedalla – and ending it with scarcely less enthusiastic endorsements of George VI. Doped by the magic of royalty, the Argus-eyes of democracy all but shut.

Since the war the press, and still more the electronic media, have been slow to take a more detached view of the monarchy. Journalists see themselves as being somehow bound up in the apparatus of the state, instead of being independent observers whose first loyalty is to the truth. This did not, of course, prevent Commander Colville, royal press secretary between 1947 and 1968, from harbouring the direst suspicions about the press. As the writer Tim Heald put it, Colville 'lived by the principle that any reporting other than the verbatim repetition of the Court Circular, was virtually treasonable'. Yet for the first decade of Colville's reign, it could not have been more sycophantic. This was the time when, as Lord Altrincham said, fawning editors and broadcasters assumed that 'the public shared the official, quasi-religious view of the Queen'. Not until the 1960s, when the satire industry and the permissive society boomed, was there any real break in the servility of the media. Even when that happened, it meant little more than the publication of photographs and articles about the royals' personal lives which would previously have been considered intrusive. There were some mildly irreverent squibs and cartoons, though most of these (even the ones in *Private Eye*) were more affectionate than subversive.

Partly in self-defence, partly as a deliberate attempt to rejuvenate an institution whose arteries were visibly hardening, the royal family took to 'marketing' itself much more aggressively in the later 1960s. Princess Alexandra said: 'Don't forget that nowadays we have to compete with Elizabeth Taylor and the Beatles.' Thus the television film *Royal Family* had them behaving almost like normal human beings instead of regal automata. The Prince of Wales's investiture was promoted with the help of Aristotle Onassis's adviser, Nigel Neilson, whose public relations company, incidentally, has had a long association with Major Ronnie Ferguson, Sarah's father. The press responded by adopting a somewhat less awe-struck tone towards the monarchy, which, though a 'unique selling proposition', was obviously a commodity like any other.

In 1871 *The Times* declared on the wedding of Queen Victoria's daughter, Princess Louise, to the Marquess of Lorne:

To-day a ray of sunshine will gladden every habitation in this island, and force its way even where uninvited. A daughter of the people in the truest sense of the word is to be married to one of ourselves. The mother is ours, and the daughter is ours. We honour and obey the Queen; we crown her and do her homage, we pray for her and work for her, and fight for her; we accept her as the dispenser of blessings and favours, dignity and honours; we share her joys and are cheered by her consolations.

There was more in this grandiloquent vein, so much more that at least one working man claimed that such '"gushing" articles were especially effective in intensifying the ill-feeling towards royalty'. The press has to some extent learnt this lesson, at least in recent years. *The Times*'s welcome for the engagement between Prince Andrew and Sarah Ferguson was no less loyal but a good deal more down-to-earth. The 'unaffected and palpably sincere' public rejoicing, it stated, is

almost wholly prompted by sentiment, not least the enduring affection of the British people for the whole Royal Family. It is a paradoxical affection in certain respects since we admire them both for performing their duties so well and for presenting an image of normality to the world.

The tabloids, to be sure, gushed like so many oil wells. However, even they tended to temper their enthusiasm for the match with a slightly quizzical air, as if to show that they and their readers were not so naïve as to swallow the royal myth hook, line and sinker. Thus in the *Daily Mail* Ann Leslie remarked: 'If he had chosen from the typing pool we wouldn't have been happy. . . . Royal Sloane-brides are tailormade to satisfy the customer's desire for the Royal Family to be up-to-date – and, at the same time, thoroughly traditional.'

There was a similar flavour about some of the sixtieth-birthday greetings which the press lavished on the Queen. Amid the cries of 'Happy Birthday, Ma'am!' and the toasts of 'Long To Reign Over Us!', amid the ballyhoo about 'the best-loved woman in the world' and variations on the theme that the monarch herself is 'the jewel in the crown', there was a note of worldly wisdom, a dash of sour to make the sweet taste sweeter. To quote the *Mail* again: 'We have grown accustomed to her smile. And to her down-in-the-dumps look, when not amused. Our Queen at 60 is much loved and, in an age of unease, wonderfully reassuring.'

Only the *Guardian*, something of a maverick on the monarchy, went so far as to suggest that the interminable anniversaries of 'this most televisual and media oriented Royal House ... while pleasant enough in themselves, are now something of a contrivance to reboost the ratings upon which the family – and the media – are now so mutually dependent'. But even the *Guardian* half apologized for such cynical speculations. It declared that although a new constitution would not include a monarchy, the devising of such a constitution was 'simply not a relevant exercise in Britain today'. Its sage conclusion was that 'there are a lot of things worse than a monarchy and that a lot of surprising things can be done under monarchy's wide umbrella'.

Photographers are more intrusive, or less easily kept at bay, than print journalists. But, though loathed by the Palace, they too are censored in British newspapers, which seldom if ever print unflattering pictures of royalty. The shots of the pregnant Princess Diana wearing a bikini ('Bahama Mama' in the *Sun's* argot) were condemned as tasteless by the Palace, by parliament and by the Press Council – always quick to spring to the defence of royalty though notoriously sluggish about righting the wrongs of ordinary people. But this was because the pictures were deemed to be a violation of royal privacy, not because there was anything indecent about them. In fact, they were rather beautiful in a fuzzy sort of way. There was much hypocritical prating, mainly by the chagrined rivals of the *Sun* and the *Star*, about how indefensible it was to publish such photographs. And Lord Matthews, recently ennobled chairman of the *Star*, was apparently embarrassed by the episode – the paper's photos were eventually locked in the editor's safe. All told, there were few in Fleet Street to agree with the 'senior executive', quoted by the *Guardian*, who said that the Prince and Princess of Wales were show business personalities and 'If they can be shown getting married, they can be shown picking their noses or scratching their bums.'

Needless to say, such pictures are never published, though photographers often catch royalty in some fairly risible poses. Instead newspapers print interminable chocolate-box photos whose news content is virtually nil. *The Times*, in particular, despite its proprietor's rumoured republicanism and its claims to be a newspaper of record, seems to regard itself as a pictorial supplement to the Court Circular. It behaves as though its readers will develop withdrawal symptoms unless presented with front-page photographs of royalty at least once or twice a week. There is, of course, no chance that royalty will be subjected to the deliberately slanted pictorial treatment which lesser mortals have to endure. The Duke of Windsor's Nazi salutes were presented as waves by the British press; Arthur Scargill's waves have been presented as Nazi salutes.

Essentially, then, there is a royalist consensus in the British press. Over the last century or so national and provincial newspapers, aided and abetted in recent years by radio and television, have been engaged in an unremitting campaign to promote the monarchy. Sometimes this has involved their maintaining a polite silence, thus encouraging the British disease of secrecy. Sometimes it has meant that journalists pander to the public appetite for snobbery, fantasy or triviality. Often their propagandist incentive is more obviously political. They are fostering conservatism and patriotism in the shape of loyalty to a dynasty. They are peddling optimism, which not only sells newspapers but helps to keep the capitalist mill turning. They are endeavouring to confirm the legitimacy of the existing order and of its ruling Establishment. They are trying to win the hearts and minds of the masses in the interests of social control. But does all this amount to an insidious conspiracy to brainwash the British people?

No. By and large the controllers of the press do not consult one another, let alone act in concert. Dog is too busy eating dog. William Deedes, former editor of the *Daily Telegraph*, will not even allow that there was a real conspiracy of silence over Edward VIII and Mrs Simpson. He finds *The Times*'s account more persuasive:

> The Crown of England touches atavistic, often subconscious springs of human emotion. The leaders of opinion, when they saw the Crown threatened, spontaneously coalesced to contain the explosion and ensure that it did as little damage as possible.

This is too pious, but it does suggest the way in which journalists can fall into the trap of self-censorship. In the interests of some supposedly higher duty they can easily persuade themselves that *suppressio veri* and *suggestio falsi* are justified. The press has not been engaged in a long conspiracy. But proprietors, editors and journalists have certainly been guilty of betraying their trust – which is to keep the wells of knowledge pure – out of loyalty to the Crown.

Even if there is only a 'gentleman's agreement' to portray the royal family in a favourable light, has this not had its effect on popular opinion? Is not the monarchy a happy hallucination which the press, and now television, projects onto the public mind? Perhaps. It must be said, though, that newspapers tend to reflect, not to direct, the views of their readers. As the American columnist Arthur Brisbane shrewdly remarked, his readers did not want to know what he thought but what they thought. Where propaganda is unpalatable it is either ignored (as in Beaverbrook's *Express*) or it ruins the paper (as in the late-lamented *Herald*). On the other hand, a sustained advertising campaign lasting over several generations, and seldom if ever challenged by dissentient voices, must have its impact on public opinion. Obviously sellers of less attractive commodities than royalty think so, otherwise the likes of Saatchi & Saatchi would go out of business.

Moreover it is significant that the revolution in the public view of the monarchy which has occurred since the Victorian period just about coincides with the birth of the popular and truly national press. Other factors, such as the growth of pageantry, contributed to this revolution, but it could never have been so complete without the insistent propaganda. The present Queen's press secretary, Michael Shea (himself, incidentally, a writer of fiction), is inclined to say that newspapers need the monarchy more than the monarchy needs newspapers. But, as Philip Ziegler has shown, public enthusiasm for royal events, wedding, investitures, coronations and so on, is initially small and only waxes when they are puffed by the media. This suggests that royal popularity depends to a considerable extent on royal publicity, that it is a bubble inflated by the press and television, an essentially spurious creation. As Suzanne Lowry wrote, 'Without press coverage, the Royal Family would be little more than rich overdressed people in big houses.' The royal family themselves apparently recognize this, though they would hardly express it in these terms. Prince Charles told Douglas Keay that 'the size of crowd he would expect to see at the start of a provincial tour was directly commensurate with the amount of publicity he or the other members of the Royal Family had received in the day or two prior to the visit'. Keay himself thinks that if – a big if – the press were ever to make a concerted effort to denigrate the royal family the very existence of the monarchy might be threatened.

It might be more plausibly suggested that, as the logic of democracy works itself out in Britain, the press and television may gradually abandon their role as royal corgis, yapping loyally in their mistress's praise and administering sharp nips to anyone impertinent enough to commit lèse-majesté. If the media begin to operate more as the people's watchdog, take their duties as the fourth estate seriously, and adopt an objective tone towards the monarchy, its mystique might gradually start to disappear. Conditions would then be ripe for a more rational approach towards constitutional reform. Assisted by one or other of the royal scandals which are doubtless germinating in the womb of time, a British republic might somehow struggle to be born.

For this to happen, though, the revolution would have to extend beyond the news media and into the whole realm – in Britain a kingdom not a republic – of letters. As Frederic Harrison intimated, sycophancy towards royalty is by no means the sole prerogative of journalists. Countless books appear which are little more than the hard-bound editions of magazines like *Majesty*, *Young Royals*, and *Royalty Monthly*. These exercises in literary toadyism need not, perhaps, be taken very seriously. Tom Nairn, writing in the *Guardian*, is admirably clear-eyed about the proliferation of what he calls 'Monarchic slosh', clouds of incense wafted towards 'a tribe of household gods, never more utterly extraordinary than when at their most banal':

> Each season sees 20 or so additions to the Windsor book-mountain, amassed for handy inspection on the 'Royal' shelves of any decent-sized W. H. Smiths. They cover a wide spectrum of discourses; mainly pictorial 'tributes' around particular events (Visits, Births, etc.); wordier musings on the latest rumours about paddock and nursery; rehashed popular biographies whose every intimate disclosure is grey with re-handling (1985's speciality is the fine 'Queen Mother' display); and stately official or semi-official argosies, with their huge and grovelling Prefaces and prim economy of illustration. ... The aim is reassurance; the cloning of a magic essence enriched with 'fascinating' details so that its perpetuity is guaranteed. Each new, candid, glazed look helps to keep a disenchanted world at bay.

It is easy enough to dismiss most of these books as the tawdry icons of a popular cult. A few of them, however, are written by intelligent authors who fall into what appears to be an inevitable obsequiousness. For example, Robert Lacey and Anthony Holden, both good journalists, have dealt with the Queen and the Prince of Wales respectively. Their books reek with what George Orwell called 'the smell of the bug'. With an elaborate show of frankness the authors seem to give a rounded view of royalty. But they evidently know how to be as ingratiating as professional courtiers. For example, Robert Lacey talks about the Queen's 'fierce sympathy with the humble'. In a similar vein, Basil Boothroyd has put not only his pen but his wit (or what passes for wit in *Punch*) at the service of Prince Philip. His biography is full of coy, and ever-so-slightly barbed, little compliments to its subject – as when he extols Philip's 'almost pathological honesty'. Boothroyd relishes royalty's endearing oddities, but he also makes fun of the eccentrics who write to the Palace and fail to share his (and by implication his readers') cosy, suburban view of its inmates. Finally, there is the curious case of Lady Longford. Her biography of Queen Victoria, though eminently respectful, is excellent, but her biography of Queen Elizabeth II is a work of the purest hagiography. How an author who has proved herself to be so clever and well-informed could pen such adulation, no doubt all of it quite sincere, is a mystery. Presumably the monarch addled her critical faculties.

This, alas, is what the monarchy seems to have done to almost the entire writing profession and to nearly everyone engaged in the mass media. Members of the fourth estate, who act as touts for royalty, and hug themselves at the proximity they have attained to these superior beings, flagrantly betray their calling. What is more, by their eager resort to harsh and archaic libel laws, they inhibit frank discussion of their own activities and further debase the currency of candour. The corrupting effect of royalty is nowhere more sadly apparent than in the modern treason of the clerks.

Twelve

Command Performance

The only thing that history proves, it is often said, is that history proves nothing at all. Still, the history of the British monarchy suggests, to put it no more strongly, that the institution is a pernicious anachronism. When the Crown exercised power it seldom did so in anything less than a reactionary fashion. When its power waned, to be replaced by an arcane influence on national affairs which has survived to this day, the continuing conservatism of monarchs was also apparent. From George III, who opposed the abolition of the slave trade, to George VI, who opposed the foundation of the welfare state, there is an essential continuity. From the appointment of William Pitt the Younger to the appointment of Lord Home, there is a fundamental identity of royal interest. In short, the sovereign is an entrenched foe of progress.

It would be odd if he were not, and the argument that he actually 'makes change easier', by lending his 'authority to the government of the day', is perverse. For it implies that the government of the day is always bent on change, when often it is not – in which case the monarch presumably makes change more difficult. Furthermore, it suggests that the monarch is a complete cipher. But, as Prince Albert said, the Crown could never be apolitical. As the career of, say, George V indicates, for all their studious pretence of neutrality British sovereigns have done their best to protect their vested interest in the status quo. Moreover the present Queen's remaining constitutional prerogatives, her long experience at the centre of affairs, the prestige attaching to her position, and the fact that she is the fount of much patronage, all give her unique leverage. There is no doubt that Queen Elizabeth could and would exert all the pressure at her command to resist the abolition of the House of Lords – a fate which Winston Churchill himself advocated for that 'lingering relic of a feudal order' as long ago as 1910. Of course, where the monarchy's own popularity or survival is concerned, successive sovereigns have been willing to countenance modest reforms. But usually they regard change as something to be embraced only in the last resort – in other words, as the royal old Duke of Cambridge used to say, 'when you can't help it'.

It is impossible to say how much influence the present Queen wields because of the pathological secrecy which surrounds the monarch's role. Sometimes, though, the supposedly sovereign people are vouchsafed a glimpse behind the sovereign's veil. Despite a massive effort, officialdom was unable to suppress publication of Richard Crossman's diaries, which recorded, among other things, the fact that the Queen urged a willing Harold Wilson to maintain censorship of the theatre in 1967. Even American archivists, under pressure from their government, pay some attention to British susceptibilities. Yet the curious student may discover the occasional revealing snippet, such as President Eisenhower's memorandum to John Foster Dulles saying that Prince Philip possessed 'a certain amount of political influence'.

A few others blow the gaff, by design or by accident. It emerges, for example, that Queen Elizabeth, like Queen Victoria, exercises a vestigial influence over the appointment of ministers, though this is apparently a matter of the nods and winks by which members of the Establishment conduct so much of their business. Willie Hamilton has revealed that he was told by the Labour Whips that his views on the monarchy would preclude him from the ministerial office which he was otherwise well qualified to hold. John Silkin informed him that 'Even if you were a junior minister you'd meet royalty and you couldn't be relied on to keep a civil tongue in your head.' And if Harold Wilson is to be believed, the Crown's wishes have to be taken into account over the choice of prime minister. In 1980 Wilson confided to Lady Longford that 'Tony [Benn] will never be leader [of the Labour Party]. We should have to select someone the Queen could send for.' Yet, like so many on the left, Benn is anything but a committed and consistent republican. Still, it is nothing short of astonishing that a democracy should permit the retention of such influence in the hands of a sovereign who may now be, to paraphrase Frederick Harrison, an 'irreproachable lady', but who could just as easily be a 'debauched booby'.

In the normal course of events, to be sure, there is little fear that the 'irreproachable lady' will behave unconstitutionally, as Queen Victoria did and as Edward VIII threatened to do. Such meagre evidence as is available suggests that she is scrupulous in her determination to act impartially and to go no further than advising, encouraging and warning the government. However, the constitutional boundaries are not precisely drawn and even the most self-effacing monarch enjoys incalculable authority simply by virtue of his prestige. A royal wish may not be a command but it can scarcely be ignored, and for loyalists even a sovereign hint takes on the character of a ukase. Thus, for example, in 1978 Prince Charles took exception to some aspect of Labour's economic policy, about which he had read in the cabinet papers, and, against the advice of his staff, he wrote a 'strongly-worded note' to the prime minister. Instead of resenting this intrusion, Mr Callaghan obsequiously invited him to lunch. According to Anthony Holden, Charles, though surprisingly liberal-minded in most spheres, is in private 'an inveterate and impassioned union-basher' and he 'injected a dash of his own brand of conservatism into the Labour Government's approach to a long winter of industrial unrest'.

Such direct and personal interventions are apparently rare. But the Palace bureaucracy, however barnacle-encrusted, knows all too well whose elbow to grasp, whose palate to tickle, whose back to scratch and whose lever to pull. Similarly, the Queen's vast experience of men and affairs must signally enhance her authority. No one has better cause to appreciate the fact that strength comes through knowledge. Queen Elizabeth laments the inadequacy of her education and, like her uncle Edward, she tries to augment it by learning from life. By all accounts – R. A. Butler's and Jim Callaghan's – she has a well-developed appetite for political gossip. There is ample testimony, from premiers as various as Winston Churchill and Harold Wilson, to the Queen's conscientiousness, hard work and attention to detail. Even Margaret Thatcher, driven on by an over-active thyroid and an overweening will to power, is not more meticulous about 'doing her boxes'. For nearly thirty-five years the Queen has been privy to every state secret, to every important aspect of domestic and foreign policy, to every crucial political development. She would be inhuman if occasionally, perhaps even habitually, she did not trade on her position.

Furthermore, the power of the monarch's remaining patronage cannot be underestimated. She has 120 grace-and-favour residences at her disposal and may choose whom she likes as tenants. They live rent-free; the taxpayer foots the bill; the Queen reaps the prestige; and the Establishment is strengthened. Only its members, retired senior officers, courtiers and the like, qualify for such privileges. Willie Hamilton's suggestion that people seriously affected by the housing shortage might be considered fell on the stoniest of ground. More important, the Queen has a number of honours in her own gift. They range from the Order of Merit (which means what it says) and the Order of the Garter (which Lord Melbourne liked because there was no damned merit about it), to the Royal Victorian Order and membership of the Royal Warrant Holders Association. The sovereign may personally bestow these and other awards, such as the Order of the Thistle or the Companion of Honour, on her subjects, but she also invests her majesty in the entire honours system. As John Walker's recent book on the subject * shows, this is at best an unedifying scramble for meretricious distinctions and at worst a disreputable exchange of cash for kudos. How much of a say the Queen has in distributing the baubles of rank, Orders of the (now defunct) British Empire to popular entertainers, knighthoods to accommodating journalists, peerages to generous tycoons, is unknown. So is the extent to which the Queen, as head of the Church of England (in Scotland, of course, she is miraculously transmogrified into a Presbyterian), interests herself in top ecclesiastical preferments. Nor is it possible to say whether she is concerned, as monarchs traditionally have been, with high-ranking promotions in the armed services, though she is known to be a stickler for punctilio, like her forebears, in military dress and address.

There is simply no information about serious matters, about what Edmund Burke once called 'those innumerable methods of clandestine corruption which are abundantly in the hands of the

* *The Queen Has Been Pleased* (1986).

court'. Indeed, the Queen's popularity to some extent derives from people's ignorance, or rather their belief that the sovereign is above the sordid fray of politics. Like God, she is a figurehead who may be praised for any good that occurs to her subjects but is mysteriously immune from blame for their ills. She is added to the state's pluses and subtracted from its minuses. No wonder Marx liked to quote William Cobbett's sardonic contrast between the *Royal* Mint and the *National* Debt. The Queen is the embodiment of the Establishment, of its wealth and social superiority and unknowable power, yet she appears to bear no responsibility for how it operates. As Churchill said, when the British win a battle they shout 'God Save the Queen'; when they lose one they vote out the prime minister. It is surely absurd and pernicious that at the heart of an allegedly democratic and open society there is an hereditary institution whose most crucial activities are secret and unaccountable.

Yet for all its lack of logic the system works, so its defenders claim. It has adapted to meet modern needs and circumstances. It provides a last-ditch defence against the possible dictatorship of politicians; Mrs Thatcher could not, in a sudden access of megalomania, declare herself Empress while the Queen is on the throne. To Lady Longford, the Watergate scandal 'suggested that a constitutional monarch may be a more principled head of state than a president'. No doubt the hereditary principle is archaic and unfair, but any other system will have its built-in disadvantages and inequities. To elect a head of state, for example, would cause division and instability. An astoundingly high proportion of the population favour the present régime, and in a democracy that should be enough to ensure its continuation. Republicanism in Britain is a caprice of cranks, sectarians and subversives. At best it is a shallow, mechanistic philosophy which ignores the subtle, organic nature of the body politic. At worst it is a dangerous, revolutionary creed, a form of atheism in politics which flies in the face of the crystallized wisdom of the ages and lays irreverent hands on the delicate fabric of society. It is a type of modern Jacobinism, excoriated by Matthew Arnold as a 'violent indignation with the past, abstract systems of renovation applied wholesale, a new doctrine drawn up in black and white for elaborating down to the very smallest details a rational society of the future'. How can the case for the defence be answered?

In the normal course of events, it is true, the royal system does work, largely because the sovereign's main business is to act as a national figurehead and a political rubber stamp. But at times of crisis or controversy the monarchy has by no means always worked well. To go back no further than 1910, George V emerged badly out of almost every contretemps. During the Peers *v*. People struggle he behaved as though he should mediate between the two political parties and then decide for himself. Asquith had to warn him against this then, and again over Home Rule in 1914, when the King seemed to give aid and comfort to the disloyal loyalists of Ulster and to the divisive Unionists in England. During the war George supported the 'Brasshats' against the 'Frocks', with results which are incalculable but may have proved.fatal to not a few of his subjects. By sustaining Ramsay MacDonald in 1931 he assisted in – what was surely predictable at the time – splitting, demoralizing and defeating the Labour Party. Had circumstances been different, his successor, Edward VIII, might easily have lent his majesty to the fascist dictatorship of Oswald Mosley, just as the Italian monarch lent his to that of Benito Mussolini. Certainly Edward's political sympathies inclined Hitler to think he would make an ideal Quisling king. The Crown might then have helped to engender stability, unity and loyalty to . . . a Nazi Britain. George VI's insistence that 'India must be governed' and his evident distaste for Socialist measures were hardly calculated to help Attlee's administration.

That Queen Elizabeth has not always used her prerogative wisely and well is suggested by her appointment of the hawkish Macmillan and, still more, the patrician Home, fully paid-up, card-carrying members of the 'magic circle'. And a moment's thought about the Suez crisis might suggest to Lady Longford that the Watergate scandal by no means indicates the superiority of a constitutional monarchy over a republic. Even after foreign disclosures, official British liars continued to deny that there had been collusion between Britain, France and Israel to invade Egypt. The Duke of Devonshire said that members of a 'wicked canaille' had suggested such a thing. Questioned about it on television, Macmillan talked complete gobbledegook, and since a deferential interviewer failed to press him the public was none the wiser. Even now the full story has not been told, sensitive documents are withheld from the Public Record Office, and civil servants have doubtless 'weeded' the files that do appear of anything damaging to the powers that be. Nothing is known of the Queen's conduct except that Eden said she was kept informed and did not protest. Eden himself retired with his dignity, if not his reputation, intact, and received the Queen's personal seal of approval in the shape of the Garter.

In the United States, by contrast, the press investigated without fear or favour, it was not stifled by false notions of patriotism, and it exposed as much of the Watergate scandal as it could. The chief conspirators were arraigned before the courts, convicted and imprisoned. Threatened with impeachment by Congress, President Nixon was forced to resign in disgrace. The British system scarcely emerges well out of the comparison. The excuse that the royal role, however minimal, must be concealed, provides a perfect justification for refusing to reveal the springs of government action. Lest the holy of holies be defiled by unbelieving eyes, the entire tabernacle must be kept locked. Acton's warning is pertinent: 'Everything secret degenerates; nothing is safe that does not show it can bear discussion and publicity.' The monarchy is an entrenched obstacle to freedom of information in Britain.

Royalists seem to agree that if the Crown were stripped of its remaining prerogatives and left simply as a decorative symbol, there would be little point in preserving it. An elected Lord Mayor of England might lack the charisma of royalty but he could perform the ceremonial functions just as well, and at a fraction of the cost. So it is the sovereign's political role which justifies the existence of a hereditary monarchy. Yet the very fact that the office is hereditary guarantees that its occupants will be unable to carry out their political functions satisfactorily. Bagehot once wrote: 'It has been said, not truly, but with a possible approximation of truth, "that in 1802 every hereditary monarch was insane".' The point is that inevitably, in the course of time, idiots, or children, or rakes, or numskulls, or rogues are going to sit on the throne. As Tom Paine observed, 'Hereditary succession is a burlesque upon monarchy. It puts it in the most ridiculous light by presenting it as an office' which any knave or fool may fill. Whatever the merits of the present Queen and her successor, and they are considerable, there can be no doubt that the House of Windsor will in due course throw up another George III, or George IV, or Edward VII, or Edward VIII. To award the crown by accident of birth, to make it the winning prize in a genetic lottery, is to consecrate an absurdity.

Of course, an elective system also promotes villains and nit-wits, as a glance at any representative assembly in the world shows. Very often, too, it gives unfair advantage to those with wealth, or high social status, or a privileged education, or even good looks. But this is not considered a sound reason for abandoning the ballot box and the polling booth, or relying on a caucus of decrepit dukes, moth-eaten marquises and fourteenth earls to run the country. Englishmen love lords only slightly less than they love monarchs, but they have happily acquiesced in reducing the power of the peerage since 1910, and long before that they generally accepted the paramountcy of the Commons. Flawed though it may be as a method of choosing a government, universal suffrage is the best technique yet evolved of harmonizing the interests of rulers and ruled. For the nominal head of the state to remain unelected and unaccountable is to thwart the purposes of democracy at the very centre of affairs.

But what if the sovereign people choose to keep the hereditary sovereign? Marxists would claim that for generations the populace has been brainwashed by royal propaganda, and, as the previous chapter indicated, there is obviously some truth in this. But to argue that the masses are the innocent victims of 'false consciousness' is to deny an essential premise of democracy, namely that each individual is the best judge of what is good for him.

What the British people want, at least for the moment, is the monarchy. Of course, they have never actually had the opportunity to choose. English kings owed their throne not to election but, as Professor Norman Stone trenchantly remarks, 'to the usual processes of murder and fornication'. Still, if consulted now the British people would presumably vote for a monarchy and they would naturally be entitled to have it. But although the will of the majority should prevail in such a matter, it is not necessarily right. Indeed, the conventional wisdom from Plato to Carlyle was that majority decisions were invariably wrong because they reflected the ignorance, passion, prejudice and venality of the masses rather than the wisdom of the few.

The democratic case can look after itself. But there is no denying the fact that public opinion may be sadly misguided. The massive popular support for appeasement in England, for Nazism in Germany, and for Prohibition in America, are cases in point. The democratic republican in Britain has no recourse but to put his faith in the justice of his cause, to educate others in the merit of his arguments, and to bear in mind John Stuart Mill's maxim that 'the real security of good government is "un peuple éclairé", which is not always the fruit of popular institutions'.

Although republicans believe that the monarchy is an obstruction on the road to progress they do not, in the light of developments elsewhere in the world, consider it immovable. Perhaps they are too idealistic; but universal suffrage itself once seemed a Utopian fantasy. And if no one else believes that republicanism will be realized in Britain successive sovereigns have certainly not shared the general incredulity. Indeed, it is quite striking that every monarch since Queen Victoria has been haunted by apocalyptic fears that a republic was at hand. Taboo though the subject is, there is no absolute ban on proselytizing for a republic. Indeed, the patriotism of republicans – a real patriotism, based on love of the country's virtues not its vices – depends on their freedom to campaign for the abolition of the monarchical system. As Frederic Harrison wrote in 1870, republicans 'are loyal in that they respect the laws of their country, be they made by them or not: they will abide by them until they are changed; but their right to change them is the condition of their loyal abiding.' After all, it is not republicans who interpret patriotism, at its best a noble spirit, as devotion to a particular dynasty. True patriots may well consider that their duty lies in working, by all democratic means, to rid their country of the crowned relic of ancient superstition.

Apologists for the monarchy say that it appeals to the atavistic instincts of human beings. Without some such potent, unifying symbol, they maintain, the community would be in danger of disintegrating. The sovereign is the god in the governmental machine, the soul of society. The institution cannot be removed without doing irreparable damage to the body politic. According to royalists, Walter Bagehot correctly understood that the monarchy's role lay in satisfying the irrational appetites of the community. As he put it, the masses deferred to 'what we may

call the "theatrical show" of society . . . a certain charmed spectacle which imposes on the many and guides their fancies as it
will'. But Bagehot was surely thus trying to transform into a
national glory what Tom Paine had revealed as a national disgrace – the fact that the common people, who ought themselves
to be sovereign, were treated as 'a herd of beings, that must be
governed by fraud, effigy and show'. There may, indeed, have
been a time in Britain when it was necessary to achieve social
cohesion by means of royal thaumaturgy and theocratic kingship.
But an affluent, educated people needs no such conjurations.
They are perpetuated because a perennially suspicious Establishment has never really believed in democracy or learnt to trust
the patriotism of the masses. As Leonard Woolf wrote: 'All the
paraphernalia of royalty, the ceremony and the snobbery, the
kissings of the hand and the deep bows and deeper curtsies are
kept alive by, and help to keep alive, the same primitive belief in
the divinity of kings.'

States which rely on such idolatry as a means of social control are
implicitly acknowledging that they lack more rational grounds for
securing the allegiance of their citizens. The most repulsive manifestations of official mystagoguery, a straightforward reversion to
savagery, were those practised by the Nazis. At Nuremberg Hitler
hypnotized his supporters with colossal displays of marching men,
massed bands, blazing torches, waving banners and thunderous
responses. Of course royalist manifestations have little in common
with these brutal extravaganzas. They are a pantomime of pomp
rather than a theatre of power. But they share the irrational element,
and there is always the danger that Britain's cosy monarchy could
be converted into something more sinister. This potential was
perhaps indicated by Berliners' response to the Queen's visit in
1965. In an access of enthusiasm they chanted 'Elizabeth, Elizabeth'. Their shouts were terribly reminiscent of the ritual 'Sieg
Heils' of Hitler's day and the Queen was visibly discomposed.
Government mystification is an expression of ancient barbarism
or new corruption. Republican government is demystified
government, public government in the public interest. Once
again Leonard Woolf is the voice of sanity:

The irrational and uncivilized attitude towards the king and the
royal family . . . is a symptom that mentally and emotionally we

remain savages . . . if our Morris car will not start, we do not expect to put it right by waving flags and muttering incantations over it. But we teach the children in elementary schools that they cannot be good and loyal Englishmen unless they approach the more important political questions in the flag-waving, incantation, medicine-man frame of mind.

Is not republicanism, though, a soulless creed, one which reduces individuals to cogs in a state machine? Surely society is a delicate growth, to be nurtured and cherished. The neat blueprints of radical theorists take no account of the complexities and the nuances of human affairs, which can only be apprehended by intuition. The crude tinkerings of social engineers ignore the generations of human wisdom which are embodied in tradition. This is the conservative case, classically expounded by Burke. It is based on the assumption that the supporters of vested interests and private privilege have established a monopoly of tradition and taken out a patent on patriotism. It assumes, too, that those who aspire to improve society are Benthamite logic-choppers, builders of abstract systems who are devoid of imagination and unrealistic about human nature.

These assumptions are false. Republicans do take note of the past, though they approach it with critical regard not know-nothing reverence. They see it as a foundation on which to build, not a ruin to romanticize. They temper imagination with reason. For, to paraphrase Mill, those who make imagination alone the criterion of truth might enthrone man's wildest dreams in the chair of philosophy.

Paradoxically, though, it is not the republicans who are the automata, but the worshippers of tradition. The latter condemn themselves to a sterile re-enactment of old routines, to a pathetic recapitulation of former glories. Their response to royalty is literally to knee jerk, whereas republicans feel a love of country which is broader and deeper than mere dynastic loyalty. Republicans believe that history is a key not a padlock, that the living cannot be shackled by the decisions of the dead. As Paine said, 'The vanity of governing beyond the grave is the most ridiculous and insolent of all tyrannies.' Experience is a good map but it can only be read in the light of reason. Of course, reason by itself, even when inspired by the brightest of contemporary ideas, is no infallible guide. But it is more reliable than intuition, which, to quote Mill again, is 'the great intellectual support of false doctrines and bad institutions. . . . There never was such an instrument devised for consecrating all deep-seated prejudices.' No prejudice is more deep-seated in Britain than the infatuation with royalty.

Nevertheless, uprooting it need not cause turmoil under current conditions and among a people committed to the ideal of equal citizenship. Other modern states have calmly embraced republicanism without social damage, let alone bloody revolution. Nor do their citizens have noticeably less national loyalty than the British. Many of them, indeed, have created new rituals and symbols of devotion, national anthems, honours based on merit rather than status, commemorations of national heroes like Gandhi, pledging allegiance to the flag. The flag, incidentally, however curious American reverence for it may seem to the British, has the supreme merit of being genuinely above party and incapable of interfering in politics. Switzerland, with its linguistic and other diversities and its federal system of government, attracts the patriotism of its citizens without any monarchical mumbo-jumbo. Although monarchies are everywhere on the retreat few republics show signs of wanting to revert to royalism. Spain is a notable exception, but while King Juan Carlos has valiantly assisted his country to return to democracy, doubtless securing his own future in the process, there is no escaping the fact that his constitutional monarchy was grafted onto the Spanish body politic by a fascist dictator – which at least has the merit of showing that even monarchies are human contrivances. In short, then, republicanism is the wave of the future. It could wash Britain free of the feudal accretions which hamper her progress. It could sluice out the aristocratic privilege enshrined at the heart of Britain's national life. And it need have none of the evil consequences forecast by royalist shamans.

Would it not, though, lead to a disastrous disintegration of the Commonwealth? The fact is, of course, that the Commonwealth has little reality and less homogeneousness. Even when a quarter of the globe was painted red on the map, notions of imperial federation were wholly chimerical. Such political ties as have remained since the Empire shrank to a few outposts are more of a hindrance to Britain than a help. Witness the difficulties caused between Britain and countries like Canada and Australia over the past decade or so, not to mention the Falklands. Britain herself has much more to hope for from the Atlantic alliance, which is based on present need rather than past sentiment. And Commonwealth countries are wisely looking to their own security by local means rather than putting their trust in any Commonwealth bond. Imperial preference, too, was always a lost cause, something amply demonstrated by its long espousal in the *Daily Express*. Now, for better or for worse, it is clear that Britain's future lies within the European Economic Community. Moreover, the countries of the Commonwealth – an odd name for an association which contains such palpable discrepancies of wealth – are forging their own economic links elsewhere, especially with Japan. In recent years royal efforts to boost British trade with Commonwealth states have been notable for their lack of success. Only thirteen per cent of Britain's trade is conducted with the Commonwealth and it is a symptom of Britain's hopelessly archaic approach to imagine that this figure will rise in response to royal drum-beating rather than improved products and competitive prices.

Nothing illustrates the factitiousness of the Commonwealth better than the American invasion of Grenada in October 1983. Evidently President Reagan did not know or did not care that the island was a member of this organization and, doubtless because of that, its head was plausibly reported to be furious. However, the Grenadians had been for years tormented by corrupt and rapacious governments and they were prepared to welcome anybody who would intervene on their behalf. Unlike many states in the region, they were pleased to come into the American sphere of influence, especially as the injection of dollars into an economy which the Commonwealth had done nothing to help would relieve the crippling unemployment. Their feeling that the British connection is virtually defunct was demonstrated by the muted welcome which a normally ebullient people gave to the Queen when she opened the refurbished parliament building in 1985.

It is often said that the Queen gets on particularly well with black Commonwealth leaders. This is encouraging, though there seems to be little royal enthusiasm for blacks closer to home and it is perhaps significant that the Queen was very fond of 'The

Black and White Ministrel Show' on television. No black has a place in the Palace hierarchy. There are few, if any, to be seen among the royal guards and, as even the Conservative peer Lord Onslow recently told the upper house, 'It is unarguable that there is passive discrimination in the Household Brigade Regiments.' ('Passive discrimination' is an interesting term, roughly corresponding in meaning, presumably, to 'active discrimination'.) Prince Philip floundered desperately when asked in an interview what his response would be if one of his children wanted to marry a black. And there has been a deafening royal silence about race relations in Britain, though Prince Charles apparently does sterling work to improve them behind the scenes. Hopes that the Commonwealth might constitute a model multiracial community have been dashed. Under Mrs Thatcher's government British aid to Commonwealth countries has been drastically reduced, while the fees of overseas students have been raised so high that the number coming to British universities has declined. Worse still, Britain has virtually isolated herself in refusing to impose comprehensive sanctions on South Africa. Various leaks in the press suggest that the Queen is doing her utmost to change government policy in order to keep the Commonwealth together. But although, on this occasion, she may be on the side of the angels, this does not invalidate the principle that secret, unaccountable influence at the centre of affairs, however ineffectual it is, has no place in a democracy.

Apologists for the Commonwealth like 'Sonny' Ramphal, its secretary general, maintain that throughout its length and breadth the Queen exerts a 'moral influence' and that she is 'a unifying force of great symbolic value'. The very vagueness of these claims makes them difficult to gauge. Still, it is clear that such influence as she does possess in the Commonwealth is on the wane – a healthy sign. In places like Zimbabwe, as even *The Times* admits, the Queen is regarded as 'a symbol of colonial oppression'. There is a similar feeling in the old dominions. In Canada, for example, the Queen is not welcomed by the more militant French-speaking population – a fact recognized in 1984 when her tour was carefully arranged to avoid embarrassing demonstrations. She means little to the one third of the Canadian population whose ancestral ties are neither British nor French. This was perhaps why Pierre Trudeau effectively made the governor general the country's head of state, though the Queen has that title when she is actually in Canada. There is a widespread belief among Canadians that changing values among the young and impatience with a connection which is at best a picturesque irrelevance and at worst a divisive nuisance will eventually lead to a complete break with the Commonwealth and its head.

In Australia that feeling of alienation is expressed by over forty per cent of the population. Under half of all Australians are of British descent and even many who do come from the 'old country' (especially the young) would like to see the Commonwealth link severed. As one said, what he wanted was the establishment of normal relations between Australia and Britain without 'echoes of past overlordship'. Nothing has stuck in Australian memories, and gullets, like the grotesque speech which a misty-eyed Robert Menzies delivered at Parliament House, Canberra, to welcome the Queen and Prince Philip on their Australian tour in 1963. It reached its climax when he applied the lines of an obscure Elizabethan poet, Barnabe Googe, to the Queen:

> There is a lady sweet and kind,
> Was never face so pleased my mind;
> I did but see her passing by,
> And yet I love her till I die.

Most Australians winced (though there was spontaneous applause in the assembly), and even the Queen blushed. But apparently no flattery can be too fulsome when it is applied to royalty. Soon afterwards the Australian prime minister was offered a Knighthood of the Thistle, an order in the sovereign's personal gift. Despite his previous protestations about its being 'better to be plain Mr Menzies' he was delighted to become Sir Robert.

Australian republicanism received an even greater fillip when the governor general, Sir John Kerr, used the 'reserve powers' of the royal prerogative to dismiss the democratically elected Labour prime minister Gough Whitlam (who had abolished the British honours system) in 1975. Whitlam was unpopular at the time and Conservatives thought that Kerr's action was vindicated by Labour's defeat in the subsequent election. But half Australia was appalled by the governor general's arbitrary act. The Nobel

Prize-winning novelist Patrick White, a staunch republican, spoke for them: 'This supposedly sophisticated country is still, alas, a colonial sheep-run.' There was some talk of Prince Charles's becoming Kerr's successor (something he apparently wanted) but only twenty per cent of Australians favoured the idea. Instead, there was an increasing tendency to reject the relics of 'Pom snobbery' and to create a genuine national identity. As the BBC's correspondent, Red Harrison, said in 1983, 'The tide of history, however slowly it might move, is against the survival of Australia's royal links with Britain.'

Members of the Commonwealth will work out their own salvation. However ramshackle and riddled with anomalies the organization becomes, many will doubtless remain inside it for sentimental reasons. Others, wishing to forge their national identity and determine their own destiny free from the imperial hangover, will leave. They will put away what their citizens increasingly come to regard as childish things, the fawning paraphenalia that accompany a royal tour, the obsolete attitude of deference to the former mother country and its great white Queen, the neo-colonial tutelage which is a badge of immaturity. Quitting the Commonwealth for these states will be a notable emancipation.

The Victorians were, Lady Longford wrote, dizzily infatuated 'with an inferior dream, the dream of Colonial Empire'. Actually, though, it is the Commonwealth which is a dream. But just as Queen Victoria became the focus for imperial loyalty, so Queen Elizabeth gives the Commonwealth its modicum of plausibility. If Britain herself became a republic the structure of the Commonwealth would be weakened, if not damaged beyond repair. Little that is really worthwhile would be lost, though some (in Britain, sad to say, all too few) would regret the passing of an organization which might perhaps help to improve global race relations. What would be gained, at least for Britain, is the dissolution of those trailing clouds of imperial glory which obscure her vision of herself and give her an inflated idea of her position in the world. Without the Commonwealth illusion the British people might recognize that their fate depends not on conjurations with a colourful past but on the present implementation of sensible and enlightened policies.

As a matter of fact, pressure is growing for Britain to put her constitutional house in order. It used to be axiomatic that Britain's lack of a written constitution was not just an advantage but a glory. As the constitutional lawyer A. V. Dicey wrote, although the Habeas Corpus Acts 'declare no principle and define no rights, they are for practical purposes worth a hundred constitutional articles guaranteeing individual liberty'. In recent years, however, it has become sadly apparent that individual liberties are not guaranteed as well in Britain as in countries which have a comprehensive Bill of Rights enshrined in their constitutions. Hence Britons are having to seek remedies in the European Court of Human Rights – for example, over the systematic maltreatment of detainees in Northern Ireland, the deprivation of the right of British Asians to enter their only country of citizenship, judicial interference with freedom of expression, sexual discrimination over the age of retirement and so on. It is clear that, *pace* Thomas Hobbes, the freedom of the individual does not rest in 'the silence of the law'.

Nor, by the same token, is good government fostered by the secretive, ill-defined, precedent-ridden, conservative-inclined system – the monarch at its centre – which prevails in Britain at the moment. A written constitution would help to eliminate hidden, hereditary influence from politics as being incompatible with democratic principles. It would transform the House of Lords into a representative assembly, perhaps elected by a different method from that which sends MPs to Westminster. And the monarchy should, at the very least, become a proper department of state, duly accountable to parliament. Any more fundamental reform, one which involved the total abolition of the monarchy, seems at present a remote eventuality. Indeed, it is about as much of a pipe-dream as Voltaire's ambition to strangle the last king with the entrails of the last priest. On the other hand, the time will surely come when a mature, democratic nation realizes that in a scientific age it does not need to gravitate round a human ju-ju located variously at Buckingham Palace, Windsor Castle, Sandringham and Balmoral. When the British have been educated out of their besotted monarchism, a simple, enlightened, egalitarian alternative exists. There are plenty of good republican models to follow – West Germany's seems a particularly sophisticated and effective one. A possible solution is to have an elected president, a figurehead whose duties are almost entirely ornamental though he may have well-defined and extremely limited functions as a political longstop. Such a president might be able, for example, to argue the Queen's case for Commonwealth sanctions against South Africa with more vigour and openness, and might be replaced by a better candidate if he failed to do so.

Sir Edmund Hillary conquered Everest at about the same time as Queen Elizabeth was crowned. He and Tenzing climbed the mountain, apparently, because it was there, and the British really have no better reason for keeping the monarchy. This reactionary, self-perpetuating institution has become increasingly anomalous over the last century or so. During that time a collection of kings and queens, some of them singularly unattractive, has reigned over a country in steep decline. They have contributed little more than a few sententious views, some playboy princes, a somewhat spurious tradition of pageantry and an expensive round of ornamental triviality. They have steadfastly opposed most of the social and political advances made over the last few generations. They have offered virtually nothing in terms of intelligence and creativity. Instead they have sustained an old-fashioned, hierarchical, deferential society. They have encouraged their subjects to dwell in a world of superstition and fantasy. They have helped to obfuscate the processes of rule, to justify undemocratic practices and to consecrate the system of closed government which prevails in Britain. And they have fostered a quite new degree of sycophancy, especially in the media, which can only be bad for the nation's health. The House of Windsor is a balloon kept aloft by a constant stream of hot air. Dean Acheson memorably remarked that postwar Britain had lost an Empire but had not found a role. The nation might find that role if it lost the monarchy. As a republic Britain could experience a renaissance. At the very least she would purge herself of the archaic influences which today corrupt her character, deform her society and retard her progress.

Further reading

Lord Altrincham, 'The Monarchy Today' in *The National and English Review* (August 1957)

'American Resident', *The Twilight of the British Monarchy* (1937)

S. E. Ayling, *George the Third* (1972)

W. Bagehot, *The English Constitution*, edited by R. H. S. Crossman (1964)

M. Bloch (editor), *Wallis and Edward: Letters 1931–1937* (1986)

B. Boothroyd, *Philip: An Informal Biography* (1971)

J. Brooke, *King George III* (1972)

D. Cannadine, 'The Context, Performance and Meaning of Ritual: The British Monarchy and the "Invention of Tradition"', c. 1820–1977' in *The Invention of Tradition*, edited by E. Hobsbawm and T. Ranger (1983)

H. Channon, *'Chips': The Diaries of Sir Henry Channon*, edited by R. Rhodes James (1967)

M. Crawford, *The Little Princesses* (1950)

F. Donaldson, *Edward VII* (1974)

A. Duncan, *The Reality of Monarchy* (1970)

J. Gore, *King George V, A Personal Memoir* (1941)

W. Hamilton, *My Queen and I* (1975)

F. Harrison, 'The Monarchy' in *Fortnightly Review* (1 June 1872)

F. Hardie, *The Political Influence of the British Monarchy 1868–1952* (1970)

R. Harrison, *Before the Socialists* (1965)

C. Hibbert, *The Court at Windsor* (1977)

——, *George IV* (1972–3)

A. Holden, *Charles, Prince of Wales* (1979)

P. Howard, *The British Monarchy in the Twentieth Century* (1977)

E. Hughes, *The Prince, the Crown and the Cash* (1969)

R. Rhodes James, *Albert, Prince Consort* (1983)

D. Judd, *King George VI 1895–1952* (1982)

D. Keay, *Royal Pursuit: The Media and the Monarchy in Conflict and Compromise* (1984)

R. Lacey, *Majesty: Elizabeth II and the House of Windsor* (1977)

D. Laird, *How the Queen Reigns* (1959)

H. Laski, *Parliamentary Government in England* (1938)

E. Longford, *Elizabeth R.* (1983)

——, *Queen Victoria* (1964)

P. Magnus, *King Edward VII* (1964)

K. Martin, *The Crown and the Establishment* (1962)

B. Masters, *Dreams about H. M. The Queen and Other Members of the Royal Family* (1972)

D. Morrah, *The Work of the Queen* (1958)

M. Muggeridge, 'Does England Really Need a Queen?' in *Saturday Evening Post* (19 October 1957)

J. Murray-Brown (editor), *The Monarchy and its Future* (1969)

H. Nicolson, *King George V* (1952)

T. Paine, *The Rights of Man* (1791)

C. Petrie, *The Modern British Monarchy* (1961)

J. Pope-Hennessy, *Queen Mary* (1959)

The Queen (A Penguin Special) (1977)

K. Rose, *King George V* (1983)

S. Temple (i.e. G. O. Trevelyan), *What Does She Do With It?* (1871)

J. A. Thompson and A. Mejia, *The Modern British Monarchy* (1971)

M. Thornton, *Royal Feud* (1983)

J. Wheeler-Bennett, *King George VI* (1958)

Duke of Windsor, *A King's Story* (1951)

C. Woodham-Smith, *Queen Victoria* (1975)

P. Ziegler, *Crown and People* (1978)

——, *King William IV* (1971)

Index